T0342976

CONTENTS

Targeting Homework
Year 6 New Edition

Copyright © 2024 Blake Education
ISBN: 978 1 92572 648 0

Published by Pascal Press
PO Box 250
Glebe NSW 2037
www.pascalpress.com.au
contact@pascalpress.com.au

Authors: Peter Alford, Edward Connor
Publisher: Lynn Dickinson
Editors: Marie Theodore & Ruth Schultz
Cover and Text Designer: Leanne Nobilio
Typesetters: Ruth Schultz
Proofreader: Tim Learner
Images & Illustrations: Dreamstime (unless otherwise indicated)
Printed by Wai Man Book Binding (China) Ltd

Acknowledgements
Thank you to the publishers, authors and illustrators
who generously granted permission for their work
to be reproduced in this book.

Introduction

Targeting Homework aims to build and reinforce English and Maths skills. This book supports the ACARA Australian Curriculum for Year 6 and helps children to revise and consolidate what has been taught in the classroom. ACARA codes are shown on each unit and a chart explaining their content descriptions is on pages v and vi. The inside back cover (Maths) and front cover (English) show the topics in each unit.

The structure of this book

This book has 32 carefully graded double-page units on English and Maths. The English units are divided into three sections:

★ Grammar and Punctuation

★ Spelling and Phonic Knowledge

★ Reading and Comprehension — includes a wide variety of literary and cross-curriculum texts.

This also includes a Reading Review segment for children to record and rate their home reading books.

The Maths units are divided between:

★ Number and Algebra

★ Measurement and Space

★ Statistics and Probability

★ Problem Solving.

My Book Review

Title _____

Author _____

Rating ☆ ☆ ☆ ☆ ☆

Comment _____
_____

Assessment

Term Reviews follow Units 1–8, 9–16, 17–24 and 25–32 to test work covered during the term, and allow parents and carers to monitor their child's progress. Children are encouraged to mark each unit as it is completed and to colour in the traffic lights at the end of each segment. These results are then transferred to the Marking Grid. Parents and carers can see at a glance if their child is excelling or struggling!

● **Green** = Excellent — 2 or fewer questions incorrect
● **Orange** = Passing — 50% or more questions answered correctly
● **Red** = Struggling — fewer than 50% correct and needs help

SCORE **/18** (0-6) (8-14) (16-18)   *Score 2 points for each correct answer!*

How to Use This Book

The activities in this book are specifically designed to be used at home with minimal resources and support. Helpful explanations of key concepts and skills are provided throughout the book to help understand the tasks. Useful examples of how to do the activities are provided.

Regular practice of key concepts and skills will support the work your child does in school and will enable you to monitor their progress throughout the year. It is recommended that children complete 8 units per school term (one a week) and then the Term Review. Every unit has a Traffic Light scoreboard at the end of each section.

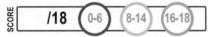

Score 2 points for each correct answer!

You or your child should mark each completed unit and then colour the traffic light that corresponds to the number of correct questions. This process will enable you to see at a glance how your child is progressing and to identify weak spots. The results should be recorded at the end of each term on the Marking Grid on page 1. The Term Review results are important for tracking progress and identifying any improvements in performance. If you find that certain questions are repeatedly

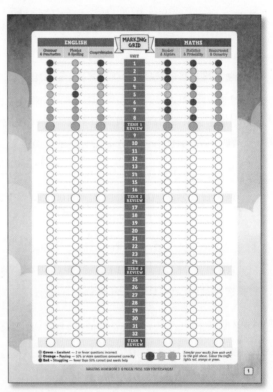

NOTE: The Maths Problem Solving questions do not appear on the Marking Grid as they often have multiple or subjective answers that cannot be easily scored.

causing difficulties and errors, then there is a good reason to discuss this with your child's teacher and arrange for extra instruction in that problem area.

Home Reading Journal

Each English unit provides space for your child to log, review and rate a book they have read during the week. These details can then be transferred to the handy Reading Journal Summary on page 146, which can be photocopied and shared with their teacher or kept as a record.

Answers

The answer section on pages 147–162 can be removed, stapled together and kept somewhere safe. Use it to check answers when your child has completed each unit. Encourage your child to colour in the Traffic Light boxes when the answers have been calculated.

TARGETING HOMEWORK 6 © PASCAL PRESS ISBN 9781925726480

Australian Curriculum Correlations: Year 6 English

CODE	CODE DESCRIPTION	Grammar & Punctuation UNITS	Phonic Knowledge & Spelling UNITS	Reading Comprehension UNITS
LANGUAGE				
AC9E6LA01	Understand that language varies as levels of formality and social distance increase			8
AC9E6LA02	Understand the uses of objective and subjective language, and identify bias			5, 17, 26
AC9E6LA03	Explain how texts across the curriculum are typically organised into characteristic stages and phases depending on purposes, recognising how authors often adapt text structures and language features			14, 26, 29, 31
AC9E6LA04	Understand that cohesion can be created by the intentional use of repetition, and the use of word associations	14, 20		
AC9E6LA05	Understand how embedded clauses can expand the variety of complex sentences to elaborate, extend and explain ideas	1, 2, 5, 6, 11, 19, 21, 29, 30, 32		
AC9E6LA06	Understand how ideas can be expanded and sharpened through careful choice of verbs, elaborated tenses and a range of adverb groups	1, 2, 3, 4, 5, 7, 8, 11, 12, 13, 14, 15, 16, 17, 18, 20, 21, 22, 23, 24, 25, 26, 27, 28, 30, 31		
AC9E6LA08	Identify authors' use of vivid, emotive vocabulary, such as metaphors, similes, personification, idioms, imagery and hyperbole			5, 8, 11, 23, 29, 31
AC9E6LA09	Understand how to use the comma for lists, to separate a dependent clause from an independent clause, and in dialogue	1, 2, 9, 10, 12, 28, 30, 32		1
LITERATURE				
AC9E6LE01	Identify responses to characters and events in literary texts, drawn from historical, social or cultural contexts, by First Nations Australian, and wide-ranging Australian and world authors			2, 3, 4, 7, 13, 19
AC9E6LE02	Identify similarities and differences in literary texts on similar topics, themes or plots			8, 14, 23, 26
AC9E6LE03	Identify and explain characteristics that define an author's individual style			8
LITERACY				
AC9E6LY03	Analyse how text structures and language features work together to meet the purpose of a text, and engage and influence audiences			5, 6, 7, 8, 11, 14, 15, 17, 20, 23, 29, 31
AC9E6LY04	Select, navigate and read texts for a range of purposes, monitoring meaning and evaluating the use of structural features; for example, table of contents, glossary, chapters, headings and subheadings		2, 3	5, 8, 14, 17, 26
AC9E6LY05	Use comprehension strategies such as visualising, predicting, connecting, summarising, monitoring and questioning to build literal and inferred meaning, and to connect and compare content from a variety of sources			ALL UNITS
AC9E6LY08	Use phonic knowledge of common and less common grapheme–phoneme relationships to read and write increasingly complex words		10, 12, 14, 18, 19, 22, 23, 24, 25, 27, 28, 30	
AC9E6LY09	Use knowledge of known words, word origins including some Latin and Greek roots, base words, prefixes, suffixes, letter patterns and spelling generalisations to spell new words including technical words		ALL UNITS	
CROSS CURRICULAR COMPREHENSION TEXTS				
HASS SKILLS				
AC9HS6S01	Develop questions to investigate people, events, developments, places and systems			20
HISTORY				
AC9HS6K01	Significant individuals, events and ideas that led to Australia's Federation, the Constitution and democratic system of government			2
AC9HS6K02	Changes in Australia's political system and to Australian citizenship after Federation and throughout the 20th century that impacted First Nations Australians, migrants, women and children			4
AC9HS6K03	The motivation of people migrating to Australia since Federation and throughout the 20th century, their stories and effects on Australian society, including migrants from the Asia region			2, 7, 25
GEOGRAPHY				
AC9HS6K04	The geographical diversity and location of places in the Asia region, and its location in relation to Australia			1, 16
AC9HS6K05	Australia's interconnections with other countries and how these change people and places			3, 4, 7, 13

Australian Curriculum Correlations: Year 6 Maths

ACARA CODE	CONTENT DESCRIPTION	Number & Algebra UNITS	Statistics & Probability UNITS	Measurement & Space UNITS	Problem Solving UNITS
NUMBER					
AC9M6N01	Recognise situations, including financial contexts, that use integers; locate and represent integers on a number line and as coordinates on the Cartesian plane	1, 3, 8			3, 8
AC9M6N02	Identify and describe the properties of prime, composite and square numbers and use these properties to solve problems and simplify calculations	1, 7			1
AC9M6N03	Apply knowledge of equivalence to compare, order and represent common fractions including halves, thirds and quarters on the same number line and justify their order	4, 5, 9, 21			4
AC9M6N04	Apply knowledge of place value to add and subtract decimals, using digital tools where appropriate; use estimation and rounding to check the reasonableness of answers	12, 13			12, 13
AC9M6N05	Solve problems involving addition and subtraction of fractions using knowledge of equivalent fractions	10, 11, 14, 21, 22, 31	31		9, 10, 14, 22, 31
AC9M6N06	Multiply and divide decimals by multiples of powers of 10 without a calculator, applying knowledge of place value and proficiency with multiplication facts; using estimation and rounding to check the reasonableness of answers	24, 25			24
AC9M6N07	Solve problems that require finding a familiar fraction, decimal or percentage of a quantity, including percentage discounts, choosing efficient calculation strategies and using digital tools where appropriate	15, 17, 18, 23, 26			7, 11, 15, 22, 23
AC9M6N08	Approximate numerical solutions to problems involving rational numbers and percentages, including financial contexts, using appropriate estimation strategies		28	29	20
AC9M6N09	Use mathematical modelling to solve practical problems, involving rational numbers and percentages, including in financial contexts; formulate the problems, choosing operations and efficient calculation strategies, and using digital tools where appropriate; interpret and communicate solutions in terms of the situation, justifying the choices made	6, 19, 23			18, 19, 23, 25, 32
ALGEBRA					
AC9M6A01	Recognise and use rules that generate visually growing patterns and number patterns involving rational numbers	27, 28			27, 28
AC9M6A02	Find unknown values in numerical equations involving brackets and combinations of arithmetic operations, using the properties of numbers and operations	20, 29, 30, 32			17
AC9M6A03	Create and use algorithms involving a sequence of steps and decisions that use rules to generate sets of numbers; identify, interpret and explain emerging patterns	2, 16			2, 16
MEASUREMENT					
AC9M6M01	convert between common metric units of length, mass and capacity; choose and use decimal representations of metric measurements relevant to the context of a problem			1, 2, 4, 5, 6, 9, 16	2, 5, 6, 9
AC9M6M02	establish the formula for the area of a rectangle and use it to solve practical problems			3, 7, 19, 20	19
AC9M6M03	interpret and use timetables and itineraries to plan activities and determine the duration of events and journeys			10, 14, 23, 30	10, 30
AC9M6M04	identify the relationships between angles on a straight line, angles at a point and vertically opposite angles; use these to determine unknown angles, communicating reasoning			16, 17, 18, 21, 22, 25, 28, 29	17, 25, 28, 29, 31
SPACE					
AC9M6SP01	compare the parallel cross-sections of objects and recognise their relationships to right prisms			8, 11, 12, 31	11, 27
AC9M6SP02	locate points in the 4 quadrants of a Cartesian plane; describe changes to the coordinates when a point is moved to a different position in the plane			15, 26, 27, 32	26
AC9M6SP03	recognise and use combinations of transformations to create tessellations and other geometric patterns, using dynamic geometric software where appropriate			13, 15	
STATISTICS					
AC9M6ST01	interpret and compare data sets for ordinal and nominal categorical, discrete and continuous numerical variables using comparative displays or visualisations and digital tools; compare distributions in terms of mode, range and shape		7, 8, 10, 13, 16, 18, 19, 22, 24, 25, 32		7, 8, 18, 26
AC9M6ST02	identify statistically informed arguments presented in traditional and digital media; discuss and critique methods, data representations and conclusions		11, 14, 30		
AC9M6ST03	plan and conduct statistical investigations by posing and refining questions or identifying a problem and collecting relevant data; analyse and interpret the data and communicate findings within the context of the investigation		31		9
PROBABILITY					
AC9M6P01	recognise that probabilities lie on numerical scales of 0 – 1 or 0% – 100% and use estimation to assign probabilities that events occur in a given context, using common fractions, percentages and decimals		1, 3, 4, 5, 6, 12, 15, 20, 21, 24, 28, 29		3, 4, 5, 15, 20, 29
AC9M6P02	conduct repeated chance experiments and run simulations with an increasing number of trials using digital tools; compare observations with expected results and discuss the effect on variation of increasing the number of trials		2, 23, 26, 27		24, 27

Australian CURRICULUM

TARGETING HOMEWORK 6 © PASCAL PRESS ISBN 9781925726480

MARKING GRID

ENGLISH			UNIT	MATHS		
Grammar & Punctuation	Phonics & Spelling	Comprehension		Number & Algebra	Statistics & Probability	Measurement & Space
○	○	○	1	○	○	○
○	○	○	2	○	○	○
○	○	○	3	○	○	○
○	○	○	4	○	○	○
○	○	○	5	○	○	○
○	○	○	6	○	○	○
○	○	○	7	○	○	○
○	○	○	8	○	○	○
○	○	○	TERM 1 REVIEW	○	○	○
○	○	○	9	○	○	○
○	○	○	10	○	○	○
○	○	○	11	○	○	○
○	○	○	12	○	○	○
○	○	○	13	○	○	○
○	○	○	14	○	○	○
○	○	○	15	○	○	○
○	○	○	16	○	○	○
○	○	○	TERM 2 REVIEW	○	○	○
○	○	○	17	○	○	○
○	○	○	18	○	○	○
○	○	○	19	○	○	○
○	○	○	20	○	○	○
○	○	○	21	○	○	○
○	○	○	22	○	○	○
○	○	○	23	○	○	○
○	○	○	24	○	○	○
○	○	○	TERM 3 REVIEW	○	○	○
○	○	○	25	○	○	○
○	○	○	26	○	○	○
○	○	○	27	○	○	○
○	○	○	28	○	○	○
○	○	○	29	○	○	○
○	○	○	30	○	○	○
○	○	○	31	○	○	○
○	○	○	32	○	○	○
○	○	○	TERM 4 REVIEW	○	○	○

● **Green** = Excellent — 2 or fewer questions incorrect
● **Orange** = Passing — 50% or more questions answered correctly
● **Red** = Struggling — fewer than 50% correct and needs help

Transfer your results from each unit to the grid above. Colour the traffic lights red, orange or green.

Grammar & Punctuation

AC9E6LA05, AC9E6LA06, AC9E6LA09

Complex sentences

A **complex sentence** has two (or more) clauses: a <u>main clause</u> which has the main idea, and a subordinate clause which gives more information about the main idea. A subordinate clause cannot stand on its own.
Example:

main clause

<u>The class was having a party</u> **because it was the end of the year.** — subordinate clause

Underline the main clauses in the sentences below.

① Luke was voted captain this year because he is a great runner.

② We aren't allowed to eat the apples hanging over the fence until they are ripe.

③ Although Jess is fantastic at cycling, she has fallen off her bike three times.

Commas in complex sentences

A **comma (,)** is used to indicate a pause between words. We usually add a comma when the subordinate clause is first in a complex sentence.
Example:

subordinate clause   comma

While we watch the fireworks display, we'll eat our dinner. — main clause

Write the missing commas to separate the clauses in these sentences.

④ Although we woke up late we still caught the bus.

⑤ When we have beach holidays my family swims in the surf every day.

⑥ While the scones are baking in the oven Jack will wash the dishes.

Conjunctions

Conjunctions can join ideas and clauses to make complex sentences. Some examples are: although, because, unless, when, while.
Example: conjunction   subordinate clause

Unless we get a bigger yard, <u>we can't get a pony</u>.   main clause

Circle the conjunctions in these sentences.

⑦ Because some old people find it difficult to walk, they use the bus.

⑧ Since we usually make a huge mess in art classes, we have to clean up.

⑨ I usually sleep in even though my dog barks loudly each morning.

Score 2 points for each correct answer! SCORE **/18** (0-6) (8-14) (16-18)

Phonic Knowledge & Spelling

AC9E6LY09

Prefixes

A **prefix** is a short word part added to the beginning of a word. It changes the meaning of a word. *Example:* **dis**agree means **not** agree.

Prefix	Meaning
dis–	apart, not
inter–	between
mis–	wrong, bad, fault
pro–	before, supporting
semi–	half
trans–	across

Choose a prefix from above to complete each word.

① _____port   ③ _____gram

② _____circle   ④ _____state

Suffixes

A **suffix** is a short word part added to the end of a word. It changes the way the word is used.
Example: care, care**less**, care**ful**, care**fully**

Suffix	Meaning
–y/–ly	like/in a manner of
–ism	belief
–ant	one/a person who
–ise	become
–ship	profession
–less	without

Choose a suffix from the box to complete each word.

⑤ My teacher was asked to organ_____ the school choir.

⑥ The inform_____ was taken to the police station.

⑦ Lucy was about to start her apprentice_____.

Score 2 points for each correct answer! SCORE **/14** (0-4) (6-10) (12-14)

TARGETING HOMEWORK 6 © PASCAL PRESS ISBN 9781925726480

Asia

Informative text – Report
Author – Nicholas Brasch

Asia is the largest continent in the world and has more people than all the other continents put together.

Asia is very diverse. It has **sparsely** populated areas in the north-east, while some cities are the most crowded on Earth. It has mountain ranges, rainforests, deserts and subarctic **tundra**. It has beach resorts, slums and bustling cities. Just about every religion on Earth is practised in Asia.

There are great differences in wealth and living standards. South Korea's **gross domestic product** (GDP) is almost 20 times greater than that of its neighbour, North Korea.

Asia has experienced just about every form of government. **Feudal** systems operated in China and Japan for many centuries. **Monarchies** ruled China and the ancient Khmer and Cham kingdoms (modern day Vietnam and Cambodia). From the 15th century European powers controlled many

countries, particularly in South-East Asia (only Thailand remained independent). In the 20th century, **communist** governments ruled in Cambodia, Mongolia, North Korea, China, Vietnam and Laos (Cambodia and Mongolia are no longer communist). Parliamentary **democracy** spread from the West and is now a feature of many Asian countries such as Japan, Indonesia and South Korea.

Source: *Asia*, Go Facts, Blake Education.

Write or circle the correct answers.

① **What is the meaning of tundra?**

  a warm, dry and rainless

  b flat, treeless and frozen

  c wet and warm

② **What were Vietnam and Cambodia known as when they were ruled by monarchies?**

_____

_____

③ **What do the words slums and bustling have in common?**

  a They both have something to do with government.

  b They both refer to types of buildings.

  c They are both about cities.

What are the four types of government mentioned in the report?

④ _____

⑤ _____

⑥ _____

⑦ _____

⑧ **GDP stands for Gross Domestic Product. Which Korea has the greater GDP?**

_____

⑨ **Name two countries which have parliamentary democracy.**

_____

_____

⑩ **When did European countries first control Asian countries?**

_____

Score 2 points for each correct answer!

SCORE **/20** (0-8) (10-14) (16-20)

My Book Review

Title _____

Author _____

Rating ☆☆☆☆☆

Comment _____

_____

Number & Algebra

AC9M6N01, AC9M6N02

Whole numbers, integers, composite numbers and prime numbers

Circle the correct answers.

① Which set of numbers is not made up only of **whole numbers**?

a {55, 60, 65, 70, 75, 80, 85. 90, 100.}

b {0, 1, 2, 3, 4, 5, 6, 7, 8, 9, 10.}

c {40, $40\frac{1}{2}$, 50, $50\frac{1}{2}$, 60, $60\frac{1}{2}$, 70, $70\frac{1}{2}$.}

② Which set of numbers is not made up of only **integers**?

a {-6, -5, -4, -3, -2, -1, 0, 1, 2, 3, 4, 5, 6.}

b {0, 2, 4, 6, 8, 10, 12.}

c {$-2\frac{1}{2}$, -2, $-1\frac{1}{2}$, -1, $-\frac{1}{2}$, 0, $\frac{1}{2}$, 1, $1\frac{1}{2}$, 2, $2\frac{1}{2}$.}

③ Which number is not a **whole number**?

a 7

b 156

c 19.5

d 1 000 000

④ Which number is not a **whole number**?

a 1 234 256

b -32

c 100

d 4

⑤ Which definition for a **composite number** is wrong?

a a number that is divisible by three or more factors

b a whole number that can be divided evenly by numbers other than 1 or itself

c a number that is a decimal fraction but not a common fraction

⑥ What **composite number** do the factors 15 and 3 make up?

a 18   b 12   c 5   d 45

⑦ Which statement about **prime numbers** is not correct?

a A prime number has no factors other than 1 and itself.

b A prime number is a number that can be divided by 2 without a remainder.

c A prime number can be divided evenly only by 1 or itself.

⑧ Which number is a **prime number**?

a 9   b 10   c 11   d 12

Score 2 points for each correct answer! SCORE **/16** (0-6) (8-12) (14-16)

Statistics & Probability

AC9M6P01

Common fractions in probability

Circle the correct answers.

① A coin has two sides, head (H) and tail (T).

With **all things being equal**, what is the chance of the coin coming up head when it is tossed?

a 2 in 2

b 1 in 1

c 2 in 1

d 1 in 2

② Which statement is correct and most descriptive in explaining the chance of the coin in Question 1 coming up tail when tossed?

a the same as the chance of the coin coming up tail because coins are round

b half the chance of the coin coming up tail because it is on the other side

c twice as much as the chance of the coin coming up tail because it is on the other side

d the same as the chance of the coin coming up tail because there are only two sides

③ Why were the words **all things being equal** included in Question 1?

a to make it sound better

b to rule out the possibility of cheating

c to rule out the possibility of a defect or fault in the coin, as well as cheating

d to rule out the possibility of a defect in the coin, as well as cheating and anything else that might affect the coin toss

④ Which common fraction represents a probability of 1 out of 4?

a $\frac{4}{1}$ b $\frac{2}{4}$ c $\frac{1}{4}$ d $\frac{1}{2}$

⑤ What is the probability of a 1 coming up when a regular six-sided die is rolled? (From now on, we'll assume that **all things are equal**.)

a one in six

b six in one

c 6 out of 1

d 6 out of 6

⑥ What is the probability of a 6 coming up when a regular die is rolled?

a $\frac{6}{1}$ b $\frac{1}{6}$ c $\frac{6}{6}$ d $\frac{1}{1}$

TARGETING HOMEWORK 6 © PASCAL PRESS ISBN 9781925726480

⑦ In a bag there are five different coloured marbles: white, black, red, yellow and green. Without looking, what is the chance of picking a red marble?

a $\frac{1}{2}$ b $\frac{1}{3}$ c $\frac{1}{5}$ d $\frac{1}{1}$

⑧ Song picked a red marble out of the bag in Question 7 and then placed it back in the bag. What is the chance of picking a red marble on her next go?

a the same as the first go

b better than the first go

c slightly worse than the first go

d a lot worse than the first go

Score 2 points for each correct answer!   SCORE **/16** ⟨0-6⟩ ⟨8-12⟩ ⟨14-16⟩

Measurement & Space

AC9M6M01

The metric system

Circle the correct answer.

① Which set of abbreviations of metric lengths is correct?

a {mm = macrometre, cm = centimetre, m = millimetre, km = kilometre.}

b {mm = millimetre, cm = centimetre, m = metre, km = kilometre.}

c {nm = nanometre, cm = centimetre, m = mile, lm = longmetre.}

② Which set of abbreviations of metric weights (mass) is correct?

a {mg = multigrain, g = grain, kg = kilograin, t = tonne.}

b {mg = megagram, g = gram, kg = kilogram, t = ton.}

c {mg = milligram, g = gram, kg = kilogram, t = tonne.}

③ Which set of abbreviations of metric capacity is correct?

a {mL = millilitre, C = cup, mg = megalitre, P = pint.}

b {L = litre, mL = millilitre, cL = centilitre, ML = megalitre.}

c {dl = decalitre, l = litre, mL = milllitre, cL = centilitre.}

This table shows commonly used metric prefixes. Write the missing entries below.

Prefix	Symbol	Numerically	Name
giga	G	1 000 000 000	4
mega	M	5	million
6	k	1000	thousand
centi	c	0.01	7
milli	8	0.001	thousandth
micro	μ	0.000 001	9
nano	n	0.000 000 001	billionth

④ _____

⑤ _____

⑥ _____

⑦ _____

⑧ _____

⑨ _____

Score 2 points for each correct answer!   SCORE **/18** ⟨0-6⟩ ⟨8-14⟩ ⟨16-18⟩

Problem Solving

AC9M6N02

Whole number problems

① The number 241 is made up of three digits that add up to 7: **2 + 4 + 1 = 7.**

What even whole number is <30 and made up of digits that add up to 10?

_____

② What two whole numbers are >100, <200 and made up of different odd digits that add up to 9?

_____   _____

③ On her next birthday, Julie's age will be the fifth prime number. How old is she now?

_____

④ What prime number is <30 and has digits that add up to 5?

_____

⑤ Even numbers added together will always equal an even number. True or false?

_____

⑥ Odd numbers added together will always equal an odd number. True or false?

_____

⑦ Which odd number when doubled is >24 and <30?

_____

Grammar & Punctuation

AC9E6LA05, AC9E6LA06, AC9E6LA09

Compound sentences

> A compound sentence has two **main clauses** — both clauses make sense on their own.
>
> *Example:*
>
>   main clause   conjunction
>
> <u>James went to school with a headache</u> **yet** <u>he didn't complain.</u>
>
>   main clause
>
> The two main clauses are joined together with a **conjunction**: and, so, but, or, yet.

Choose a conjunction from above to complete each compound sentence.

1. My brother used to love climbing trees, _____ he fell and broke his arm.

2. Baking cakes at school is easy, _____ when I got home I tried a recipe.

3. Fishing off the rocks is great fun _____ I also like beach fishing.

4. These holidays I could go to vacation care, _____ I could stay at Nana's place.

Commas in compound sentences

> In a compound sentence, a **comma** is usually placed before **so, but** and **or**.
>
> *Example:* Easter is my favourite time of the year, so my family gives me lots of chocolate.
>
> When **and** is used in a compound sentence, use a comma when the subjects are different.
>
> *Examples:*
>
> **My head** is aching, and **my feet** are sore. (subjects are different – use comma)
>
> **Emma** is running fast and **she** is not looking back. (subjects are the same – no comma)

Write the missing comma to separate the two main clauses in each sentence.

5. Our family has a boat near the river so we try to catch crabs during crabbing season.

6. Summer is becoming hotter but some people don't believe it's because of global warming.

7. Serina is learning ballet and her younger sister is learning hip-hop.

8. Our black stallion was a racehorse and he won lots of races.

9. Eric could go surfing with Dad on Sunday or he could go to the movies with Mum.

Phonic Knowledge & Spelling

AC9E6LY09, AC9E6LY04

Homophones

> **Homophones** are words that sound the same but have different spelling and meanings.
>
> *Example*: **waist** and **waste** are homophones. **Waist** is the area around the centre of the body and **waste** means rubbish.

Word Bank

Homophone	Meaning
band	a group of musical instruments
banned	something that may not be used or done
caught	to catch (past tense)
court	a place where people are judged
lesson	learn something
lessen	to reduce or take away
great	important or big
grate	to shred
pact	an agreement
packed	storing things together in a container

Choose the correct homophone from the word bank to complete each sentence.

1. The farmer decided to _____ the weight on his truck.

2. When we make pizza, we _____ lots of cheese to put on top.

3. Before I left to go skiing, I _____ a woollen jumper.

4. He broke the law and had to appear in _____.

Match the homophones in the box with their meanings.

allowed / aloud	horse / hoarse
board / bored	cheep / cheap
cereal / serial	write / right

5. a voice that has become worn: _____

6. a plank of wood: _____

7. an item that costs little money: _____

8. a grain e.g. wheat: _____

9. correct: _____

TARGETING HOMEWORK 6 © PASCAL PRESS ISBN 9781925726480

AC9E6LE01, AC9E6LY05, AC9HS6K01, AC9HS6K03

Federation

Informative text – Report
Author – Nicholas Brasch

In 1788, Great Britain established the colony of New South Wales (NSW) in Australia. The colony was somewhere to send British prisoners. There was no thought that the colony would become an independent nation. Everything about the new colony was British.

It was not only the running of NSW that had its roots in Great Britain — so did just about every aspect of daily life. Christianity was the main religion, with Catholics and Protestants clashing with each other as they did back home. The colonists tried to grow the same crops they grew in England.

Soon other colonies were founded: Western Australia (1829), South Australia (1836), Victoria (1851), Tasmania (1856) and Queensland (1859).

In their early days, each colony was run by a governor. Later they formed their own governments who passed laws for each colony. While the laws had to be approved by the British Government, they did not have to be the same as those of the other colonies.

Source: *Federation*, Go Facts, Blake Education.

Write or circle the correct answers.

① **Why did Great Britain start the colony of NSW?**

_____

_____

② **What were the last two colonies to be founded in Australia?**

_____

_____

③ **What were the main two religions in the colony?**

_____

_____

④ **What does established mean in this text?**

a made

b built and created

c ordered

⑤ **The most important person in the colonies was the ...**

a farmer.

b builder.

c governor.

⑥ **The words independent nation say what Australia became when there was a federation of the colonies. Which sentence below says what this means?**

a The colonies decided to remain separate.

b A few colonies decided to join together to make a country.

c All of the colonies joined to form our country, Australia.

⑦ **Did people who were Catholic and Protestant get along in the new colony?**

a Yes   b No

Score 2 points for each correct answer!   SCORE **/14** (0-4) (6-10) (12-14)

My Book Review

Title _____

Author _____

Rating ☆☆☆☆☆

Comment _____

_____

Number & Algebra

AC9M6A03

Mental strategies

① Which pairs of numbers between 1 and 9 **inclusive** add up to 10?

Note: **inclusive** means include both 1 and 9. There are four such pairs, not counting 5 + 5.

_____

Circle the sets of **juxtaposed** numbers that add up to 10. There can be two or three numbers in a set. Find two sets of numbers in each row.

Note: **juxtaposed** means 'side-by-side'.

②	5	3	2	4	5	3	7	8	4	3	8	2	3	6
③	9	0	6	4	2	5	6	1	4	7	8	1	1	2
④	1	7	5	2	3	8	6	2	6	5	0	8	3	7
⑤	3	8	2	1	6	5	0	6	2	2	7	5	9	8
⑥	4	4	6	4	0	4	2	4	8	9	3	2	5	1
⑦	8	1	6	3	2	8	4	2	9	1	7	6	2	5
⑧	4	5	1	7	1	8	9	6	0	0	2	5	2	3
⑨	8	1	8	2	6	5	8	2	4	1	7	9	2	3
⑩	0	5	7	2	4	2	4	5	0	3	9	3	1	6
⑪	3	3	3	1	6	8	2	9	0	5	2	4	7	5
⑫	1	0	1	4	0	6	7	2	5	8	9	0	1	3
⑬	2	2	6	5	4	8	3	7	9	0	2	4	7	2
⑭	9	8	7	6	5	4	3	2	1	7	8	9	0	1

⑮ Which three sets of numbers between 1 and 9 inclusive add up to 10? _Hint_: there are four sets to choose from.

_____ _____ _____

Score 2 points for each correct answer!

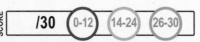

SCORE /30 (0-12) (14-24) (26-30)

Statistics & Probability

AC9M6P02

Chance experiments

Write or circle the correct answers.

① Scientists conducted a chance experiment called **X-Event**.
They did the experiment five times.
The result was positive three times.
What is the probability that the next result will be positive?

a $\frac{1}{5}$ c $\frac{5}{3}$

b $\frac{3}{5}$ d $\frac{1}{3}$

② How sure can the scientists be that their estimation of the probability of the next result is accurate?

a perfectly sure c fairly sure
b very sure d not sure

③ Scientists conducted the chance experiment **X-Event** 50 times.
The result was positive 40 times.
What is the probability that the next result will be positive?

a $\frac{1}{40}$ b $\frac{5}{4}$ c $\frac{4}{5}$ d $\frac{1}{50}$

④ Can the scientists be more confident of their estimation of the probability after Question 3 than they were after Question 1? Answer **yes** or **no** and say why.

_____

_____

⑤ How sure can the scientists be that their estimation of the **X-Event** probability is accurate now?

a perfectly sure c fairly sure
b very sure d not sure

⑥ Scientists conducted the chance experiment **X-Event** 1000 times.
The result was positive 800 times.
What is the probability that the next result will be positive?

a $\frac{1}{40}$ b $\frac{5}{4}$ c $\frac{4}{5}$ d $\frac{1}{50}$

⑦ Can the scientists be more confident of their estimation of the probability now than they were after Question 1? Answer **yes** or **no** and say why.

_____

_____

⑧ How sure can the scientists be that their estimation of the **X-Event** probability is accurate after 10 000 tries?

a perfectly sure c fairly sure
b very sure d not sure

Score 2 points for each correct answer!

SCORE /16 (0-6) (8-12) (14-16)

Measurement & Space

AC9M6M01

Equivalent measurements

Write or circle the correct answers.

1. How many metres in 3.5 km?

   a 350 m   c 35 000 m

   b 3.500 m   d 3500 m

2. How many centimetres in 3.5 metres?

   a 3.50 cm   c 3500.0 cm

   b 350 cm   d 3500 cm

3. How many millimetres in 6.5 centimetres?

   a 650 mm   c 65 mm

   b 60.5 mm   d 6500 mm

4. How many centimetres in 2.25 kilometres?

   a 225 cm   c 22 500 cm

   b 225 000 cm   d 2250 cm

5. How many millimetres in 1.5 metres?

   a 1500 mm   c 150 000 mm

   b 150 mm   d 15 000 mm

6. How many kilometres in 500 metres?

   a 5 km   c 0.005 km

   b 0.05 km   d 0.5 km

7. How many kilometres in 7250 metres?

   a 72.5 km   c 7.25 km

   b 7.205 km   d 7.025 km

8. Seventeen and a quarter kilometres is the same as which of the following?

   a 17.14 km   c 17.4 km

   b 17.25 km   d 17.025 km

9. Three and three quarters centimetres is the same as which of the following?

   a 3.75 cm   c 3.075 cm

   b 37.5 cm   d 3.705 cm

10. How many grams in 4.85 kilograms?

    a 485 g   c 48 500 g

    b 48.5 g   d 4850 g

11. How many milligrams in 1.55 kilograms?

    a 150.50 mg   c 155 000 mg

    b 1550 mg   d 1 550 000 mg

12. How many kilograms in 4736 grams?

    a 0.4736 kg   c 47.36 kg

    b 473.6 kg   d 4.736 kg

13. How many milligrams in 1.2 kilograms?

    a 120 000 mg   c 1 200 000 mg

    b 12 000 mg   d 120 000 000 mg

14. How many millilitres in 2.34 litres?

    a 2340 mL   c 234.0 mL

    b 234 mL   d 234 000 mL

15. How many millilitres in 1 cubic centimetre (1 cm^3)?

    a 10 mL   c 100 mL

    b 1 mL   d 1000 mL

Score 2 points for each correct answer!   SCORE /30   0-12   14-24   26-30

Problem Solving

AC9M6A03, AC9M6M01

Number and metric system problems

Circle the sets of **three** numbers that add up to 20. There could be more than one set in a row.

1	2	7	13	0	9	4	12	3	16	5	17
2	17	2	9	13	8	2	6	12	4	1	14
3	6	6	0	17	9	11	3	1	16	8	3
4	14	7	6	9	5	8	2	11	9	3	8
5	1	18	1	14	2	4	9	7	4	13	0

6. An ant walked straight across a sheet of paper, taking steps that were 0.5 mm long.

   It took the ant 400 steps to make the journey. Then it turned around and made the trip back.

   In total, how many centimetres did the ant walk?

   _____

7. A worker ant weighs 5 milligrams and it can lift 500 times its own weight. How much can the worker ant lift? Answer in grams.

   _____

8. Hans shared a 1 litre bottle of orange juice equally between himself and three of his friends. How much juice did each of them get? Answer in millilitres.

   _____

Grammar & Punctuation

AC9E6LA06

Adverbs

Adverbs tell **how**, **where**, **when** and **why** about the verb.

Example: **Yesterday**, Sarah watched **closely** as her dance teacher **quickly** showed her the next step.

①–⑦ **Circle the 7 adverbs in the box.**

loudly	quickly	rode
hear	tomorrow	secretly
cheerfully	speedily	now

Adverbial phrases

Adverbial phrases are a group of words that take the place of the adverb. Adverbial phrases tell about **when**, **where** and **how**.
Example:
I do all my homework **before dinner**.

Underline the adverbial phrase that tells you when things happened.

⑧ After lunch, Dan ran to join his friends on the basketball court.

⑨ Rabbits ran around the paddock during the night.

⑩ Lightning cracked directly above our heads during the fierce storm.

Underline the adverbial phrase that tells where something happened.

⑪ Monstrous squid live kilometres below the ocean surface.

⑫ Tigers in the zoo pace their cages from dawn until dusk.

⑬ We race around our town when our annual bicycle race is held.

Underline the adverbial phrase which tells how something happened.

⑭ The last swimmer pulled herself out of the water very slowly.

⑮ With great difficulty, the mountain climber climbed up the rock wall.

⑯ Riding very carefully, the girl nursed the tired horse home.

Phonic Knowledge & Spelling

AC9E6LY04, AC9E6LY09

Letter teams

Letter Teams have sounds that do not match the letters. These patterns are often at the end of the word.
Examples: informa**tion**, con**scious**, fa**cial**

–tion (says *shon*)	**–tient** (says *shunt*)
–tial (says *shall*)	**–cial** (says *shall*)
–scious (says *shus*)	**–ise** (says *ice*)
–ience (says *shens*)	

Use the Letter Teams in the box to finish the listed words.

① pa_____

② direc_____

③ parad_____

④ spe_____

Root words

English uses parts of words from other languages. These word parts help give the meaning of the words. They are called **root words**. *Examples:* **dent**al, **octo**gon, **bio**graphy

Word Bank

Root Word	Meaning	Example
denti	tooth	dentist
mono	one	monorail
hydro	water	hydroelectricity
geo	world	geography
oct	eight	octopus
bio	life	biology

Complete the words using the word roots from above.

⑤ When searching for rocks, the _____logist made an exciting discovery.

⑥ The clown showed great balance riding a _____cycle.

⑦ The _____logist found a new type of orchid in the rainforests of Queensland.

First Peoples

Informative text – Report
Author – Caroline Tate

First peoples are the **indigenous** peoples of the world. They are **descended** from the first people to live in their land.

There are more than 370 million indigenous people in the world, belonging to 5000 people groups, from every continent except Antarctica. They belong to thousands of nations or tribes, many with their own language and customs.

European nations sent ships all over the world between the 1400s and the 1700s. People from countries such as Great Britain, France, Spain and Portugal landed throughout Africa, **Oceania**, Asia and the Americas. They set up colonies and **penal settlements**. They took the land, food, gold and silver they found, usually by force. They introduced diseases that killed millions of indigenous people. They introduced their own customs and religion.

Indigenous peoples confronted the foreigners in their land. Many fought back. They lost their land and thousands died from conflict and disease.

Source: *First Peoples*, Go Facts, Blake Education.

Write or circle the correct answer.

① **What is the only continent to not have indigenous people?**

_____

② **What was brought to the continents that was harmful to the indigenous peoples?**

_____

③ **What does the phrase 'usually by force' mean in this text?**

a paying for gold and silver

b taking gold and silver using weapons

c stealing gold and silver

④ **What four things were taken from indigenous people?**

_____

_____

_____

_____

⑤ **Which four countries sent ships to these new lands?**

_____

_____

_____

⑥ **Which phrase explains what 'confronted the foreigners' means?**

a welcomed the foreigners

b hid from the foreigners

c fought the foreigners

⑦ **When did countries send ships all over the world?**

_____

⑧ **What does descended mean in the text?**

a related to

b to know

c to be friends with

Score 2 points for each correct answer!

SCORE /16   0-6   8-12   14-16

My Book Review

Title _____

Author _____

Rating ☆☆☆☆☆

Comment _____

_____

TERM 1 MATHS

Number & Algebra

AC9M6N01

Understanding integers

Use the number line at the right to answer the following questions.

- -8 • A
- -7 • B
- -6 • C
- -5 •
- -4 •
- -3 • D
- -2 • E
- -1 •
- 0 • F
- 1 •
- 2 • G
- 3 • H
- 4 •
- 5 • I
- 6 • J
- 7 • K
- 8 • L

① What is the midpoint of the number line? _____

② What are numbers with a minus sign in front of them called?

_____

③ What are numbers without a minus sign in front of them called?

_____

What is the difference between the two given points?

④ points F and H _____
⑤ points K and L _____
⑥ points G and K _____
⑦ points F and D _____
⑧ points F and C _____
⑨ points D and B _____
⑩ points E and I _____
⑪ points B and J _____
⑫ points A and L _____

⑬ What happens when two numbers with plus signs in front of them are combined?

   a They are multiplied.
   b They are added.
   c They are subtracted.
   d They are divided.

⑭ What happens when a number with a plus sign in front of it is combined with a number with a minus sign in front of it?

   a They are multiplied.
   b They are added.
   c They are subtracted.
   d They are divided.

⑮ What happens when two numbers with minus signs in front of them are combined?

   a They are multiplied.
   b They are added.
   c They are subtracted.
   d They are divided.

Statistics & Probability

AC9M6P01

Describing probabilities

Circle the correct answer.

① What is another way of saying that an event has a $\frac{1}{2}$ chance of occurring?

   a 1.2 chance   c 0.12 chance
   b 0.5 chance   d 2.1 chance

② What is another way of saying that an event has a three out of four chance of happening?

   a 50% chance.   c 43% chance.
   b 34% chance.   d 75% chance.

③ What is another way of saying that an event has a four out of five chance of occurring?

   a 0.8 chance   c 0.4 chance
   b 4.5 chance   d 8.0 chance

④ Which of these is the same as a 25% probability of an event happening?

   a a one in twenty-five probability
   b a two in five probability
   c a one in four probability
   d a twenty-five to one probability

⑤ Which of these is the same as a 0.4 probability of an event happening?

   a a one out of four probability
   b two in five probability
   c a zero in four probability
   d a two out of four probability

⑥ Which expression of probability is different to the others?

   a $\frac{1}{10}$ probability
   b a ten in one chance
   c 10% probability
   d 0.1 probability

⑦ Which expression of a chance event happening is different to the others?

   a $\frac{1}{5}$ chance
   b a one in five chance
   c 5% probability
   d 0.2 probability

Score 2 points for each correct answer!

SCORE /30   (0-12) (14-24) (26-30)

TARGETING HOMEWORK 6 © PASCAL PRESS ISBN 9781925726480

8 Which expression of a random event happening is different to the others?

a $\frac{5}{20}$ probability

b a one in four chance

c 25% chance

d 0.4 probability

Score 2 points for each correct answer! SCORE **/16** (0-6) (8-12) (14-16)

Measurement & Space

AC9M6M02

Comparing lengths and areas

Use these shapes to answer the following questions.

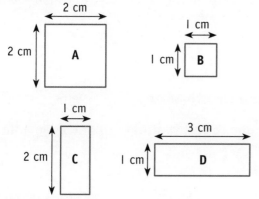

① Which shape has the smallest area? ____

② Which shape has the largest area? ____

③ Do any shapes have the same area?
a yes   b no

④ Which shape has the shortest perimeter? ___

⑤ Which two shapes have the longest perimeter? _____

⑥ Which shape has an area of 2 cm²? ____

⑦ Which shape has an area of 1 cm²? ____

⑧ What is the area of shape A? _____

⑨ What is the area of shape B? _____

⑩ Which shape has a perimeter of 4 cm? ____

⑪ Which shapes have a perimeter of 8 cm? _____

⑫ What is the perimeter of shape A? _____

⑬ What is the perimeter of shape C? _____

⑭ What is the sum of the perimeters of all the shapes?

_____

Score 2 points for each correct answer! SCORE **/28** (0-12) (14-22) (24-28)

Problem Solving

AC9M6N01, AC9M6P01

Number line and spinner problems

Use this number line to answer the following questions.

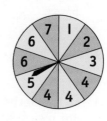

① Start at point B. Plus 4, minus 2. What number are you on?

_____

② Begin at point C. Add 4, subtract 6, add 2. What number are you on?

_____

③ Commence at point D. Subtract 6, plus 5, minus 9. What number are you on? _____

④ Enter at point A. Add 10, subtract 3, take away 5, plus 6. What number are you on?

_____

⑤ Start at point C. Go negative 7, positive 11, negative 3. What number are you on?

_____

⑥ Begin at point A. Go positive 4, repeat, repeat, negative 8.
How many steps must you move to reach zero? _____
Are the steps positive or negative?

_____

⑦ Enter at point D. Go positive 1, negative 9, positive 7. Repeat all the steps.
How many steps must you move to reach zero? _____
Are the steps positive or negative?

_____

Use this spinner to answer the following questions.

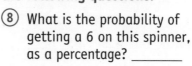

⑧ What is the probability of getting a 6 on this spinner, as a percentage? _____

⑨ What is the probability of getting a 5, as a decimal? _____

⑩ What is the probability of getting a 4, as a common fraction? _____

⑪ What is the probability of getting a 4 or a 6, as a percentage? _____

⑫ What is the probability of getting a 1, 2 or 3, as a decimal? _____

Grammar & Punctuation

AC9E6LA06

Verbs

Verbs tell what is 'going on' in a sentence. They tell us what people or things are doing, thinking and saying.
Example: Billy **rode** his bike home.
The same action can be described by many verbs.
Example: run – sprint, plod, race, jog

Choose a verb from the box to replace the bold verb.

| babble   plod   spotted   gazed |

① As the children moved to art class they began to **talk**.

_____

② Because it was old, the horse could only **walk**.

_____

③ Through his telescope he **saw** a new planet.

_____

④ We **looked** at the million stars in the night sky.

_____

Write the verb from the list into the correct space.

| weeping   giggle   yelling   running |

⑤ Will went _____ to see his football hero.

⑥ At the news of the terrible accident she began _____ .

⑦ People were _____ because their tickets could not be used.

⑧ She began to _____ at the comedy.

Match the verbs in the box with verbs of similar meaning.

| chase   cry   talk   grab |

⑨ follow   pursue   _____

⑩ natter   gabble   _____

⑪ grasp   grip   _____

⑫ weep   bawl   _____

Phonic Knowledge & Spelling

AC9E6LY09

Root words

Root words can help you understand the meaning of new words. For example, auto**graph** means to write your name.

Word Bank

Root	Meaning	Root	Meaning
graph	write	sub	under
mille	thousand	fore	before
centrum	one hundred	omni	all

Use the roots in the word bank to finish the words. Use the meanings as a clue.

① an animal that eats all types of food: _____vorous

② the lower part of the arm: _____arm

③ go under the water: _____merge

Write the correct root word from the box into the spaces.

| dict (say / tell)   tri (three)
| mit (let go / send) |

④ tell the future: pre_____

⑤ three-legged stand: _____pod

⑥ let the truth go: ad_____

Plurals

In words that end with **–f**, change the **f** to **v** and add **–es**. *Example:* loa**f** – loa**ves**

Make these words plural.

⑦ shelf   _____

⑧ roof   _____

⑨ scarf   _____

⑩ wolf   _____

Silent letters

Circle the silent letter in these words.

⑪ spaghetti

⑫ calm

⑬ lamb

⑭ soften

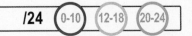

Indigenous Australian Peoples

Informative text – Report
Author – Caroline Tate

Aboriginal and Torres Strait Islander peoples (Indigenous Australians) lived in Australia for as many as 70 000 years before the British arrived.

British **colonisation** forced Indigenous Australians from their country and sources of food. Tens of thousands of Aboriginal people died fighting to keep what was theirs. Aboriginal and Torres Strait Islander culture suffered greatly. Families were separated. Without access to country and family, Indigenous Australians could not pass on their law and language.

Today, Indigenous Australians face many challenges. Compared to non-indigenous Australians, they are three times more likely to suffer **diabetes**. Their **life expectancy** is 10 years less than non-indigenous Australians. They are about half as likely to have a job as non-indigenous Australians.

Despite these challenges, Indigenous Australian culture — probably the oldest continuous culture on Earth — continues to thrive. Many Indigenous Australians live on their country. They manage how it is used and get income from it.

Source: *First Peoples*, Go Facts, Blake Education.

Write or circle the correct answer.

1. Who were the first people to live in Australia?

_____

2. What is the oldest culture in the world?

_____

3. What is one challenge that Indigenous Australians face today?

_____

_____

4. Where do many Indigenous Australians live?

_____

_____

5. What did British colonisation mean for Indigenous peoples?

    a They could not build their houses.

    b They found it hard to see each other.

    c They could not use their country to find food.

6. How many Aboriginal people died in fighting?

_____

7. What were two things Aboriginal and Torres Strait Islanders could not pass on?

_____

_____

8. What does 'continues to thrive' mean in the text?

    a Still happens and is going well.

    b Does not happen anymore.

    c Was happening and has started again.

Score 2 points for each correct answer!

SCORE /16 0-6 8-12 14-16

My Book Review

Title _____

Author _____

Rating ☆☆☆☆☆

Comment _____

_____

Number & Algebra

AC9M6N03

Comparing fractions with related denominators

Use these diagrams to answer the following questions.

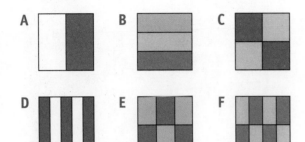

① Which statement about the way these shapes are coloured is totally correct?

a $A = \frac{1}{2}$, $B = \frac{1}{4}$, $C = \frac{1}{4}$, $D = \frac{1}{5}$

b $B = \frac{1}{3}$, $C = \frac{1}{2}$, $E = \frac{1}{6}$, $F = \frac{1}{8}$

c $A = \frac{1}{2}$, $C = \frac{1}{3}$, $D = \frac{1}{5}$, $E = \frac{1}{6}$

d $A = \frac{1}{2}$, $B = \frac{1}{3}$, $D = \frac{1}{5}$, $E = \frac{1}{6}$

Write the correct answers.

② How many parts of C are equal to one part of A?

_____

③ How many parts of F are equal to one part of A?

_____

④ How many parts of A are equal to five parts of D?

_____

⑤ How many parts of F are equal to two parts of C?

_____

⑥ How many parts of E are equal to two parts of B?

_____

Which is larger? Circle the correct answer.

⑦ a one part of A

  b two parts of D

⑧ a two parts of C

  b two parts of E plus one part of F

⑨ a one part of B?

  b three parts of F

Write <, > or = to make the statements true.

⑩ $\frac{3}{4}$ —— $\frac{6}{8}$ ⑬ $\frac{1}{4}$ —— $\frac{2}{5}$

⑪ $\frac{4}{5}$ —— $\frac{2}{2}$ ⑭ $\frac{4}{5}$ —— $\frac{2}{3}$

⑫ $\frac{2}{3}$ —— $\frac{4}{6}$

Score 2 points for each correct answer! SCORE **/28** (0-12) (14-22) (24-28)

Statistics & Probability

AC9M6P01

Games of chance

The Plains Cree people in North America play a game called **Kutepuchkunuputuk**. They get an odd number of sticks. In secret, one player puts the sticks in two groups so that one group has one stick more than the other group. The other player looks at the two groups and guesses which has more sticks.

Write or circle the correct answers.

① Is Kutepuchkunuputuk entirely a game of chance?

  a yes   b no

② Could the eyesight of the players affect the outcome of the game?

  a yes   b no

③ If Kutepuchkunuputuk was entirely a game of chance, the second player has a 0.5 chance of guessing correctly.

  What is this probability as a fraction?

_____

④ To win Kutepuchkunuputuk, a player has to guess correctly four times in a row.

  If they were playing entirely by chance, what chance does a player have of winning?

  a $\frac{1}{4}$ b $\frac{1}{8}$ c $\frac{1}{16}$ d $\frac{1}{20}$

⑤ If a player makes two correct consecutive guesses, what is that player's chance then?

  a 20%   b 25%   c 40%   d 45%

⑥ If a player makes three correct consecutive guesses, what is their chance then?

  a 0.333   b 0.125   c 0.103   d 0.03

Score 2 points for each correct answer! SCORE **/12** (0-4) (6-8) (10-12)

TARGETING HOMEWORK 6 © PASCAL PRESS ISBN 9781925726480

Measurement & Space

AC9M6M01

Converting metric units

The following table shows conversions for some units of length.

Some spaces have been shaded grey because the values are too large or too small to be useful for this activity.

Fill in the spaces numbered from 1 to 8.

Millimetres (mm)	Centimetres (cm)	Metres (m)	Kilometres (km)
100	10	①	
5	②	0.005	
③	3	0.03	
25	2.5	④	
⑤	400	4	0.004
5250	⑥	5.25	0.005 25
	200 000	2000	⑦
	125 000	1250	⑧

The following table shows conversions for some units of mass (weight).

Some spaces have been shaded grey because the values are too large or too small to be useful for this activity.

Fill in the spaces numbered from 9 to 15.

Milligrams (mg)	Grams (g)	Kilograms (kg)	Tonnes (t)
25	⑨		
⑩	5	0.005	
1300	1.3	⑪	
10 000 000	⑫	10	0.01
50 000 000	50 000	50	⑬
	1 000 000	⑭	1
		1200	⑮

Problem Solving

UNIT 4

AC9M6N03, AC9M6P01

Fraction problems

Use this rod to answer the following questions.

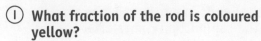

① **What fraction of the rod is coloured yellow?**

  a $\frac{2}{12}$ b $\frac{1}{2}$ c $\frac{6}{24}$ d $\frac{2}{24}$

② **What fraction of the rod is coloured blue?**

  a $\frac{1}{4}$ b $\frac{2}{12}$ c $\frac{6}{12}$ d $\frac{2}{24}$

③ **What fraction of the rod is coloured red?**

  a $\frac{1}{4}$ b $\frac{1}{3}$ c $\frac{3}{21}$ d $\frac{1}{8}$

④ **What fraction of the rod is coloured green?**

  a $\frac{1}{9}$ b $\frac{3}{12}$ c $\frac{3}{9}$ d $\frac{1}{8}$

⑤ **What fraction of the rod is coloured white?**

  a $\frac{1}{12}$ b $\frac{1}{24}$ c $\frac{1}{1}$ d 1

⑥ **Which two colours combined make up half of the rod?**

_____

⑦ **Which three colours combined make up half of the rod?**

_____

⑧ **Which two colours combined make up $\frac{1}{6}$ of the rod?**

_____

Write the correct answers.

⑨ A teacher had five different coloured pieces of paper. She told Samuel to close his eyes while she held up one of the papers.

What chance did Samuel have of guessing the right colour? Answer as a fraction.

_____

⑩ If Samuel was wrong and the teacher asked him to guess again, what chance did he have then? Answer as a decimal.

_____

⑪ How many guesses would Samuel have to make before he could be certain that he would get it right on his next guess?

_____

Score 2 points for each correct answer!

SCORE /30   0-12   14-24   26-30

Grammar & Punctuation

AC9E6LA05, AC9E6LA06

TERM 1 ENGLISH

Conjunctions in compound sentences

> A compound sentence has two **main clauses**. The two clauses are joined with a **conjunction**: so, and, but, for, or, nor, yet.

Write the words in brackets in the correct order. The conjunction comes after the comma.

① Ali loves his skateboard, _____ not allowed to ride it on the road.
(he is **but**)

② We can go and watch a movie, _____ go out and have dinner.
(can we **or**)

③ They happily pulled up the boat anchor, _____ didn't catch any fish on that trip. (they **yet**)

Choose a conjunction from the box to complete each sentence.

> nor   or   but   yet

④ Oscar waited for the plane at the airport, _____ his flight was very late.

⑤ Matt doesn't like playing soccer, _____ does he like cricket.

⑥ Rock climbing can be a dangerous sport, _____ people still do it.

⑦ Jemma has to score this goal, _____ her team won't get into the finals.

Circle the correct conjunction.

⑧ Sheri always trained hard at swimming (yet   so) she had not been rewarded.

⑨ I dislike free diving, (nor   but) I would like to try diving with a scuba tank.

⑩ We have to learn first aid (for   so) we don't know when this skill might be needed.

⑪ She had the voice of an angel, (but   so) of course she got the lead role in the musical.

Phonic Knowledge & Spelling

AC9E6IY09

Synonyms

> **Synonyms** are words which have the same or a similar meaning. Some words have many synonyms. Synonyms can help make our writing more interesting and expressive.
> *Example*: old – aged, ancient, vulnerable

Word Bank

Common word	Synonyms		
do	achieve	effect	finish
have	hold	own	possess
get	gain	obtain	gather
put	place	set	attach
take	remove	seize	grasp

Find the synonym in each sentence. Then find the matching common word in the word bank and write it in the space.

① The gold miner wanted to possess a piece of gold. _____

② We needed to obtain a passport for our trip. _____

③ Do not remove sand from the beach. _____

④ People were asked to place their jewellery in the box. _____

Antonyms

> **Antonyms** are words which are opposite in meaning to each other.
> *Example*: big – small, tiny, minute

Match the words in the box with their antonyms.

> cheap   cheerful   cruel   absent
> arrive   calm   combine   bent

⑤ sad   _____
⑥ kind   _____
⑦ windy   _____
⑧ depart   _____
⑨ expensive _____
⑩ straight   _____
⑪ present   _____
⑫ separate   _____

Score 2 points for each correct answer! **SCORE** **/22** (0-8) (10-16) (18-22)

Score 2 points for each correct answer! **SCORE** **/24** (0-10) (12-18) (20-24)

TARGETING HOMEWORK 6 © PASCAL PRESS ISBN 9781925726480

AC9E6LA02, AC9E6LA08, AC9E6LY03, AC9E6LY04, AC9E6LY05

Should Zoos Take Gorillas out of their Natural Environments?

Persuasive text – Discussion
Author – Merryn Whitfield

There are three subspecies of gorillas living in Africa — the western lowland, eastern lowland and mountain — and all are endangered. To ensure their continued existence, it is important for us to take action. Many zoos which conduct gorilla-breeding programs use the gorillas they already hold in captivity. This might sound like a good idea, but is zoo breeding the only way to guarantee their survival?

Unfortunately, one of the main problems facing gorillas is that the species has a slow rate of reproduction. In 1995, a cooperative project between two zoos using in vitro fertilisation and embryo transfer resulted in the birth of a lowland gorilla baby. While one birth may not seem important, if more gorillas were kept in zoos, scientists could improve these techniques to hopefully increase the rate of reproduction even in the wild.

One significant advantage of working with captive gorillas is the increase in their life span. In the wild it is only 30–40 years, whereas under the nurturing care of zookeepers a gorilla can live to the ripe old age of 60! As zoos continue to research these primates, knowledge of their ideal living conditions will improve and it is expected that gorillas' life spans will increase further.

On the other hand, animal activists claim that taking a gorilla out of its natural environment means that their diet will be altered. Gorillas are mainly herbivorous and eat 200 types of leaves, funghi, fruits and even some insects. While replicating this range of food in a zoo is almost impossible, it is also quite unnecessary. You and I are able to eat a wide range of foods but we don't need to eat all of them all of the time to stay happy and healthy.

So it appears that while zoos cannot reproduce the natural environment of gorillas, it is essential that at least some are kept in captivity so that they continue to breed and so that the species continues to exist past our own generation.

Source: *Writing Centres: Persuasive Texts*, Upper Primary, Blake Education.

Write or circle the correct answer.

① **What are the three subspecies of gorilla living in Africa?**

_____

_____

_____

② **What is one of the main problems facing gorillas?**

_____

_____

③ **What advantage is there in keeping gorillas in captivity?**

_____

_____

_____

④ **How long can gorillas live in captivity?**

_____

⑤ **What does herbivorous mean?**
   a only eats insects
   b eats insects and plants
   c only eats plants

⑥ **Replicate means to …**
   a copy something.
   b change something.
   c create something.

⑦ **This text suggests that gorillas are better off in the wild.**
   a True   b False

My Book Review

Title _____

Author _____

Rating ☆☆☆☆☆

Comment _____

_____

Score 2 points for each correct answer!   SCORE   **/14**   (0-4) (6-10) (12-14)

Number & Algebra

AC9M6N03

Comparing fractions

Use the fractions number line at the right to answer the following questions.

0	A
$\frac{1}{4}$	B
$\frac{1}{2}$	C
$\frac{3}{4}$	D
1	E
$1\frac{1}{4}$	F
$1\frac{1}{2}$	G
$1\frac{3}{4}$	H
2	I
$2\frac{1}{4}$	J
$2\frac{1}{2}$	K
$2\frac{3}{4}$	L
3	M
$3\frac{1}{4}$	N
$3\frac{1}{2}$	O
$3\frac{3}{4}$	P
4	Q

① Which point is $1\frac{1}{2}$ more than point D on the number line?

_____

② Which point is $1\frac{1}{2}$ less than point M?

_____

③ How much more than point F is point L?

_____

④ How much less than point G is point C?

_____

⑤ If point C was added on to point E, which point would they land on?

_____

⑥ If point D was subtracted from point K, which point would they land on?

_____

⑦ How far apart are points F and L?

_____

⑧ Which two points are $1\frac{3}{4}$ removed from point I?

_____

⑨ Which point is halfway between points D and L?

_____

⑩ Which point is at the three-quarter mark between points F and J?

_____

⑪ Which point is $2\frac{3}{4}$ more than point D?

_____

⑫ Which point is $2\frac{3}{4}$ less than point L?

_____

⑬ How much more than point F is point O?

_____

⑭ How much less than point N is point C?

_____

⑮ What point is three times more than point D?

_____

Statistics & Probability

AC9M6P01

Comparing the probability of events

Label the events in order from 1 (**most likely** to happen) to 4 (**least** likely to happen).

① a ☐ Humans will one day land on Mars.

b ☐ Humans will one day land on the moon again.

c ☐ Humans will one day vacation on Mars.

d ☐ Humans will turn Mars into a jungle.

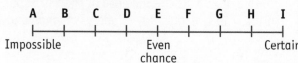

② a ☐ Aliens from another planet are secretly in control of the Earth.

b ☐ There are aliens from another planet observing us.

c ☐ Movies about aliens will always be popular with some people.

d ☐ Aliens from other planets will come to Earth one day.

Use this **probability scale** to answer the following questions.

```
    A   B   C   D   E   F   G   H   I
    |---|---|---|---|---|---|---|---|
Impossible          Even           Certain
                   chance
```

What points along the **probability scale** would these events be? Write the matching letters in the boxes.

③ ☐ Next winter, it's going to rain four days in a row, three times.

④ ☐ Next summer, there are going to be at least four days of 40 °C or higher.

⑤ ☐ Next spring, no roses will bloom.

⑥ ☐ Next autumn, most deciduous trees will lose their leaves.

⑦ ☐ Next summer, there are going to be eight consecutive days of 40 °C or higher.

⑧ ☐ Next winter, it's going to rain at least ten days in a row, three times.

⑨ ☐ Late next spring, it's going to be hot enough to go swimming.

⑩ If this probability scale was a fractional probability scale, what fraction would be at the **even chance** point?

_____

Score 2 points for each correct answer!   SCORE **/30** (0-12) (14-24) (26-30)

TARGETING HOMEWORK 6 © PASCAL PRESS ISBN 9781925726480

⑪ If this probability scale was a percentage probability scale, what percentage would be at point C?

_____

Score 2 points for each correct answer!

Measurement & Space

AC9M6M01

Converting metric units

The following table shows conversions for some units of volume.

Some spaces have been shaded grey because the values are too large or too small to be useful for this activity.

Fill in the spaces numbered from 1 to 7.

Millilitres (mL)	Litres (L)	Kilolitres (kL)	Megalitres (ML)
100	①	0.000 01	
1000	1	②	
③	20	0.02	0.000 02
80 000	80	④	0.000 08
	⑤	10	0.01
	1 000 000	1000	⑥
	500 000	⑦	0.5

Write the correct answers.

⑧ How many centimetres are in two and a half metres? _____

⑨ How many millimetres are in one and a quarter centimetres? _____

⑩ How many metres are in five and three-quarters kilometres? _____

⑪ How many kilometres are in ten thousand and sixty-five metres?

_____

⑫ How many milligrams are in one and a quarter grams? _____

⑬ How many grams are in two and a fifth kilograms? _____

⑭ How many kilograms are in half a tonne?

_____

Score 2 points for each correct answer!

Problem Solving

UNIT **5**

AC9M6M01, AC9M6P01

Probability and metric unit problems

Circle the correct answers.

① Jim had 80 baseball cards that he wanted to divide equally among his four friends. What fraction of the cards would he give to each of them?

a $\frac{1}{80}$ b $\frac{1}{8}$ c $\frac{1}{4}$ d $\frac{1}{12}$

② Jim changed his mind and thought he'd give his best friend, Habib, twice as many cards as each of the other three friends. What fraction of his cards would Jim give Habib?

a $\frac{2}{4}$ b $\frac{2}{3}$ c $\frac{2}{1}$ d $\frac{2}{5}$

③ On reflection, Jim decided he'd rather give Habib three times as many cards as each of the other three friends. What fraction of his cards would Jim give Habib?

a $\frac{1}{2}$ b $\frac{5}{3}$ c $\frac{3}{4}$ d $\frac{4}{2}$

④ Finally Jim gave Habib half of his cards and he shared the rest equally among his other three friends. What fraction of what was left of the cards after Habib had received his did each of Jim's other three friends get?

a $\frac{1}{4}$ b $\frac{3}{4}$ c $\frac{1}{3}$ d $\frac{2}{3}$

⑤ In question 4, what fraction of the original total number of cards did each of Jim's other three friends get?

a $\frac{1}{3}$ b $\frac{1}{4}$ c $\frac{1}{5}$ d $\frac{1}{6}$

Write the correct answers to these metric unit problems.

⑥ A flea moved five centimetres with each hop. At that rate, how many hops would it need to cover one metre?

_____

⑦ A kangaroo moved 10 metres with each jump. At that rate, how many jumps would it need to cover half a kilometre?

_____

⑧ A cat swallowed 10 millilitres of milk each time it lapped at its bowl. At that rate, how many laps would it need to lap up a quarter of a litre of milk?

_____

⑨ A lion swallowed 50 millilitres of water each time it lapped water out of a river. At that rate, how many laps would it need to lap up two litres of water?

_____

Grammar & Punctuation

AC9E6LA05

Conjunctions

Conjunctions are words that join ideas in sentences.

They can join words that are the same. *Example:* rain **or** shine

They can join phrases. *Example:* Emily ran down the bank **and** into the river.

They can also join simple sentences to make compound sentences. *Example:* It's starting to rain, **so** I'll go home now.

Other **conjunctions** can link a subordinate clause with the main clause in complex sentences. *Example:* I'll stay here **until** my parents pick me up.

Choose conjunctions from the box to complete the sentences. The first letter has been given.

after	because	although	and
before	as	but	if
once	then	though	therefore
until	unless	where	whenever
when	wherever	while	whilst

① B_____ she slept in, Abbey was late for the bus.

② All seemed calm u_____ the lightning began.

③ We looked at the swans w_____ we waited for the bus.

④ Eve was invited to the party, b_____ she couldn't go.

⑤ O_____ we had had our lunch at the fair, we visited the horror house.

⑥ There was little rain this year, t_____ farmers planted fewer crops.

Use the conjunctions in the box to complete the sentences.

although	before	unless	while

⑦ _____ the bike race is dangerous, we will let you compete.

⑧ Come to the forest centre _____ you are visiting the area.

⑨ You can't do the mountain climb _____ you have trained first.

⑩ Amy was taken to the doctor _____ her cough got any worse.

Phonic Knowledge & Spelling

AC9E6LY09

Spelling with ie and ei

The rule **i before e except after c** is only when there is the sound of **ee** in the word (the sound in tr**ee**). *Example:* rec**ei**ve

In some words where the **ie** has a **long e sound** the **i** is usually before the **e**. *Example:* f**ie**ld

Add ie or ei to finish the words below.

① bel____ve

② th____f

③ c____ling

④ rec____pt

⑤ ach____ve

⑥ ch____f

Spelling with g

When **g** is followed by the letters **e** or **i**, it has a **j** sound. *Examples:* jud**ge**, **gi**ant

Write the words below with i or e.
Example: judg__   judge

⑦ stag__   _____

⑧ g__nger   _____

⑨ languag__   _____

⑩ allerg__c   _____

Silent letters

Some words have silent letters that are not heard when said aloud.
Examples: clim**b**, mus**c**le

Circle the silent letters.

⑪ knight   ⑬ salmon

⑫ gnaw   ⑭ edge

Match the antonyms in the box to the correct sentences.

crooked	complex	innocent

⑮ Mathematics is quite **simple** really.

_____

⑯ Every line she marked was **straight**.

_____

⑰ In court the criminal was found **guilty**.

_____

Prissy

Imaginative text – Narrative
Author – Peter Alford, **Illustrator** – Paul Lennon

Prissy could be the loveliest, sweetest and best mannered girl. For people who didn't matter or were not important, she had a razor tongue and spat venom. 'How lovely you look', 'Thank you so much', 'You are so kind', 'You are wonderful', 'You are so clever', 'What an amazing person you are' — all phrases she slimily aimed at adults. 'Get out of my way', 'Idiot', 'You're dumb' and 'Stupid person' were comments thrown at everyone else.

Being new to the school, Meg was trying so hard to be liked. She was very lonely. Perhaps she was trying too hard. Little witches needed to make friends because they had so many enemies. Meg hadn't learnt to change form, so she was stuck with peculiar birds' nest hair and long bony witch fingers. She

definitely looked different to every other student which made finding friends really difficult.

"Hello, can I play with you?" Meg asked Prissy.

"Go away, you horrid thing," was the reply from Prissy. Meg trudged off, more than a little hurt.

Prissy saw the principal and thought that she needed to win her attention.

"Good mor ...," was all she managed before a stream of green, slimy goop spewed from her mouth, covering the startled principal from head to toe. All that mess caused by one tiny, magical wink that no-one had noticed.

Write or circle the correct answer.

1. **What does 'she had a razor tongue and spat venom' say about Prissy?**

    a She was nice to everyone.

    b She spoke nastily.

    c She was kind to some people.

2. **What does 'change form' mean?**

    a change her body

    b change classes

    c perform

3. **Which two words tell you that Meg was perhaps able to place a spell on someone?**

    _____

4. **What does the phrase 'win her attention' mean?**

    a play a game with her

    b be her friend

    c make sure she was seen and heard

5. **What sentence says that Meg was upset with Prissy?**

    _____

    _____

    _____

6. **Why was Meg trying hard to make friends at her new school?**

    _____

    _____

7. **What does 'slimily aimed at adults' say about Prissy's behaviour with adults.**

    a She was overly nice to adults.

    b She slimed adults.

    c She was kind to adults.

8. **Which phrase tells you why Meg found it difficult to find friends?**

    _____

Score 2 points for each correct answer!   SCORE **/16** (0-6) (8-12) (14-16)

My Book Review

Title _____

Author _____

Rating ☆☆☆☆☆

Comment _____

_____

Number & Algebra

AC9M6N09

Solving everyday addition problems

Use the number line at the right to answer the following questions.

If the answer is in between two points, write both points as the answer.

Example: if the answer is **30**, write **C/D**.

① What point is at 15 + 90? _____

② What point is at 15 + 35? _____

③ What point is at 125 – 20? _____

④ What point is at 15 + 30 + 45?

_____

⑤ What point is at 140 – 45? _____

⑥ What point is at 75 – 35 + 25 – 5?

_____

⑦ What point is at $55 + $20 + $45 – $20? _____

⑧ What point is at 155 km – 35 km – 40 km + 75 km? _____

⑨ What point is at 0 mL + 40 mL – 25 mL + 65 mL – 60 mL? _____

⑩ What point is 35 × 2? _____

⑪ What point is at 15 × 4? _____

⑫ What point is halfway between 60 and 100? _____

⑬ What point is halfway between 45 and 95?

_____

⑭ What point is a third of the way between 20 and 80? _____

⑮ What point is a third of the way between 75 and 90? _____

Number line:
```
10  A
20  B
    C
30  D
40  E
50  F
60  G
70  H
80  I
90  J
100 K
110 L
120 M
130 N
140 O
150 P
160 Q
```

Score 2 points for each correct answer! **SCORE /30** (0-12) (14-24) (26-30)

Statistics & Probability

AC9M6P01

Investigating likely and surprising outcomes

Circle the correct answers.

① **Which of these would be the most surprising event?**

a a dog crossing a road

b a car stopped at a traffic light

c an elephant in your garden

d an emu at the zoo

② **Which of these is a likely event?**

a a horse wearing a tutu

b a traffic light turning green

c a giraffe climbing a ladder

d a person chopping down a flagpole

③ **Which of these would be the most surprising event?**

a a horse stopped at a traffic light

b a traffic light turning red

c a giraffe wearing an Easter bonnet

d a person eating rabbit stew

④ **Which of these would be the most likely event?**

a a police officer chasing a criminal

b a doctor seeing a patient

c a firefighter visiting the school

d a fashion model eating two large pizzas

⑤ **Write the numbers 1 to 4 to rank the events in question 1 from most likely (1) to least likely (4).**

a ___   b ___   c ___   d ___

⑥ **Write the numbers 1 to 4 to rank the events in question 2 from most surprising (1) to least surprising (4).**

a ___   b ___   c ___   d ___

⑦ **Write the numbers 1 to 4 to rank the events in question 3 from common (1) to unusual (4).**

a ___   b ___   c ___   d ___

⑧ **Write the numbers 1 to 4 to rank the events in question 4 from rarely (1) to everyday (4).**

a ___   b ___   c ___   d ___

Use this spinner to answer the following questions.

Orani spun the spinner 120 times and recorded her results.

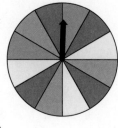

⑨ Which two colours were most likely spun the same number of times?

_____   _____

⑩ Which colour was most likely spun forty times?

_____

   TARGETING HOMEWORK 6 © PASCAL PRESS ISBN 9781925726480

(11) Which two colours combined were most likely spun half the times?

____

(12) Was red **not likely**, **likely** or **positively** spun 40 times?

____

Score 2 points for each correct answer! SCORE /24 0-10 12-18 20-24

Measurement & Space

AC9M6M01

Equivalent measurements

Are these correct? Write Y (yes) or N (no).

(1) 125 cm = 12.5 m ☐
(2) 1 000 000 g = 1 t ☐
(3) 10 001 m = 100.01 km ☐
(4) 2809 mm = 28.09 m ☐
(5) 9001 mm = 900.1 cm ☐
(6) 9001 mm = 90.01 cm ☐
(7) 125 cm = 1.25 m ☐
(8) 5 cm = 50 mm ☐
(9) 5 cm = 500 mm ☐
(10) 202 m = 20 200 cm ☐
(11) 202 m = 2020 cm ☐
(12) 1 000 000 g = 20 t ☐
(13) 100 km = 10 000 m ☐
(14) 602 mL = 0.602 L ☐
(15) 10 000 kg = 1 t ☐
(16) 1100 L = 1.1 kL ☐
(17) 4004 mg = 40.04 g ☐
(18) 1100 L = 0.11 kL ☐
(19) 4004 mg = 4.004 g ☐
(20) 6543 g = 6.543 kg ☐
(21) 6543 g = 654.3 kg ☐
(22) 0.007 kg = 7 g ☐
(23) 0.007 kg = 70 g ☐
(24) 10 000 kg = 10 t ☐
(25) 1000 kg = 10 t ☐
(26) 1 t = 1000 kg ☐

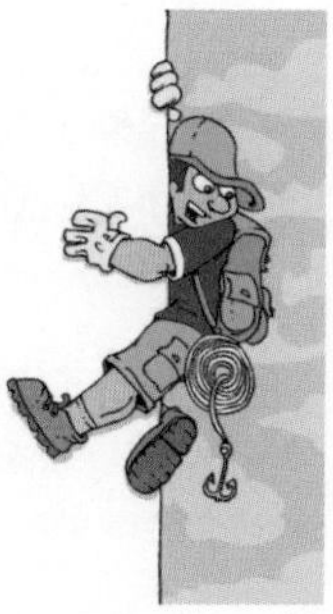

Score 2 points for each correct answer! SCORE /52 0-24 26-46 48-52

Problem Solving

AC9M6M01

Number line and volume problems

Use the number line at the right to answer the following questions.

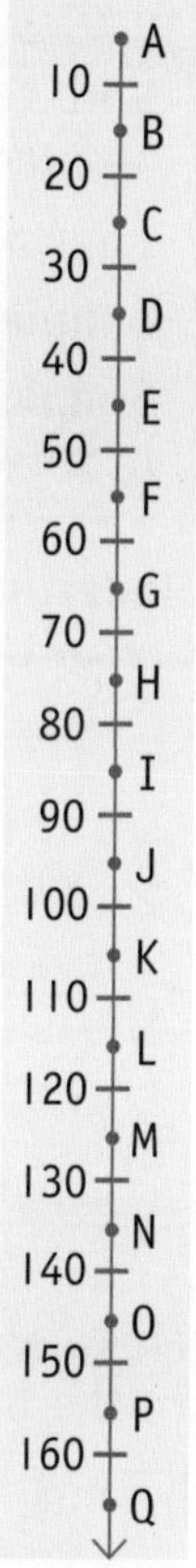

A
10
B
20
C
30
D
40
E
50
F
60
G
70
H
80
I
90
J
100
K
110
L
120
M
130
N
140
O
150
P
160
Q

(1) Phillip lived a distance in kilometres from Aiko that is equal to the space between points G and E. How far was that?

____

(2) Aiko lived a distance in kilometres from Haima that is equal to the space between points P and I. How far was that?

____

(3) What is the difference in kilometres between Phillip's distance from Aiko and Haima's distance from Aiko?

____

(4) If Aiko walked only half the distance between her house and Phillip's, what two points could she end up on if she started at point D?

____

Use this list of acids to answer the following questions. Write the letters of the acids.

A 105 mL maleic acid
B 250 mL fumaric acid
C 425 mL hydrofluoric acid
D 150 mL nicotinic acid
E 75 mL adipic acid
F 280 mL tannic acid

(5) Which three acids combined make 680 mL?

____

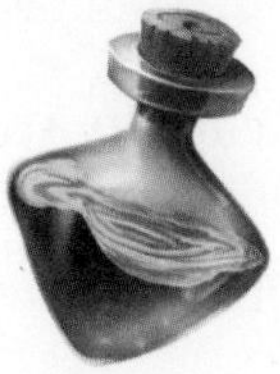

(6) Of which acid is there a quarter of a litre?

____

(7) Which acid is half as much as nicotinic acid?

____

(8) Which two acids combined make half a litre?

____

(9) Which two acids combined make 30 mL more than half a litre?

____

(10) If a chemist combined all the maleic acid and adipic acid and a third of the mixture evaporated, how much would be left?

____

UNIT 7

Grammar & Punctuation

AC9E6LA06

Verb tenses: simple present and past

> **Verb tenses** tell us **when** an action happened — present or past.
> *Examples*:
> **Simple present tense:** We **swim** at the creek.
> **Simple past tense:** Two weeks ago, we **swam** at the creek.

Underline the verb in each sentence and write present or past in the space.

① She dived in the competition.
_____

② Jenna always sleeps during the news.
_____

③ The group made the largest sandcastle in the world. _____

④ It's quite a gift that he sings so beautifully.
_____

Make each sentence past tense using a word in the box.

rode	fought	slept	told

⑤ In the past, stockmen _____ horses when droving stock.

⑥ During the war, brave soldiers _____ to keep us free.

⑦ Billy _____ the story of his narrow escape last week.

⑧ Years ago, people _____ on their verandas in summer.

Read the story and write either present or past next to the numbered verbs.

Our adventure holiday was amazing! We swam (9)_____ with dolphins and we dived (10)_____ off a bridge 80 metres high for a bungee jump. Each night we slept (11)_____ in tents in the jungle. We made (12)_____ our own breakfast each morning and at night we ate some amazing food. Now that we are back, I tell (13)_____ all my friends about the fantastic time I had. Some of my friends say (14)_____ they are signing up. We know (15)_____ the trip is well worth the money.

Phonic Knowledge & Spelling

AC9E6LY09

Contractions

> A **contraction** is when two words are shortened and combined to make one word. An **apostrophe (')** is used in place of the missing letter/s.
> *Examples:* do not – **don't**, I am – **I'm**

Write the full words for the contractions in the sentence. Use words from the box.

we had	who had	when is	we have

① We'd best be leaving, we might be late.
_____

② When's the bus arriving from swimming?
_____

③ We've had a great time in the park.
_____

④ Who'd been standing at that desk?
_____

Letter teams –tious, –cious

> Some **letter teams** have the same sound but different spelling. The sound at the end of a word ending in –tious or –cious says *shus*.

⑤–⑧ **Circle the 4 words that end in a *shus* sound.**

a delicious   d spacious
b cautious   e suspicious
c tremendous   f fabulous

Choose the aw/or sounds from the box to complete the words.

our	all	au	or

⑨ Harry loves playing indoor football in the h_____.

⑩ After the band played, the _____**dience** clapped for ages.

⑪ In ancient Rome, people did not use a f_____k to eat their food.

⑫ P_____**ing** the gold into its mould was very hot work.

⑬–⑭ **Underline the 2 compound words and then split them with a /.**
Example: post/man

a witchcraft   c wireless
b delightful   d rainbow

TERM 1 ENGLISH

Nova Peris

Informative text – Report
Author – Lisa Nicol, **Photographer:** David Munoz/AAP

Nova Peris has many firsts to her name and is a passionate spokeswoman for Indigenous peoples.

Born in Darwin, Nova Peris showed great athletic ability from an early age. She excelled at every sport, including touch football, swimming and cricket. On Saturdays, she ran at **Little Athletics** meetings and dreamed of one day running at the Olympic Games.

Peris also began playing hockey. She moved to Perth in 1992 to join the hockey program at the Western Australian Institute of Sport. By this time, Peris had a child. She juggled work, training and bringing up her daughter by herself.

Peris was selected for the national hockey team, the Hockeyroos. At the 1996 Atlanta Olympic Games, the Hockeyroos beat South Korea in the final. Peris became the first Indigenous Australian to win an Olympic gold medal.

Source: *Great Indigenous Australians*, Go Facts, Blake Education.

Write or circle the correct answer.

1. Where did Nova Peris move to to be part of a hockey program?

_____

2. How many Indigenous people had won a gold medal before 1996?

   a ten   b two   c none

3. What were 3 sports in which Nova Peris showed her excellence?

_____

_____

4. What does it mean, Nova Peris 'juggled work, training and bringing up her daughter'?

   a Nova Peris was able to juggle babies.

   b Nova Peris was able to give time to all of these things.

   c Nova Peris could take her daughter with her when working.

5. Where did Nova Peris win her first gold medal?

6. What native animal has part of its name in the name Hockeyroos?

   a wombat   b koala   c kangaroo

7. What was Nova Peris' dream as a child in Darwin?

_____

_____

8. What does **Little Athletics** probably mean?

   a athletics for small people

   b athletics for small children

   c athletics for adults to take part in

Score 2 points for each correct answer!

SCORE /16 0-6   8-12   14-16

My Book Review

Title _____

Author _____

Rating ☆☆☆☆☆

Comment _____

_____

Number & Algebra

AC9M6N02

Composite numbers and prime factors

① Which set is not made up only of prime numbers? Circle the correct answer.

a {1, 2, 3, 5, 7, 11, 13, 17.}

b {13, 17, 19, 23, 29, 31, 37, 41.}

c {17, 19, 23, 29, 31, 37, 41, 43.}

d {31, 37, 41, 43, 47, 53, 59, 61, 67.}

Write or circle the correct answers.

② Which is the nearest prime number to 84? _____

③ Which two prime numbers are adjacent to 43? _____, _____

④ What composite number is made up by the multiplication of 2, 3 and 2? _____

⑤ What composite number is made up by the multiplication of 3, 3 and 11? _____

⑥ What are the prime factors of 6?

a 6   b 1, 6   c 2, 3   d 23

⑦ What are the prime factors of 8?

b 2   b 2, 2, 2   c 2, 4   d 2, 3, 3

⑧ What are the prime factors of 24? (*Hint*: first think of 2 × 12 = 24.) _____

⑨ What are the prime factors of 30? (*Hint*: first think of 3 × 10 = 30.) _____

⑩ What are the prime factors of 28? (*Hint*: first think of 4 × 7 = 28.) _____

⑪ What are the prime factors of 40? (*Hint*: first think of 4 × 10 = 40.) _____

⑫ What are the prime factors of 81? (*Hint*: first think of 9 × 9 = 81.) _____

⑬ What are the prime factors of 180? (*Hint*: first think of 18 × 10 = 180 and then 2 × 9 × 10 = 180) _____

Write yes or no.

⑭ Can two prime numbers multiplied together equal an even number? _____

⑮ Can two prime numbers multiplied together equal an odd number? _____

⑯ Can two prime numbers multiplied together equal a prime number? _____

Statistics & Probability

AC9M6ST01

Interpreting data displays

These graphs show the number of times that the same three people were bitten by different creatures. Use the graphs to answer the following questions.

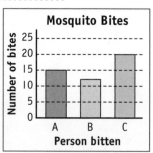
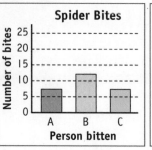
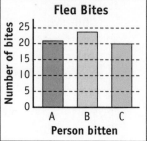

① Who was bitten the least by mosquitoes – A, B or C? ___

② Who was bitten the most by spiders? ___

③ Who was bitten the most by fleas? ___

④ Which creature inflicted most bites in total? _____

⑤ Which two people were bitten the same number of times by the same creature? ____

⑥ Which two people were bitten the same number of times by different creatures? ____

⑦ Who was bitten the same number of times by two different creatures? ____

⑧ How many times was A bitten by fleas? ____

⑨ How many times was A bitten by spiders? ____

⑩ Who was bitten the least by mosquitoes? ____

⑪ How many times in total was B bitten? ____

⑫ How many times in total was B bitten by mosquitoes, A bitten by fleas and C bitten by spiders? _____

⑬ By which creature were the people bitten most nearly the same number of times? _____

⑭ For which creature is the number of bites the three people experienced most spread out? _____

Measurement & Space

AC9M6M02

Comparing lengths and areas

Use these plan drawings to answer the following questions.

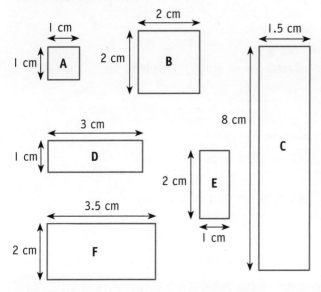

1. Which shape has the smallest area? ___
2. Which shape has the largest area? ___
3. Which shape has the smallest perimeter? ___
4. Which shape has the largest perimeter? ___
5. Which shape has an area of 1 cm²? ___
6. Which shape has a perimeter of 4 cm? ___
7. What is the area of Shape C? _____
8. What is the area of Shape F? _____
9. What two shapes have equal perimeters? _____
10. What is the combined perimeters of shapes B, D and F? _____
11. Which shape has a perimeter half that of shape D? ___
12. What is the same about shapes B and D? _____
13. How many of shape B could fit exactly into shape C? ____
14. How many of shape E could fit exactly into shape C? ____
15. The combined areas of which three shapes equals the combined areas of shapes C and E? _____

Score 2 points for each correct answer! **SCORE** **/30** (0-12) (14-24) (26-30)

Problem Solving

AC9M6N07, AC9M6ST01

Multiplication and data problems

1. Which of these is the same as 3 × 21?
   - a 3 × 20 × 3 × 1
   - b 3 × 2 × 3 × 1
   - c 3 × 3 × 7
   - d 3 × 20 × 1

2. Which of these is the same as 16 × 21?
   - a 16 × 20 × 3 × 1
   - b 16 × 2 × 3 × 1
   - c 16 × 3 × 7
   - d 16 × 20 × 1

3. Which of these is the same as 8 × 45?
   - a 8 × 3 × 3 × 5
   - b 8 × 4 × 5
   - c 8 × 40 × 5
   - d 8 × 2 × 2 × 5

4. Which of these is the same as 24 × 45?
   - a 24 × 4 × 5
   - b 24 × 4 × 10 × 5
   - c 24 × 3 × 5 × 3
   - d 24 × 4 × 24 × 5

5. Which of these is the same as 17 × 33?
   - a 17 × 3 × 1
   - b 17 × 3 × 11
   - c 17 × 3 × 10
   - d 17 × 3 × 3

Use the graphs of Mosquito, Spider and Flea Bites to answer the following questions.

6. If on the occasions when the three people were bitten by fleas, B had used repellent and wasn't bitten, how many times would B have been bitten in total by all the creatures?

   _____

7. If C had been bitten by spiders as many times as she had been as well as the number of times that A had been, how many times would C have been bitten in total by all the creatures?

   _____

8. If one of the spiders that bit the people was radioactive so that its bite made the person it bit into a superhero, who would that person most likely have been?

   _____

9. If A had been bitten twice as many times on one of the occasions so that he was bitten fourteen times in total, which was that occasion?

   _____

10. If one of the people was bitten only half as many times on two occasions so that in total they had been bitten 27 times, who would that have been?

    _____

Grammar & Punctuation

AC9E6LA06

TERM 1 ENGLISH

Simple past tense

Many verbs can be changed to the **past tense** by adding the suffix **–ed**.

Example:
Two girls **play** on that equipment.
(present tense)

Two girls **played** on that equipment.
(past tense)

Find the verbs in these sentences and make them past tense by adding –ed.

① The friends chase each other to the top of the sandhill. _____

② You cook for at least ten extra people each night. _____

③ After the storm we walk through the park.
_____

④ Builders shout to each other over the noise of the tractor. _____

Choose a verb from the box to complete each sentence. Each verb will be in the past tense.

stay	laugh	visit	wait

⑤ Lots of older people _____**ed** home over the holidays.

⑥ We _____**ed** the city museum twice.

⑦ The two friends _____**ed** at the clowns in the show.

⑧ Service was slow so we _____**ed** for an hour.

Past tense verbs ending in –e

Verbs that end in **–e** only need **d** to be added to make them past tense.
Examples: rac**e** – rac**ed**, chas**e** – chas**ed**

Change these verbs into the past tense.

⑨ Both Ali and Sara **dance**___ tonight.

⑩ After the service we **place**___ flowers at the memorial.

⑪ "I **bake**___ many thousands of cakes," the cook said proudly.

Phonic Knowledge & Spelling

AC9E6LY09

Vocabulary

Vocabulary is the words which make up our language. Some vocabulary can be grouped into subjects, or words that have the same or similar meaning.

Example:
Emotions – fearful, annoyed, angry, worried, upset, etc.

Circle the best emotion word for each sentence.

① An excited person may:
wince / whoop / howl.

② A frightened person may:
frown / smile / yawn.

③ An upset person may: cry / giggle / hesitate.

④ A happy person may: frown / laugh / cry.

Match a job from the box with its description.

acrobat	plumber	accountant	florist

⑤ A person who arranges flowers is a/an
_____.

⑥ A person who fixes pipes and installs them is a/an _____.

⑦ A person who performs rolls and tumbles is a/an _____.

⑧ A person who works with money and finance is a/an _____.

Suffixes

A suffix is a syllable added to the end of a word which changes how that word is used. When adding suffixes to words ending in **–y** the **y** becomes an **i** before the rest of the suffix is added. *Examples:*
ordinary – ordinarily, mercy – merciless

Match the suffixes with their words. Write the words in full with the correct spelling.

–ful	–ness	–ous	–cation

⑨ beauty _____

⑩ envy _____

⑪ apply _____

⑫ busy _____

Persuasive text – Letter
Author – Peter Alford

Letter 1

Deer Teecha

Please do not be angree with Sammy becos she didn't do hur homework. She done it but it was wet soe we stuck it in the uven to dri. We forgot abowt it and it cort fire. That is cos I spilt me tee on it. She is such a luvly kid and needs a good marc. PLees be kind to hur. By the way she shood be a class captin caus she's kleva.

mRs Smith

Letter 2

Dear Teacher
Please excuse Sammy for not doing her homework. Our family was out late last night and she didn't have the time for homework in the morning before school. Sammy will do the homework after school tonight. Thank you for your understanding.
Regards
Mrs Smith

Write or circle the correct answer.

① **Which of these statements is probably true?**

  a Sammy wrote letter 2.

  b Sammy's parent wrote letter 1.

  c Sammy wrote letter 1.

In letter 1 there are many spelling mistakes. Write the correct spelling for these words.

② becos _____

③ angree _____

④ luvly _____

⑤ **Which reason in letter 1 tells why Sammy should be class captain?**

  a She is honest.

  b She is clever.

  c She works well in class.

⑥ **When did Sammy not have time to do her homework?**

_____

_____

⑦ **When was Sammy going to do her missed homework?**

_____

⑧ **What was one thing that happened to Sammy's homework? Use the correct spelling.**

_____

_____

⑨ **What was the reason letter 2 gave for Sammy not doing her homework?**

_____

_____

Score 2 points for each correct answer! SCORE **/18** (0-6) (8-14) (16-18)

My Book Review

Title _____

Author _____

Rating ☆☆☆☆☆

Comment _____

_____

Number & Algebra

AC9M6N01

Positive and negative whole numbers

Use the number line at the right to answer the following questions.

If the answer is in between two points, write both points as the answer.
Example: if the answer is 21, 22, 23 or 24, write **U/V**.

Write the correct answers.

① At which point on the number line is 48?

_____

② At which point on the number line is -48?

_____

③ Is -85 shown on the number line?

_____

Where will these operations end up on the number line? Write the correct points.

④ Make 67 smaller by 40. _____

⑤ Make 49 larger by 30. _____

⑥ Make 35 smaller by 50. _____

⑦ Make -65 larger by 25. _____

⑧ Make -15 smaller by 45. _____

⑨ Make -27 smaller by 15. _____

⑩ Make -32 larger by 45. _____

⑪ Make 75 smaller by 115. _____

⑫ Make -75 larger by 115. _____

Follow these instructions and write the point you end up on.

⑬ Start at 35, make it larger by 50, make it smaller by 85, make it smaller by 75, make it larger by 60.

_____

⑭ Start at -50, make it larger by 95, larger by 25, make it smaller by 60, smaller by 75.

_____

⑮ Start at 68, make it smaller by 25, make it smaller by 85, make it larger by 15, make it larger by 45, make it larger by 60.

_____

-80	A
	B
-70	C
	D
-60	E
	F
-50	G
	H
-40	I
	J
-30	K
	L
-20	M
	N
-10	O
	P
0	Q
	R
10	S
	T
20	U
	V
30	W
	X
40	Y
	Z
50	AA
	BB
60	CC
	DD
70	EE
	FF
80	GG

Statistics & Probability

AC9M6ST01

Interpreting and comparing data displays

Use these line graphs to answer the following questions.

The values have not been put into the graphs but the graphs have been marked in sections and they have the same scale.

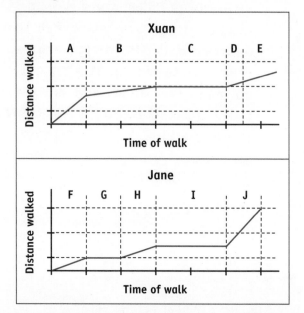

The graphs show a walk done by two people.

① Who rested more times? _____

② Who rested for longer time? _____

③ Who walked for more time? _____

④ Who walked the further distance? _____

⑤ In which section or sections was Xuan resting? _____

⑥ In which section or sections was Jane resting? _____

⑦ In which section was Xuan walking at his fastest pace? _____

⑧ In which section was Jane walking at her fastest pace? _____

⑨ In which section was Xuan walking at his slowest pace? _____

⑩ In which sections was Jane walking at her slowest pace? _____

⑪ In which section did Xuan walk for the longest time without a rest? _____

⑫ On average, who must have walked faster?

_____

Measurement & Space

AC9M6SP01

Concrete materials

Use these pictures of a house brick, a pyramid and a tin can to answer the following questions.

Write or circle the correct answers.

① Are bricks, pyramids and tin cans two-dimensional or three-dimensional objects?

_____

② How many faces does the brick have? ____

③ Which geometric shape are the faces of the brick?
  a square   d pentagon
  b triangle   e hexagon
  c rectangle   f circle

④ How many faces does the pyramid have? ___

⑤ Which two geometric shapes are the faces of the pyramid?
  a square   d pentagon
  b triangle   e hexagon
  c rectangle   f circle

⑥ How many faces does the tin can have? ___

⑦ Which two geometric shapes are the faces of the tin can?
  a square   d pentagon
  b triangle   e hexagon
  c rectangle   f circle

⑧ Are squares, triangles and rectangles two-dimensional or three-dimensional?

_____

⑨ Are pentagons, hexagons and circles two-dimensional or three-dimensional?

_____

How many edges does each object have?

⑩ brick ____   ⑫ tin can ____
⑪ pyramid ____

How many vertices does each object have?

⑬ brick ____   ⑮ tin can ____
⑭ pyramid ____

Problem Solving

AC9M6N01, AC9M6ST01

Negative numbers and distance data problems

Circle the larger number.

① a 3967   b 4001
② a -129   b 67
③ a -3958   b 3
④ a 12 700   b -999 999
⑤ a 1   b -1

Use this line graph of a journey to answer the following questions.

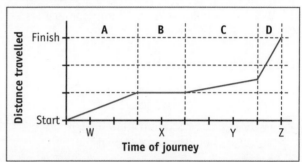

⑥ What was the traveller doing during section B of the journey?

_____

⑦ During which section of the journey was the traveller moving at the fastest speed?

_____

⑧ During which section of the journey was the traveller moving at the slowest speed?

_____

Assume that point X marks 6 hours along the journey.

⑨ How long into the journey was point W?

_____

⑩ How long into the journey was point Y?

_____

⑪ How long did the journey take?

_____

⑫ How long did the traveller spend resting?

_____

Grammar & Punctuation

Underline the main clauses in these complex sentences.

① Trish was voted as school councillor because she is now in year six.

② Over the next few weeks we will see many places as we have no school.

Write the missing commas to separate the clauses in these complex sentences.

③ Because our alarm clock doesn't always go off we miss the bus.

④ While Trent loves to go snow skiing there isn't always good snowfall.

⑤ When it is overcooked fish can sometimes become soft and mushy.

Underline the conjunctions.

⑥ Toddlers find it difficult to walk as their muscles are not strong.

⑦ Every year one student gets a book prize because they are good at maths.

⑧ Every summer the shark alarm sounds but usually the shark swims away.

Underline the verbs and write if they are present or past.

⑨ Sam walked in the race today.
_____

⑩ Mrs R Ose spent time in her garden.
_____

⑪ Jen often dozes through the news on TV.
_____

Choose verbs from the box to replace the highlighted verbs.

| observed | chatter | sprinted | dawdle |

⑫ When told to listen, the students began to **talk**. _____

⑬ Having very old legs, the ancient man could only **walk**. _____

⑭ Police **saw** the criminal committing the crime. _____

⑮ Jack **ran** to the car as it was raining.
_____

Phonic Knowledge & Spelling

Choose homophones from the box to complete the sentences.

| caught/court | waste/waist |
| great/grate | pact/packed |

① Her new dress was tight at the _____.

② The new find near the temple was of _____ importance.

③ At last we were _____ and ready to move to our new house.

④ We were _____ in a rainstorm.

Complete the words with roots from the box.

Root Word	Meaning	Example
mono	one	monorail
geo	world	geography
oct	eight	octopus
bio	life	biology

⑤ The shape has eight sides so it is an _____gon.

⑥ The actor was on stage by himself giving a _____logue.

⑦ His rock collection is being looked at by a _____logist.

⑧ The _____logist studied the samples looking for any living organisms.

Choose synonyms from the box to replace the highlighted adjectives.

| bright | awful | new | interesting |

⑨ Any accident on the road is **horrible**.
_____

⑩ Yes, that new painting is **fascinating**.
_____

⑪ I am not all that **clever** in mathematics.
_____

⑫ **Modern** cars now drive themselves.
_____

Transportation

Imaginative text – Narrative
Author – Peter Alford

Nine months on this rotting tub, the smell made me sick to my gut. Vomit from sea sickness swirled around our feet and human waste was washed back along the deck if the sea was rough. This dripped on us below the deck.

Now the sails did not fill with wind to push this hulk along, we stood quiet in the water. Fourteen hours a day we were locked beneath. Sickness had claimed many of the older convicts. Our food, if you can call it that, was rotting salted meat and biscuits that seemed they were made of wood.

My crime, the theft of three handkerchiefs. At thirteen I was going to be hanged. The judge then said I was for transportation to New South Wales. Sometimes I wish that I had met my fate in England. Caged like an animal for months at sea was worse than hanging at times. Talking back to a guard meant a whipping and soldiers bullied convicts, using their guns like clubs.

Write or circle the correct answer.

1 **What word does the writer use instead of ship or boat?**

a transportation

b hulk

c caged

2 **How old was the boy when he was sent to New South Wales?**

_____

3 **Something about the ship suggests that this was a long time ago.**

a the sea was rough

b rotting tub

c sails did not fill

4 **What was this boy's crime?**

_____

_____

5 **How did the writer give the idea that the biscuits were hard to eat?**

_____

_____

6 **What happened if a convict answered a guard back?**

_____

_____

Score 2 points for each correct answer!

SCORE **/12** 0-4 6-8 10-12

Number & Algebra

Write or circle the correct answers.

Circle the number that is not a **whole number**.

① a 2222   b 7878   c 9000   d 555.5

② a 56 666   b 00 045   c $999\frac{4}{5}$ d 1

③ a $88\frac{1}{2}$ b 591   c 1000   d 1

Circle the **adjoining** pairs of numbers that add up to 15. There could be more than one pair in each row.

④ | 7 | 9 | 14 | 0 | 3 | 8 | 7 | 6 | 1 | 3 |
|---|---|---|---|---|---|---|---|---|---|

⑤ | 6 | 9 | 4 | 4 | 8 | 6 | 5 | 10 | 4 | 11 |
|---|---|---|---|---|---|---|---|---|---|

⑥ | 11 | 8 | 13 | 2 | 12 | 5 | 1 | 14 | 9 | 5 |
|---|---|---|---|---|---|---|---|---|---|

⑦ | 13 | 2 | 2 | 9 | 6 | 4 | 10 | 6 | 15 | 0 |
|---|---|---|---|---|---|---|---|---|---|

⑧ | 14 | 7 | 5 | 8 | 11 | 4 | 0 | 9 | 3 | 6 |
|---|---|---|---|---|---|---|---|---|---|

⑨ | 3 | 5 | 9 | 6 | 8 | 4 | 3 | 5 | 7 | 8 |
|---|---|---|---|---|---|---|---|---|---|

⑩ What happens when two numbers with minus signs in front of them are combined?

a subtraction
b addition
c There is a mistake.
d It can't be done.

⑪ What happens when a number with a plus sign in front of it is combined with a number with a minus sign in front of it?

a subtraction
b addition
c There is a mistake.
d It can't be done.

⑫ Circle the fractions that are **equal** to one another. (There could be more than two.)

a $\frac{1}{2}$ c $\frac{4}{7}$ e $\frac{2}{4}$

b $\frac{3}{8}$ d $\frac{1}{3}$ f $\frac{5}{10}$

⑬ Circle the **largest** fraction.

a $\frac{1}{2}$ c $\frac{7}{8}$ e $\frac{2}{4}$

b $\frac{6}{8}$ d $\frac{1}{4}$ f $\frac{5}{8}$

⑭ Circle the **smallest** fraction.

a $\frac{1}{2}$ c $\frac{7}{8}$ e $\frac{2}{4}$

b $\frac{6}{8}$ d $\frac{1}{4}$ f $\frac{5}{8}$

⑮ Circle the **prime numbers**.
(There could be more than two.)

a 76   c 75   e 99
b 71   d 93   f 97

Score 2 points for each correct answer! SCORE **/30** (0-12) (14-24) (26-30)

Statistics & Probability

Statistics & Probability

Write or circle the correct answers.

① When chance experiments are carried out, why are expressions like **A fair experiment** or **All things being equal** used?

a to make it sound more scientific
b to eliminate the possibility of cheating
c to eliminate the possibility of anything that makes the chance of one thing happening more likely
d to make it sound more scientific as well as attract the attention of people

There are 500 marbles in a bag.
Half of them are red, 200 are green and the rest are yellow.

② What is the chance of picking a red marble, at random?

a $\frac{1}{5}$ b $\frac{1}{2}$ c $\frac{1}{10}$ d $\frac{2}{10}$

③ What is the chance of picking a green marble, at random?
Write the answer as a common fraction.

———

④ What is the chance of picking a yellow marble, at random?
Write the answer as a decimal fraction.

———

Dodecahedron dice have twelve sides. Each side has a fair chance of landing face up. The next three questions are based on rolling a dodecahedron die.

⑤ What is the chance of a 3 being rolled?

———

⑥ What is the chance of an even number being rolled?

———

⑦ What is the chance of a multiple of 3 being rolled?

a $\frac{1}{12}$ b $\frac{1}{6}$ c $\frac{1}{3}$ d $\frac{1}{2}$

TARGETING HOMEWORK 6 © PASCAL PRESS ISBN 9781925726480

This bar graph showing the number of lollies collected by seven trick or treaters is incomplete. Numbers for the vertical scale have been left out.

Use the graph to answer the following questions.

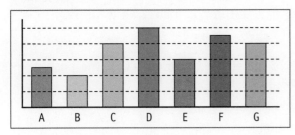

⑧ Which trick or treater collected half as many lollies as C?

_____

⑨ The numbers of lollies for which two trick or treaters can be added together to equal D's number of lollies?

_____

⑩ If E collected 75 lollies, how many did G collect?

_____

Measurement & Space

① How many centimetres in 5.07 metres?

_____

② How many millimetres in 58.85 centimetres?

_____

③ How many metres in 99.009 kilometres?

_____

④ How many litres in 200 500 millilitres?

_____

⑤ How many tonnes in 3709 kilograms?

_____

⑥ How many kilograms in 71 grams?

_____

Use these three shapes to answer the following questions.

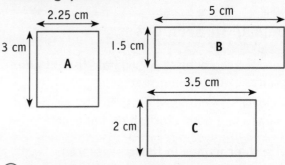

⑦ Which shape has an area of 7.5 cm² – A, B or C?

_____

⑧ Which shape has a perimeter of 11 cm?

_____

⑨ Which two shapes have a combined area of 14.25 cm²?

_____

⑩ Which two shapes have a combined perimeter of 21.5 cm?

_____

Use these three shapes to answer the following questions.

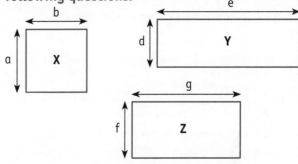

⑪ What length is **side a** if **shape X** is a square with an area of 25 m²?

_____

⑫ If **side d** is 9 mm and **shape Y** has a perimeter of 58 mm, what length is **side e**?

_____

⑬ If **shape Z** has an area of 70 cm² and **side f** is 7 cm, what length is **side g**?

_____

⑭ If **side b** is 9 mm long and **shape X** is a square, what is the area of **shape X**?

_____

⑮ If **side d** is 0.7 m and **shape Y** has an area of 2.8 m², what length is **side g**?

_____

Grammar & Punctuation

AC9E6LA09

Commas in noun groups

> Commas can be used to separate lists of **noun groups (things)** in a sentence.
> *Example:* We gathered **glass floats, cuttlefish bones** and **dead starfish** on the beach.

Write the commas in these sentences.

① Jax took his old bike gas stove and old Digger's hat to the river.

② To make steamed pudding, you need plain flour red jam a sealable tin and lots of butter.

③ Dragsters have huge rear wheels a powerful motor and a parachute to stop.

Commas in verb groups

> Commas can be used to separate lists of **verb groups (actions)** in a sentence.
> *Example:* The kangaroo **jumped the fence, hopped through the paddock** and **escaped into the bush.**

Write the commas in these sentences.

④ The witch added bat wings stirred the cauldron said a spell and then drank the potion.

⑤ She sandpapered the wood sawed another piece and then screwed them together.

⑥ After swimming in the pool, she climbed the tree tied a rope to a branch and swung across the water.

Commas with names in direct speech

> Commas can be used to separate the **name of a person** spoken to from the rest of a sentence.
> *Examples:* "Come on, **Mel,** let's take our time."
> "**Brendon,** would you like to jump next?"

Write the commas in the speech below.

⑦ "Well Mr Simms may I have that large watermelon please?" asked Jin.

⑧ "Gracie please take out the garbage," asked Mum.

⑨ "Look Miah it is not that your dog smells," commented Sam.

⑩ "Are you well Tran?" asked Sia.

Phonic Knowledge & Spelling

AC9E6LY09

Base words

> Base words are the simplest form of a word.
> *Examples:* run**ning** – base word **run**
> **read**able – base word **read**

Circle the suffix that doesn't fit the base word.

① accident   –ly   –al   –s   –ed

② laugh   –ing   –ed   –or   –able

Circle the base words in the words below.

③ training

④ controller

⑤ wonderful

⑥ juices

Synonyms

> **Synonyms** are words that have the same or similar meaning.
> *Example:* help – assist   small – minute

Circle the synonym from the group of words which matches the first word in the column.

⑦ **usual:**   common   unusual   take

⑧ **neat:**   untidy   funny   tidy

Derivatives

> Some words are made up of two words. These are called **derivatives**.
> *Example:*
> **Motel** is made up of **mo**tor and ho**tel**.

Choose a word from the box that makes the derivative.

| breakfast   fog   parade |

⑨ **br**unch   lunch   _____

⑩ **motor**cade   motor   _____

⑪ **sm**og   smoke   _____

Cave In

Imaginative text – Narrative
Author – Peter Alford

They ignored what they had been told by their father a hundred times.

As they dug, tears made tracks down the black dust on their cheeks. Wishing so hard that they had listened, their digging was furious. Underground cubbies are great fun — a place to light fires, hide, store all your valuables and drink soft drink.

Number one rule! Never dig and have sand or clay over your head. It falls in, smothering you in an instant. Ringing in their ears,

those words spelt out to Mina and Renee that their brother was in trouble. If only they could turn back time. Life or death was now in those shaking, frightened, shovelling hands. Collapsing sand was never going to help them, it just reminded them of their lousy choices.

Fingers wriggling in front of their strained eyes told them something too good to be true. Police and ambulance sirens were getting closer …

TERM 2 ENGLISH

Write or circle the correct answer.

① What are two reasons these children decided to dig an underground cubby?

_____

_____

② What could happen if you dig and have sand or clay above your head?

_____

_____

③ What does 'smothering you in an instant' mean in this story?

a You are able to breathe.

b You may die because there is no air.

c You may get very sick.

④ What told them that their brother may be all right?

_____

⑤ Who was coming to help them rescue their brother?

_____

_____

⑥ What was the name of the two girls in the story?

_____

_____

⑦ How do you think the two girls were feeling while digging for their brother?

a happy   b relaxed   c fearful

⑧ How many times had their father told them that digging can be dangerous?

_____

⑨ What does 'ringing in their ears' mean?

a They were remembering it.

b They had a telephone.

c They had sore ears.

My Book Review

Title _____

Author _____

Rating ☆☆☆☆☆

Comment _____

_____

Score 2 points for each correct answer!

SCORE /18   0-6   8-14   16-18

Number & Algebra

AC9M6N03

Equivalent fractions

Write the correct answers.

Are these fractions proper or improper?

① $\frac{3}{5}$ _____

② $\frac{7}{9}$ _____

③ $\frac{11}{9}$ _____

④ $\frac{6}{5}$ _____

⑤ $\frac{4}{4}$ _____

⑥ $\frac{8}{3}$ _____

Convert these improper fractions to mixed numbers.

⑦ $\frac{18}{3}$ = _____

⑧ $\frac{10}{2}$ = _____

⑨ $\frac{37}{6}$ = _____

⑩ $\frac{27}{8}$ = _____

⑪ $\frac{19}{3}$ = _____

⑫ $\frac{7}{6}$ = _____

⑬ $\frac{55}{4}$ = _____

⑭ $\frac{99}{5}$ = _____

Simplify these fractions.

⑮ $\frac{16}{20}$ = _____

⑯ $\frac{4}{128}$ = _____

⑰ $\frac{10}{15}$ = _____

⑱ $\frac{9}{81}$ = _____

⑲ $\frac{16}{20}$ = _____

⑳ $\frac{30}{445}$ = _____

Simplify these improper fractions and then convert them to mixed numbers.

Improper fraction		Simplified fraction		Mixed number
$\frac{26}{8}$	=	㉑	=	㉒
$\frac{45}{10}$	=	㉓	=	㉔
$\frac{33}{22}$	=	㉕	=	㉖
$\frac{32}{6}$	=	㉗	=	㉘
$\frac{28}{12}$	=	㉙	=	㉚
$\frac{63}{18}$	=	㉛	=	㉜

Score 2 points for each correct answer! **SCORE** **/64**

Statistics & Probability

AC9M6ST03

Graphs with broken axes

This bar graph displays **My Friends' Wealth** and it includes broken axes. Use the graph to answer the following questions.

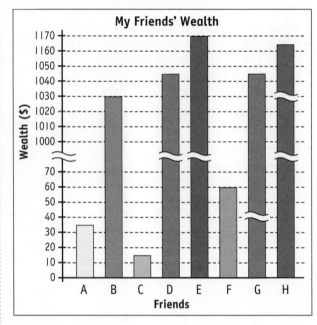

① Why was this graph drawn with broken axes?

_____

_____

② If the graph didn't have broken axes, what would the broken bars look like?

_____

_____

③ What is wrong with bar B?

_____

④ What is wrong with bar G?

_____

⑤ What is wrong with bar H?

_____

⑥ What is the value of bar A? _____

⑦ What is the value of bar E? _____

⑧ What is the value of bar D? _____

⑨ What is the approximate difference in value between bars A and C? _____

⑩ What is the approximate difference in value between bars D and E? _____

⑪ What is the difference in value between bars A and D? _____

⑫ What is the difference in value between bars C and E? _____

Score 2 points for each correct answer! **SCORE** **/24**

TARGETING HOMEWORK 6 © PASCAL PRESS ISBN 9781925726480

Measurement & Space

AC9M6M01

Converting metric units

Complete these metric unit conversions.

① 1.5 L = _____ mL

② 335 g = _____ kg

③ 1567 mm = _____ m

④ 2.7 km = _____ m

⑤ 1345 mm = _____ m

⑥ 2.6 m = _____ mm

⑦ 3.6 kg = _____ g

⑧ $2\frac{3}{4}$ kg = _____ g

⑨ 1.25 L = _____ mL

⑩ 375 mL = _____ L

Convert to centimetres.

⑪ 5270 mm = _____

⑫ 34.04 m = _____

⑬ 0.001 m = _____

⑭ 86.9 mm = _____

Convert to litres.

⑮ 1.5 mL = _____

⑯ 1000 kL = _____

⑰ 1257 mL = _____

⑱ 54.69 kL = _____

Problem Solving

AC9M6N05, AC9M6ST03, AC9M6M01

Fraction, data and volume problems

Reverse the simplification.

Improper fraction		Simplified fraction		Mixed number
①	=	② $\frac{}{8}$	=	$2\frac{3}{4}$
③	=	④ $\frac{}{14}$	=	$4\frac{1}{2}$
⑤	=	⑥ $\frac{}{9}$	=	2
⑦	=	⑧ $\frac{}{6}$	=	$5\frac{1}{2}$
⑨	=	⑩ $\frac{}{56}$	=	3

Use the bar graph in **Statistics & Probability** to answer the following questions.

If you had to construct a bar graph to display the following data, at which point along the *y*-axis would you place the breaks?

You need to give values for two points. For example, the breaks in the graph **My Friends' Wealth** are at $70 and $1000.

⑪ Data for **My Friends Marble Collection**:
Jill 3789, Kavinka 281, Mei 101, Bert 2912 and Freyja 112.

_____

⑫ Data for **Highways and Streets**:
Rathdown St 23 km, Eyre Hwy 1660 Km, Anne Beadell Highway 1325 km and Princes St 1.25 km.

_____

⑬ Data for **Heights of Animals**:
Mouse 4 cm, Snail 2.5 cm, Giraffe 5.85 m, Guinea pig 8 cm and Elephant 3.25 m.

_____

Write the correct answers to these measurement problems.

⑭ Jack had a two-litre bottle of apple juice. He's already drunk 1.2 L from it.
How much does he have left, in millilitres?

_____

⑮ Tailors work in centimetres and carpenters work in millimetres.
How would each express 2.75 metres?
a Tailors: _____
b Carpenters: _____

⑯ A recipe requires half as much sugar as fruit. The fruit weighs $2\frac{1}{4}$ kg.
How much sugar is needed?
Answer in grams.

_____

Grammar & Punctuation

AC9E6LA09

Commas in direct speech

Commas separate direct speech from the speaker.

When the direct speech is written first, the **comma** is inside the speech marks.

Example: "Sit," said the man to his dog.

When the speaker is written first, the **comma** is outside the speech marks.

Example: The man said, "Fetch the ball!"

When the speaker is in the middle of the spoken text, there are **two commas**.

Example: "It's still raining," whinged May, "and our game is about to start."

Add a comma and speech marks to each sentence.

① Come over here said Kyle.

② Don't forget reminded Georgia's father.

③ His manners were poor commented Coach.

④ The giant pink rabbit said This really isn't a dream.

Add two commas to each sentence.

⑤ "It isn't fair" complained Ryan "that Josh can sit up front."

⑥ "Can I have a turn" asked Shari "after you're finished?"

⑦ "Yep" Jeff replied "I'm up for that."

⑧ "Wherever or however" the captain commanded "we will be there."

Add commas to these statements.

⑨ Flying down the sandhill, he yelled "This is fantastic fun!"

⑩ "Everything has changed" reminded the coach.

⑪ She swam the river and gasped "That was the hardest thing I've ever done."

⑫ "No" Billy shouted "I don't want to go!"

Score 2 points for each correct answer! **SCORE** **/24** (0-10) (12-18) (20-24)

Phonic Knowledge & Spelling

AC9E6LY08, AC9E6LY09

Letter teams – 'f' sound

Some **letter teams** have the same sound but different spelling. The sound **f** can be spelt as **f, ph, ff, gh**.

Choose a f sound from the box to spell the words.

| f | ph | ff | gh |

① My grandfather answered the tele____one.

② Maths is a di____icult subject for me.

③ To win the gold medal she had to jump per____ectly.

④ During English we were asked to write a paragra____.

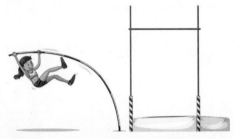

Choose missing letters from the box to complete the –ant words.

| vac | dist | import | pl |

⑤ ___ ___ ___ ant

⑥ ___ ___ ___ ___ ___ ___ ant

⑦ ___ ___ ant

⑧ ___ ___ ___ ___ ant

American English

Some words in American English are spelt differently to Australian English.

Examples:
thea**ter** (American), thea**tre** (Australian)
cen**ter** (American), cen**tre** (Australian)

Rewrite the American spelling into Australian spelling.

⑨ fiber _____

⑩ liter _____

⑪ meter _____

⑫ luster _____

Score 2 points for each correct answer! **SCORE** **/24** (0-10) (12-18) (20-24)

What is Weather Forecasting?

Informative text – Report
Author – Janette Ellis

Since ancient times, people have tried to predict or forecast the weather. It is not an exact science.

Forecasting today uses the best 21st century technology — **artificial satellites**, ground-based instruments and the fastest computers in the world. They take weather measurements every moment of every day.

Satellites track the bigger picture from above, whilst temperature, rainfall, **humidity** and wind speed are recorded locally. Meteorologists (people who study weather) and mathematicians create complex computer systems to make the most accurate forecasts.

Weather forecasts are important for many reasons. For example, air and sea travel can be dangerous in poor weather; farmers need to know what season to expect; and people use weather forecasts to plan their daily activities.

Source: *Forecasting*, Go Facts, Blake Education.

TERM 2 ENGLISH

Write or circle the correct answer.

① What is meant by forecasting is 'not an exact science'?

a Forecasting is not science.

b Forecasting is difficult to get right.

c Scientists are always right.

② What four things are measured locally and not by satellites?

_____ _____

_____ _____

③ Are the computers that measure weather turned off at night? Write the sentence that answers this question.

_____

_____

_____

④ Which two people below need the weather forecasts to be correct?

a the captain of an aircraft

b a hairdresser

c an artist

d a ship's captain

⑤ Name two of the technologies that are used today for forecasting weather.

_____

_____

⑥ What do meteorologists do?

_____

_____

⑦ What do farmers need to know from forecasters?

_____

_____

Score 2 points for each correct answer! SCORE **/14** 0-4 6-10 12-14

My Book Review

Title _____

Author _____

Rating ☆☆☆☆☆

Comment _____

_____

Number & Algebra

AC9M6N05

Adding fractions

Work out these equations. Convert any answers that are improper fractions to mixed numbers.

① $5\frac{3}{4} + 4\frac{1}{4}$

= _____

② $\frac{7}{8} + \frac{5}{8} + \frac{5}{8}$

= _____

③ $6\frac{2}{6} + \frac{4}{6}$

= _____

④ $9\frac{3}{5} + 9\frac{4}{5} + \frac{2}{5}$

= _____

⑤ $7\frac{4}{9} + \frac{6}{9} + 1\frac{4}{9}$

= _____

⑥ $\frac{8}{10} + 3\frac{3}{10} + 6\frac{2}{10}$

= _____

⑦ $\frac{1}{2} + 2\frac{1}{2} + 9 + 3\frac{1}{2}$

= _____

⑧ $12 + \frac{5}{12} + 3\frac{7}{12}$

= _____

⑨ $\frac{6}{8} + \frac{6}{8} + \frac{6}{8} + \frac{6}{8}$

= _____

⑩ $4\frac{4}{5} + 2\frac{2}{5} + 6\frac{1}{5}$

= _____

⑪ $13\frac{2}{7} + 9\frac{1}{7} + 8 + 1\frac{4}{7}$

= _____

⑫ $\frac{4}{9} + \frac{8}{9} + \frac{5}{9} + \frac{2}{9}$

= _____

⑬ $8\frac{1}{3} + 3 + 4\frac{2}{3} + \frac{1}{3} + 6\frac{2}{3} + 7\frac{1}{3}$

= _____

Statistics & Probability

AC9M6ST01

Pie charts

These pie charts represents how much of a pumpkin pie and a chocolate cake was eaten by four people. Use it to answer the following questions.

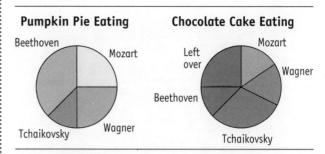

Pumpkin Pie Eating

Beethoven
Mozart
Tchaikovsky
Wagner

Chocolate Cake Eating

Mozart
Wagner
Left over
Beethoven
Tchaikovsky

① Who ate the most pumpkin pie?

_____

② Who ate the least pumpkin pie?

_____

③ Who ate the same amount of pumpkin pie as Mozart?

_____

④ Did Mozart and Wagner together eat the same amount of pumpkin pie as Beethoven?

_____

⑤ Who ate the most chocolate cake?

_____

⑥ Who ate the least chocolate cake?

_____

⑦ Which two people seem to have eaten the same amount of chocolate cake?

_____

⑧ The pie charts are the same size. Does that mean that the pie and the cake were the same size?

_____

⑨ How much chocolate cake was left over compared to the amount of chocolate cake that Beethoven ate?

_____

⑩ Which two people together ate as much chocolate cake as Tchaikovsky?

_____

⑪ About how much of the chocolate cake was left uneaten?

_____

Score 2 points for each correct answer! **SCORE** /26 (0-10) (12-20) (22-26)

Score 2 points for each correct answer! **SCORE** /22 (0-8) (10-16) (18-22)

TARGETING HOMEWORK 6 © PASCAL PRESS ISBN 9781925726480

Measurement & Space

AC9M6M03

Interpreting and using timetables

The table shows part of a timetable of the two trains that regularly travel the entire distance between Sydney and Melbourne. Use the table to answer the following questions.

Stations	Train 623	Train 621
Sydney Central	7:33 am	8:34 pm
Yass Junction	11:20 am	00:18 am
Wagga Wagga	1:54 pm	2:47 am
Albury	3:11 pm	4:03 am
Melbourne Southern Cross	6:30 pm	7:25 am

① How many stations does this timetable show?

_____

② Which train begins its journey to Melbourne first?

_____

③ Which train arrives in Melbourne on a different day than it left Sydney?

_____

④ What time does the 621 train arrive in Wagga Wagga?

_____

⑤ How long after leaving Sydney does the 623 train arrive in Yass Junction?

_____

⑥ How long after the 623 train arrives at Albury does the 621 train arrive there?

_____

⑦ How long does it take the 621 train to travel between Wagga Wagga and Albury?

_____

⑧ How long does it take the 623 train to travel between Wagga Wagga and Albury?

_____

⑨ How long is the entire journey for Train 623?

_____

⑩ How long is the entire journey for Train 621?

_____

Problem Solving

AC9M6N05, AC9M6M03

Fraction and time problems

Use the information below to answer the following questions.

Brad and Angelina took their three daughters and three sons to a movie that was two hours long. Brad stayed for two quarters of the movie while Angelina stayed for three quarters of it. Their children each managed to see only a quarter of the movie.

Mr and Mrs DiCaprio went to a movie that was four hours long. While Mrs DiCaprio saw all of it, Mr DiCaprio only stayed for a quarter of it.

Tom (an adult) went on his own to a movie that was six hours long but he could only stay for two quarters of it.

① As a mixed number, what do the fractions of movies seen by everyone add up to?

_____

② As a mixed number, how much did the females see altogether?

_____

③ As a mixed number, how much did the males see altogether?

_____

④ In total, how much did Brad, Angelina and their children see?

_____

⑤ In total, how much did the children see?

_____

Use the timetable in Measurement & Space to answer the following questions.

⑥ If a problem occurred on Train 621 at 3:18 am that delayed it for twenty-three minutes, what time would it arrive at the next station and what station was it?

_____

⑦ If a problem occurred on Train 623 at 9:45 am that forced it to stay 20 minutes longer at each station after that time, what time would it arrive in Melbourne?

_____

⑧ If someone was in Yass Junction at 8:38 am, waiting to catch the next train to Albury, how much longer did she have to wait?

_____

Score 2 points for each correct answer!

SCORE /20 0-8 10-14 16-20

Grammar & Punctuation

AC9E6LA05, AC9E6LA06

Conjunctions in compound sentences

Remember! A **conjunction** can join two simple sentences to make a **compound sentence**. The commonly used conjunctions are: **and, but, or, so**.

These conjunctions join ideas in different ways:

- to add information, e.g. Katie loves her dog **and** she loves her bird.
- to contrast ideas, e.g. Thomas fell off his bike, **but** he didn't cry.
- to compare ideas, e.g. We can drive to school, **or** we can walk.
- to show cause and effect, e.g. Lin trained hard, **so** she could be in the athletics team.

Circle the correct conjunction.

① There was no sunscreen left, (or   and) no one had any money to go and buy some.

② They went to the match early, (so   or) there weren't many people seated yet.

③ I'm trying to eat healthy, (so   but) I can't ignore the dessert you made.

④ Tom thought that he'd buy the racer, (so   but) he could ride in the race.

⑤ Gemma could study for the test today, (and   or) she could study tomorrow.

⑥ Rose is very competitive (and   but) she enjoys playing most sports.

Choose a conjunction from the box to complete each sentence.

and	but	or	so

⑦ Dogs are great pets _____ they are very loyal and become friends easily.

⑧ We have never travelled to Japan, _____ we have visited China.

⑨ Tyler felt really sick, _____ his parents took him to the hospital.

⑩ Should we go to the kart-racing track, _____ should we stand outside and wait?

Phonic Knowledge & Spelling

AC9E6LY09

Vocabulary

Vocabulary is the words which make up our language. Some words can be grouped into a subject. *Example:* Describing people's build – slight, heavy, solid, athletic

Write two words from the box to describe the parts of the body.

blond	clear	overweight
sleepy	curly	slim

① build

_____   _____

② eyes

_____   _____

③ hair

_____   _____

Choose a word from the box about weather to complete each sentence. Read all of the sentences before you begin.

muggy	blustery	scorching
chilly	overcast	

④ During winter it can be quite _____, so gloves should be worn.

⑤ Before the event there were many clouds and it became _____.

⑥ During the yacht race the wind became _____.

⑦ In some parts of Australia it is _____ during summer.

⑧ When it is hot and wet, the weather can be _____.

Antonyms

Antonyms are words which are opposite in meaning. *Example:* hot – cold

Choose an antonym from the box for each adjective.

careful	safe	costly	weak

⑨ careless   _____

⑩ strong   _____

⑪ dangerous   _____

⑫ cheap   _____

TERM 2 ENGLISH

Persuasive text – Letter of request
Author – Peter Alford

Child Drivers

Dear Madam/Sir

Every day I am forced to travel on two buses to school and I am very, very sick of having to do this! For this reason, I would ask that your government think about allowing ten-year-old children to drive cars. Think of all the extra cars that would be bought! Our car industry would get a huge boost. Think about all of those extra jobs! Think about all those extra taxes and that lovely money! Adults would thoroughly enjoy having children take themselves to school.

Of course, seats in cars would have to be higher and brake pedals longer. Both are minor costs and not really a problem. Ten-year-olds would be extremely careful drivers. There are fewer bicycle accidents compared with car crashes on the roads which proves we are safer. Because we are small, at least ten children would be able to fit into each car. Student drivers would reduce the traffic around schools. Please pass this law as I am wasting my precious life on buses.

Yours sincerely,

Bec Funnichild

Write or circle the correct answer.

1. **What does it mean that the car industry would get a 'massive boost'?**
   a There would be more booster seats in cars.
   b The car industry would like this idea.
   c More cars would be sold.

2. **What change would be needed in cars?**
   a longer pedals
   b lighter cars
   c smaller cars

3. **According to the writer, where would there be less traffic?**

   _____

4. **What does 'wasting my precious life' mean?**
   a Life is precious.
   b Bec's time is being wasted.
   c Driving cars is a waste of time.

5. **What is Bec forced to do each day?**

   _____

6. **How does Bec try to persuade readers that children are safer on the road than adults?**
   a Careless adults would no longer have accidents.
   b There are fewer bicycle accidents.
   c This would lessen the traffic around schools.

7. **What would adults enjoy?**

   _____

   _____

Score 2 points for each correct answer!

SCORE /14   0-4   6-10   12-14

My Book Review

Title _____

Author _____

Rating ☆☆☆☆☆

Comment _____

_____

Number & Algebra

AC9M6N05

Subtracting fractions

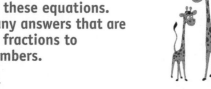

Work out these equations. Convert any answers that are improper fractions to mixed numbers.

(1) $\frac{7}{8} - \frac{4}{8}$

= _____

(2) $\frac{29}{16} - \frac{8}{16}$

= _____

(3) $3\frac{3}{5} - \frac{2}{5}$

= _____

(4) $5\frac{13}{16} - 3\frac{8}{16}$

= _____

(5) $\frac{34}{17} - \frac{9}{17}$

= _____

(6) $\frac{56}{7} - \frac{20}{7}$

= _____

(7) $23\frac{8}{9} - 16\frac{6}{9}$

= _____

(8) $100\frac{15}{23} - 99\frac{15}{23}$

= _____

(9) $32\frac{8}{13} - 16\frac{4}{13}$

= _____

(10) $\frac{44}{5} - \frac{23}{5}$

= _____

(11) $\frac{18}{2} - \frac{12}{2}$

= _____

(12) $\frac{17}{3} - \frac{11}{3}$

= _____

(13) $\frac{105}{7} - \frac{98}{7}$

= _____

Statistics & Probability

AC9M6ST02

Tables

Use the table of data to answer the following questions.

Population of Sydney (to the nearest thousand)	
1975	3 118 000
1980	3 252 000
1985	3 432 000
1990	3 632 000
1995	3 819 000
2000	4 052 000
2005	4 225 000
2010	4 364 000
2015	4 505 000

(1) How many years does this table cover?

_____

(2) What is the **trend** of the population?
(**Trend** means **change or development**.)

_____

_____

(3) What was Sydney's population at the halfway mark of this data?

_____

(4) If a bar graph of this data was constructed, what would the label on the Y axis be?

_____

(5) If a bar graph of this data was constructed, what would the label on the X axis be?

_____

(6) What is the difference in population between 1985 and 1990?

_____

(7) Which two periods have a population difference of 1 112 000?

_____

Think about the trend and the data to make your best estimates for the following questions.

(8) What was the population of Sydney halfway through 1987?

_____

(9) What will the population of Sydney be in 2020?

_____

(10) What was the population of Sydney in 1920?

_____

(11) When do you predict the population of Sydney will reach 5 million?

_____

Score 2 points for each correct answer! SCORE **/26**

Score 2 points for each correct answer! SCORE **/22**

TARGETING HOMEWORK 6 © PASCAL PRESS ISBN 9781925726480

Measurement & Space

AC9M6SP01

Constructing pyramids from nets

Some of these shapes are nets of pyramids and others are not. Use them to answer the following questions.

 A
 B
 C
 D
 E
 F

① Which of these shapes is not a net of a pyramid?

  a D   b E   c B

② How do you know?

_____

③ Which of these shapes is not a net of a pyramid?

  a C   b A   c F

④ How do you know?

_____

Use these pyramids to answer the following questions.

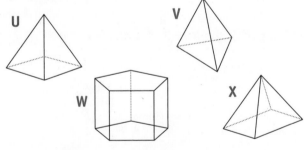

⑤ Which net constructs pyramid U? _____

⑥ Which net constructs pyramid V? _____

⑦ Which net constructs pyramid W? _____

⑧ Which net constructs pyramid X? _____

⑨ Which net constructs a square-based pyramid? _____

⑩ Which net constructs a triangle-based pyramid? _____

⑪ Which net constructs a pentagon-based pyramid? _____

⑫ Which net constructs a rectangular-based pyramid? _____

Problem Solving

AC9M6N07, AC9M6SP01

Population and pyramid problems

Use the table of data in **Statistics & Probability** to answer these problems. Use a calculator if you need to.

① In 2000, a city had a population equivalent to 200 000 less than Sydney's population in 1990. What was that city's population in 2000?

_____

② One year, a quarter of Sydney's population had the hiccups but only half of them thought it was funny. If the number of people that thought it was funny was 454 000, what year was that?

_____

③ If one-fifth of Sydney's population of 2005 had the hiccups and a fifth of them also had itchy toes, how many Sydneyites had both hiccups and itchy toes?

_____

④ One-eighth of the difference between Sydney's population of 1980 and 2010 is the number of Sydney dwellers who ate pizza last year. How many was that?

_____

⑤ If you divide a particular year's population by 8000 and then you find a third of it, you get 143. What year was that?

_____

Use the names of the different types of pyramids to answer the following questions.

• square-based pyramid	• pentagon-based pyramid
• triangle-based pyramid	• rectangular-based pyramid

⑥ What kind of pyramid has a base with four right angles but not all equal sides?

_____

⑦ What kind of pyramid has a base with internal angles that total 360° and a common side length?

_____

⑧ What kind of pyramid has a base with five internal angles?

_____

⑨ What kind of pyramid has a base with internal angles that total 180°?

_____

Grammar & Punctuation

AC9E6LA06, AC9E6LA09

Commas with adjectival clauses

> **Commas** are used to separate adjectival clauses in sentences, but **only when they add extra meaning to a sentence.**
> *Example:* Our orange tree, **which was planted years ago,** still bears fruit.

Add the commas to these sentences.

1. The snake catcher who had a limp is an expert.
2. Treehouses which can be made of wood should not be too high.
3. Deep space which is well out of the galaxy hasn't been reached by humans.
4. In her backyard which is massive there's a huge mulberry tree.

Commas with adverbial phrases

> **Commas** are used to separate **adverbial phrases** when they are at the beginning of a sentence.
> *Examples:* **Over the weekend,** my sister found fool's gold.
> **From our porch,** I could see the school.

Add the commas to these sentences.

5. From our boat we swam to see the seals.
6. Yesterday afternoon I was allowed to ride Sarah's horse.
7. With tiny steps the climber reached the peak of the mountain.
8. Because we had been well behaved our teacher took us to sport.

Commas in direct speech

> Some words are separated by a **comma** in **direct speech**: yes, no, well, oh.
> *Example:*
> "**Yes,** I do believe it is our turn," she replied.
> James commented, "**Oh,** I thought it was open."

Add the commas to these sentences.

9. "Yes I did borrow the bike," Jake admitted.
10. "Oh that was so clever," Mrs James said.
11. The scientist proclaimed, "Yes I have the answer!"
12. "No you need to do that again," demanded his father.

Score 2 points for each correct answer! **SCORE /24** (0-10) (12-18) (20-24)

Phonic Knowledge & Spelling

AC9E6LY08, AC9E6LY09

Plurals

> Most words that end in **–o** are made plural by adding **–es**. *Example:* mang**o**, mango**es**.
> Musical instruments have only **–s** added.
> *Example:* pian**o**, piano**s**

Write the plural (more than one) by adding either –es or just –s.

1. banjo _____
2. tomato _____
3. potato _____

Circle the words which have a long 'e' sound.

4. steep   guess   litre   meant
5. ankle   cheap   eight   people

Choose a sound from the box that the underlined word makes. The first one is done for you.

> **uff:** the sound in stuff   **ow:** the sound in cow
> **ew:** the sound in stew   **off:** the sound in toffee

Lost for hours, we broke the <u>bough</u> to use as shade. <u>ow</u>

6. Our small plane had a very <u>rough</u> landing. _____
7. We had to walk <u>through</u> the raging creek water. _____
8. My bad <u>cough</u> kept me awake at night. _____

Compound Words

Match the words in the box to make compound words.

| bed   life   neck   sauce   brush |

9. tooth_____
10. after_____
11. _____pan
12. _____room
13. _____lace

Score 2 points for each correct answer! **SCORE /26** (0-10) (12-20) (22-26)

TARGETING HOMEWORK 6 © PASCAL PRESS ISBN 9781925726480

Manta Ray

Imaginative text – Narrative
Author – Peter Alford

With massive wings, four metres wide, these huge animals are like graceful birds flying through the ocean. Filter feeders, vacuuming the seawater, they fill their stomachs with tiny plankton and shrimp. Like a cave, their mouth is always open. With a throat the size of a football, they threaten few creatures in the ocean. Weighing the same as your parents' car, nothing threatens them in return.

Tide changes in the north of Western Australia are up to nine metres — the height of your house. Water near the shore can become very deep. Sally saw the huge ray swimming close to shore. Quickly, she gathered her diving goggles, flippers and snorkel. Paddling wildly, she reached the back of the ray which seemingly ignored her as it

swam lazily. One thought flashed into her mind.

"Grab the tail! Grab the tail!"

It was the crazy person in her head demanding it.

She reached towards the animal as it turned in its body length and came straight for her. Seeing that two-metre-wide mouth threatening to swallow her, she panicked. At the last moment, the beast turned, flapping its mighty wing. Like a stone she plummeted down, spinning like clothes in a washing machine.

After being briefly pinned to the sea floor, she struggled to the surface. Manta rays may not smile, but that animal did.

TERM 2 ENGLISH

Write or circle the correct answer.

1. **What does 'in return' mean?**

   a in exchange or response

   b in an aggressive way

   c in a bad mood

2. **How high are the tide changes in Western Australia?**

   _____

3. **What does it mean that there was a crazy person in Sally's head?**

   a She was laughing.

   b She was asking herself.

   c She was thinking to herself.

4. **What do manta rays eat?**

   _____

5. **How heavy is a manta ray?**

   _____

6. **Which words tell you how Sally felt when the manta ray turned to face her?**

   _____

7. **How did the writer compare the way the manta ray moves with a bird?**

   _____

   _____

8. **Which words describe that Sally rolled around in the ocean?**

   _____

   _____

Score 2 points for each correct answer!

SCORE **/16** 0-6 8-12 14-16

My Book Review

Title _____

Author _____

Rating ☆☆☆☆☆

Comment _____

Number & Algebra

AC9M6N04

Adding decimals without digital technologies

Do not use calculators to do the additions in this section.

Complete these calculations mentally.

① 6.307 + 13.51 = _____

② 2.72 + 4.409 = _____

③ 4.586 + 0.71 = _____

④ 2.004 + 1.06 + 5.9 = _____

⑤ 8.13 + 20.04 + 100.6 = _____

Complete these calculations.

⑥
```
   34.03
+  17.987
    3.02
_____
```

⑨
```
    0.3474
+  10.4347
    1.3447
_____
```

⑦
```
  123.98
+  58.067
  220.15
_____
```

⑩
```
   93.07
+  10.17
   55.27
_____
```

⑧
```
    7.093
+ 913.72
   51.001
_____
```

⑪
```
  109.978
+   1.309
   50.08
_____
```

Complete these calculations. You can use pen and paper to help.

⑫ 0.450 + 13.20 + 41.008

= _____

⑬ 9.23 + 0.301 + 111.11 + 2.022 + 40

= _____

⑭ 1004 + 7.021 + 203.0102 + 0.2101 + 21

= _____

⑮ 0.9 + 9.09 + 90.009

= _____

Statistics & Probability

AC9M6P01

Predicting likely outcomes

Use this spinner to answer the following five questions.

Write your answers as common fractions.

① What is the chance of a 6 being spun on the first go?

_____

② What is the chance of a 6 being spun on the second go?

_____

③ What is the chance of an even number being spun?

_____

④ What is the chance of a factor of 12 being spun?

_____

⑤ If there is nothing wrong with the wheel and the number 7 was spun five times in a row, what is the chance that 7 will come up again on the sixth spin?

_____

⑥ What is the chance that a number greater than 3 will be spun, as a percentage?
a 55% **b** 60% **c** 75% **d** 80%

⑦ What is the chance that a number less than 5 will be spun, as a fraction?

a $\frac{1}{2}$ **b** $\frac{1}{3}$ **c** $\frac{1}{4}$ **d** $\frac{1}{5}$

⑧ What is the chance that a number greater than 9 will be spun, as a decimal?

_____

⑨ What is the chance that an odd number or an even number will come up?
a 1.0 **b** 2.0 **c** 12 **d** 1.1

⑩ If the spinner was spun 120 times, which of these results would be most likely?
a Nine never came up.
b Nine came up fifty times.
c Nine came up three times.
d Nine came up nine times.

11. If the spinner was spun 100 times, which of these results would be most likely?

    a Five and ten came up 30 times.

    b Five and ten came up 20 times.

    c Five and ten came up 8 times.

    d Five and ten came up 14 times.

12. If the spinner was spun 180 times, which of these results would be most likely?

    a Seven and ten came up 13 times.

    b Seven and ten came up 28 times.

    c Seven and ten came up 6 times.

    d Seven and ten came up 36 times.

Score 2 points for each correct answer! SCORE **/24** (0-10) (12-18) (20-24)

Measurement & Space

AC9M6SP01

Constructing 3-D objects from nets

Some of these shapes are nets of 3-D objects. Use them to answer the following questions.

A   B   C

D   E   F

Which net could make each object? Write the letter of the net in the box.

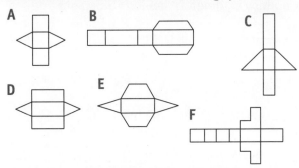

① ☐   ④ ☐

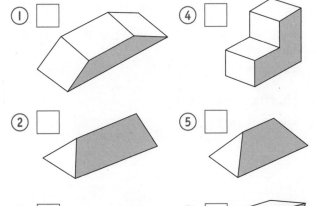

② ☐   ⑤ ☐

③ ☐   ⑥ ☐

⑦ Which object has six faces? _____

⑧ How many faces does F have? _____

⑨ How many edges does D have? _____

---

⑩ How many edges does C have? _____

⑪ How many edges does B have? Circle the correct answer.

a 8   **b** 10   **c** 12   **d** 14

⑫ How many edges does F have? Circle the correct answer

a 16   **b** 18   **c** 20   **d** 22

Score 2 points for each correct answer! SCORE **/24** (0-10) (12-18) (20-24)

Problem Solving

AC9M6N04

Number problems

Do not use calculators but you may use paper and pen.

This coded message was sent to five spies. Use it to answer the following questions.

> Robert Rooster is 7.034, in between 0.19, followed by 4.76, preceded by 1.063 and stored in 3.407.
>
> Leanne Lemur is 0.006 leaping 6.06, spinning 4.4, twirling 4.202 and hopping 3.
>
> Diane Dormouse is 6.07 throwing 6.009, tossing 3.01, hurling 3.005 and chucking 6.1.

① The first spy who got the coded message knew she had to add together all the numbers from the Robert Rooster section that were less than four to get her special number. What was it?

_____

② The second spy who got the coded message had to add together all the numbers where the last digit is a prime number to get his special number. What was it?

_____

③ The third spy needed to add all of Diane Dormouse's numbers that were larger than the largest number in Leanne Lemur's set to get his special number. What was it?

_____

④ The fourth spy needed to add the smallest number in each of the three groups to get her special number. What was it?

_____

⑤ The fifth spy had to add the middle-sized number in each of the three groups to get her special number. What was it?

_____

TARGETING HOMEWORK 6 © PASCAL PRESS · ISBN 9781925726480

Grammar & Punctuation

AC9E6LA06

Adverbial phrases

> An **adverbial phrase** says **how, when, where** and **why** something happened.
>
> *Example:*
> I usually go to football training **at 7 pm**. (when)
>
> Kate walked **through lots of cobwebs**. (where)

Underline the adverbial phrase and write how, when, where or why about the verb.

① Mum took us to the pool on the school holidays. _____

② After eating the grass, the old cow mooed. _____

③ Moonlight was streaming through my window. _____

④ I dug a huge hole with Grandma's shovel. _____

⑤ We're going there for a holiday. _____

Prepositions in adverbial phrases

> **Adverbial phrases** usually start with a **preposition**. Prepositions are words like: about, above, after, before, behind, for, on, through, until, with, within, without etc.

Choose a preposition from the box to complete each sentence.

> without   through   until
> within   behind

⑥ The lost pilot trudged slowly _____ the swamp.

⑦ _____ enough water, people can only survive two days.

⑧ The explorers dug _____ the tree and buried their treasure.

⑨ _____ seconds the drone crashed to the ground.

⑩ Both dragons stood quietly _____ one breathed fire and charged.

Score 2 points for each correct answer!   SCORE **/20**   (0-8) (10-14) (16-20)

Phonic Knowledge & Spelling

AC9E6LY09

Word origins

> Some English words come from other languages such as the French language.
> *Examples:* chic, bouquet, brunette
>
> Many Australian animal names come from Aboriginal languages.
> *Examples:* bilby, currawong, quoll

Complete these French cooking words by using the endings in the box.

> –on   –aise   –ach   –nge

① mayonn_____

② mutt_____

③ spin_____

④ ora_____

Choose an Australian animal from the box to complete each sentence.

> wallaby   dingo   galah   wombat

⑤ Living in a tunnel, the _____ has very strong claws to dig.

⑥ A _____ can be found in large flocks flying together.

⑦ Bouncing through the bush, the _____ balances with its tail.

⑧ Farmers do not like the _____ because they kill stock for food.

Suffixes

> A suffix is a syllable added to the end of a word which changes the way the word can be used.
> *Examples:* child, child**ish**   enjoy, enjoy**ment**

Suffix	Meaning
–ive	nature of
–ment	state of
–ory	place for
–ish	nature of

Choose a suffix from above to complete each word.

⑨ expens_____   ⑪ fact_____

⑩ govern_____   ⑫ short_____

Score 2 points for each correct answer!   SCORE **/24**   (0-10) (12-18) (20-24)

TARGETING HOMEWORK 6 © PASCAL PRESS ISBN 9781925726480

American Indian Wars

Informative text – Report
Author – Caroline Tate

Native Americans fought British settlers from the time they first arrived in North America. By the early 1800s, the United States Government was removing Native Americans from their land east of the Mississippi River and placing them west of the river.

After the American Civil War ended in 1865, thousands of settlers moved to the west. They demanded the protection of the United States Army. Lieutenant General William T. Sherman wrote, "Each spot of every road, and each little settlement along five thousand miles of frontier wants its regiment of cavalry or infantry to protect it against the combined power of all the Indians."

The Government and the Lakota Nation signed a **treaty** in 1868. In 1874 an Army-led expedition to the Black Hills found gold. People immediately rushed to the area illegally.

Source: *First Peoples*, Go Facts, Blake Education.

TERM 2 ENGLISH

Write or circle the correct answer.

① What happened after the American Civil War?

_____

② Who did the Native Americans fight first?

_____

③ When was gold found in the Black Hills?

_____

④ 'People immediately rushed to the area illegally.' What does this mean?

a People wanted to find gold and ignored the treaty.

b There was a treaty and this meant that people could go to the Black Hills.

c The American Army became angry after people took the gold.

⑤ Before the 1800s, were there Native Americans living east of the Mississippi River? Write the sentence that answers this question.

_____

_____

_____

⑥ Which Indian nation signed a treaty with the Government?

_____

⑦ Why did people rush to find gold in the Black Hills?

a They wanted to live in the Black Hills.

b Gold was worth lots of money.

c People loved gold for necklaces.

Score 2 points for each correct answer!

SCORE /14 (0-4) (6-10) (12-14)

My Book Review

Title _____

Author _____

Rating ☆☆☆☆☆

Comment _____

_____

Number & Algebra

AC9M6N04

Subtracting decimals without digital technologies

Do not use calculators to do the additions in this section.

Complete these calculations mentally.

① 13.51 – 6.3 = _____

② 4.249 – 4.102 = _____

③ 4.586 – 0.51 = _____

④ 5.58 – 1.24 = _____

⑤ 20.34 – 10.74 = _____

Complete these calculations.

⑥
$$- \begin{array}{r} 34.03 \\ 11.92 \end{array}$$

⑨
$$- \begin{array}{r} 10.3404 \\ 0.1141 \end{array}$$

⑦
$$- \begin{array}{r} 123.98 \\ 58.09 \end{array}$$

⑩
$$- \begin{array}{r} 93.07 \\ 10.17 \end{array}$$

⑧
$$- \begin{array}{r} 7.09 \\ 3.72 \end{array}$$

⑪
$$- \begin{array}{r} 19.07 \\ 11.38 \end{array}$$

Complete these calculations. You can use pen and paper to help.

⑫ 0.45 – 0.20

= _____

⑬ 9.03 – 4.35

= _____

⑭ 14 – 7.2

= _____

⑮ 30.9 – 9.09

= _____

SCORE **/30** (0-12) (14-24) (26-30)

Statistics & Probability

AC9M6ST01

Using a table and a bar graph

Use this table and graph of train accidents in India in 2012 to answer the following questions. They have some missing data and differences between them.

Train Accidents in India, 2012	
Date	Deaths
11/1	5
26/2	3
20/3	15
26/3	2
22/5	35
31/5	7
19/7	1
30/11	47
20/12	0

Source, viewed 13 Aug 2018: https://en.wikipedia.org/wiki/List_of_Indian_rail_accidents

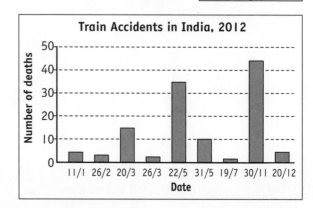

① On which date did the most deaths happen?

_____

② On which date does the graph display the fewest deaths?

_____

③ Which dates on the graph display the same number of deaths?

_____

④ Which two dates have a difference of twenty deaths, according to the table?

_____

⑤ Which two dates have a combined death toll of twelve, according to the table?

_____

⑥ Which two dates have a difference of about nine deaths, as displayed on the graph?

_____

⑦ Which two dates have a combined death toll of twenty, as displayed on the graph?

_____

⑧ Which three dates have a combined death toll of twenty-one, according to the table?

_____

⑨ Which three dates have a combined death toll of twenty-six, according to the graph?

_____

⑩ Which two dates have a difference of seven times between them, according to the table?

_____

⑪ According to the graph, what was the total number of deaths for the dates that had fewer than ten deaths each?

_____

⑫ Which two dates have discrepancies between the table and the graph?

_____

SCORE /24 0-10 12-18 20-24

Measurement & Space

AC9M6SP03

Translations, reflections and rotations

How has the first shape been transformed to get the second shape? Write **translation**, **reflection** or **rotation**.

① _____
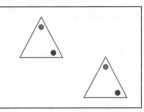

② _____
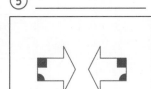

③ _____

④ _____

⑤ _____
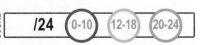

⑥ _____
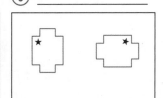

⑦ _____
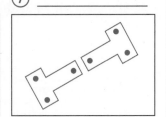

⑧ _____
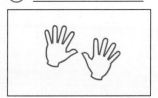

⑨ _____   ⑩ _____
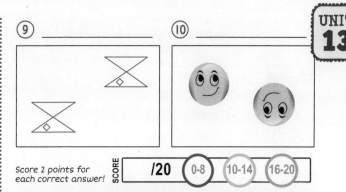

SCORE /20 0-8 10-14 16-20

Problem Solving

AC9M6N04

Number problems

Do not use calculators but you may use paper and pen.

This coded message was sent to five spies. Use it to answer the following questions.

> James can carry 8.03 or hold 66.21 or lift 0.162 or support 2.02 but not all five of them. Max can drop 6.66 or spill 1.8 or drip 1.701 or leak 88.35 but only one at a time. Jason can eat 0.028 or gobble 78.15 or guzzle 100 or consume 12.12 as often as he likes because they are nutritious.

① The first spy who got the coded message knew he had to subtract Max's smallest number from Jason's largest to get her special number. What was it?

_____

② The second spy who got the coded message had to subtract the smallest number that appeared in the coded message from the largest one to get her special number. What was it?

_____

③ The third spy had to find the difference between the number whose digits added up to four and the number whose digits added up to 10 to get her special number. What was it?

_____

④ The fourth spy had to subtract James' number that was closest to 1 from Jason's number that was closest to 45 to get her special number. What was it?

_____

⑤ The fifth spy had to subtract James' number that had a prime number for the last digit from Max's number that had a prime number for the last digit to get her special number. What was it?

_____

Grammar & Punctuation

AC9E6LA04, AC9E6LA06

Phonic Knowledge & Spelling

AC9E6LY08, AC9E6LY09

Verbs

Verbs tell us what is happening in a sentence.
- **Doing verbs** tell us what actions people and things are doing.
  Examples: run, sleep, smell, cry
- **Saying verbs** express different ways of speaking.
  Examples: whisper, shout, bark, growl
- **Feeling verbs** tell us how people and animals feel.
  Examples: love, want, need, hope

Write the missing vowels to complete these doing verbs.

① As he sat by the log, the dingo sn__ff__d the air.

② Firefighters b__rst through the locked door.

③ Our school choir s__ng beautifully at the concert.

④ Eve sh__ffl__d into the room with the plaster on her leg.

⑤ Storm chasers f__ll__w__d the huge storms across the state.

Circle the feeling verbs.

⑥ Emma admires the winner of the dance competition.

⑦ They rejoiced for hours after finding all that hidden food.

⑧ Kangaroos feared the wild dogs in the bush.

⑨ The wombats wished to grow a bill like the platypus.

⑩ The sitter loves looking after energetic toddlers.

Write the jumbled saying verbs correctly.

⑪ The bear **rgwolde** a warning before attacking. _____

⑫ Ethan **hwsiprede** as he tiptoed through the house. _____

⑬ The team **rgmubdle** after their loss.
_____

Root words

English uses parts of words from other languages. These word parts help give the meaning of the words. They are called **root words.**

Examples: **astro–** stars, **–ologist** student of, **sen–** old, **sciss–** cut, **botan–** studies plants, **sol–** the sun

Use the root words from above to complete the words.

① An adjective having to do with the sun.
_____ar

② A person who works in a zoo.
zo_____

③ One who looks after forests.
_____ist

④ One who studies the night sky.
_____nomer

⑤ An instrument used to cut things.
_____ors

⑥ An elderly person. _____ior

Choose silent letters from the box to complete the words.

l	n	s	t	c	k

⑦ sof__en

⑧ i__land

⑨ mus__le

⑩ ca__f

⑪ autum__

⑫ __nife

Choose a sound from the box to match the words.

j	k	sh	long a

⑬ h**a**y   tr**ai**n   _____

⑭ **s**ugar   ma**ch**ine   _____

⑮ du**ck**   **c**limb   _____

⑯ **j**am   we**dge**   _____

Persuasive text – Argument
Author – Peter Alford

Text 1: Make Cough Medicine Yummy

Cruelty to children — do adults ever stop? A simple cough has parents running out to buy a revolting medicine that tastes like nothing else on earth! Why is it that cough medicine has to taste like the leg of a rotting yak? Surely scientists, who seem to be able to do everything these days, could make it taste nice. Coughing is bad enough, swallowing horrible gunk is worse. Doctors and parents seem to have a plan — making medicine taste so disgusting that children try very hard not to get the cold or flu in the first place. Doctors are so very cruel!

Text 2: Cough Medicine

Without cough medicine children may become very sick indeed. Coughing can lead to a number of very dangerous illnesses. Being sent to hospital is sure to happen if coughs are ignored. Cough medicine should be used.

TERM 2 ENGLISH

Write or circle the correct answer.

① **Which word means awful?**

　a wallowing

　b revolting

　c rotting

　d cruel

② **What does the writer compare the taste of cough medicine to?**

_____

③ **What could happen to children if they cough and don't have medicine?**

_____

_____

④ **What is the parents' and doctors' plan to stop children becoming ill?**

_____

_____

_____

⑤ **Which phrase is used to say that children are made to have terrible tasting medicine?**

　a do parents ever stop

　b parents running out

　c cruelty to children

⑥ **Which word in text 2 means 'not taking notice of something'?**

_____

⑦ **What should scientists be able to do?**

_____

_____

_____

⑧ **Which text is formal and likely to have been written by a doctor?**

_____

Score 2 points for each correct answer! SCORE **/16** (0-6) (8-12) (14-16)

My Book Review

Title _____

Author _____

Rating ☆☆☆☆☆

Comment _____

_____

Number & Algebra

AC9M6N05

Adding and subtracting fractions with related denominators

Work out these equations. Convert any answers that are improper fractions to mixed numbers.

① $\frac{7}{8} + \frac{4}{8} - \frac{3}{8}$

= _____

② $\frac{9}{16} - \frac{8}{16} + \frac{12}{16}$

= _____

③ $3\frac{3}{5} + \frac{1}{5} - \frac{2}{5}$

= _____

④ $5\frac{3}{16} - 3\frac{1}{16} + 2\frac{5}{16}$

= _____

⑤ $8\frac{4}{17} - \frac{3}{17} + 4\frac{7}{17}$

= _____

⑥ $\frac{6}{7} - \frac{4}{7} + 2\frac{1}{7} - \frac{3}{7}$

= _____

⑦ $3\frac{9}{11} - 1\frac{7}{11} + 2\frac{2}{11} + 4\frac{1}{11}$

= _____

⑧ $20\frac{7}{8} - 15\frac{5}{8} + 90\frac{5}{8} + 4\frac{1}{8}$

= _____

⑨ $2\frac{8}{13} + 6\frac{4}{13} + 5\frac{3}{13} - 5\frac{1}{13}$

= _____

⑩ $\frac{14}{15} - \frac{9}{15} - \frac{3}{15} + \frac{4}{15} + \frac{8}{15} + \frac{6}{15}$

= _____

⑪ $\frac{9}{2} - \frac{7}{2} + \frac{1}{2} + \frac{6}{2} - \frac{3}{2}$

= _____

⑫ $\frac{7}{3} + \frac{11}{3} + \frac{4}{3} + \frac{5}{3} - \frac{7}{3} - \frac{7}{3}$

= _____

⑬ $8\frac{3}{5} + \frac{2}{5} - 2\frac{2}{5}$

= _____

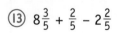

Statistics & Probability

AC9M6ST02

Using a table and a line graph

Use the table and the graph to answer the following questions.

Average Temperature in Antarctica (degrees Celsius)						
Month	Jan	Feb	Mar	Apr	May	Jun
Temp.	-2.8	-8.8	-17.3	-20.9	-23.3	-22.9
Month	Jul	Aug	Sep	Oct	Nov	Dec
Temp.	-25.8	-27.4	-25.7	-19.4	-9.7	-3.5

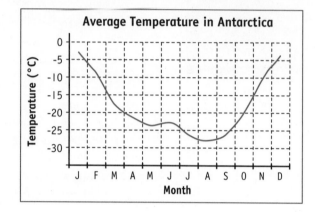

Average Temperature in Antarctica

① What is the lowest temperature in the data?

_____

② Which month has the lowest temperature?

_____

③ What is the highest temperature in the data?

_____

④ Which month has the highest temperature?

_____

⑤ What is the difference between the highest and lowest temperatures?

_____

⑥ Which two months have -18 °C?

_____

⑦ Approximately, what temperature is common to the most months?

_____

⑧ Could this data have been represented as a bar graph? _____

⑨ Give a reason for your answer to question 8.

_____

⑩ Which two months have a temperature difference of 2 °C?

_____

⑪ Which two months have a temperature difference of 17 °C?

_____

TARGETING HOMEWORK 6 © PASCAL PRESS ISBN 9781925726480

⑫ Which two months combined result in a temperature of -27 °C?

_____

⑬ The July part of the graph looks like this:

What part of the line shows the temperature in the data? Circle the correct answer.

a beginning   **b** centre   **c** end

Score 2 points for each correct answer!   SCORE **/26** (0-10) (12-20) (22-26)

Measurement & Space
AC9M6M03

Interpreting and using timetables

Use this timetable to answer the following questions.

Cruise Ships Arrival in Melbourne, November 2017						
Ship	**Arrival**			**Departure**		
	Day	**Date**	**Time**	**Day**	**Date**	**Time**
Pacific Jewel	Wed	1 Nov 2017	0900	Wed	8 Nov 2017	1600
Maasdam	Thu	9 Nov 2017	0200	Sun	12 Nov 2017	0730
Noordam	Tue	14 Nov 2017	1100	Fri	17 Nov 2017	1830
Norwegian Jewel	Sat	18 Nov 2017	1500	Wed	22 Nov 2017	0100
Pacific Jewel	Fri	24 Nov 2017	0730	Mon	27 Nov 2017	1600
Celebrity Solstice	Tue	28 Nov 2017	1300	Thu	30 Nov 2017	1900

① How many different cruise ships are featured in the timetable? _____

② In total, how many times during the timetable period do cruise ships arrive in Melbourne?

_____

③ Which ship arrives and departs in the morning?

_____

④ What is the earliest time that a cruise ship arrives?

_____

⑤ What is the latest time that a cruise ship arrives?

_____

⑥ What is the earliest time that a cruise ship departs?

_____

⑦ What is the latest time that a cruise ship departs?

_____

⑧ How many days does *Celebrity Solstice* stay in Melbourne?

_____

⑨ How long, in days and hours, does *Maasdam* stay in Melbourne?

_____

⑩ Which cruise ship stays the shortest time in Melbourne?

_____

⑪ How many days are there between the arrival of *Noordam* and the arrival of *Celebrity Solstice*?

_____

⑫ In total, which cruise ship stays the longest time in Melbourne?

_____

⑬ How many days is the longest stay in Melbourne?

_____

Score 2 points for each correct answer!   SCORE **/26** (0-10) (12-20) (22-26)

Problem Solving
AC9M6N05

Fraction and location problems

Follow the grid locations to add or subtract fractions. For example, the fraction at grid location 2B is $\frac{4}{10}$.

Convert any answers that are improper fractions to mixed numbers.

	A	B	C	D	E	F	G	H
1	$\frac{7}{7}$	$\frac{9}{16}$	$\frac{5}{9}$	$\frac{1}{9}$	$\frac{12}{16}$	$\frac{6}{10}$	$\frac{5}{7}$	$\frac{2}{7}$
2	$\frac{3}{5}$	$\frac{4}{10}$	$\frac{2}{8}$	$\frac{5}{16}$	$\frac{1}{8}$	$\frac{7}{10}$	$\frac{3}{9}$	$\frac{4}{8}$
3	$\frac{9}{10}$	$\frac{8}{16}$	$\frac{1}{10}$	$\frac{5}{8}$	$\frac{8}{10}$	$\frac{15}{16}$	$\frac{3}{10}$	$\frac{3}{7}$
4	$\frac{8}{16}$	$\frac{3}{16}$	$\frac{1}{7}$	$\frac{1}{5}$	$\frac{6}{7}$	$\frac{3}{8}$	$\frac{4}{7}$	$\frac{1}{8}$
5	$\frac{4}{5}$	$\frac{7}{10}$	$\frac{7}{9}$	$\frac{2}{10}$	$\frac{2}{5}$	$\frac{5}{10}$	$\frac{1}{16}$	$\frac{2}{16}$

① 2B + 3E − 5D + 3G = _____

② 5A − 2A + 5E + 4D = _____

③ 2B + 3G + 5B − 3E = _____

④ 3F − 5H − 3B + 5G + 1B = _____

⑤ 1A + 4C − 3H + 4C − 1G = _____

Grammar & Punctuation

AC9E6LA06

Prepositions and adverbial phrases

> **Adverbial phrases** usually start with a **preposition**. Prepositions are words like: about, above, after, at, before, behind, during, without.
>
> *Examples:*
>
> I usually watch my favourite show **at** 7 o'clock.
>
> preposition   adverbial phrase
>
> **During** the game, I fell and sprained my ankle.

Write the missing vowels to complete the prepositions.

① He lifted the bow b__f__r__ he took aim at the apple.

② D__r__ng his performance, the clown fell over his feet.

③ Jason buttered the toast __ft__r taking it from the toaster.

④ The sky was clear and the sun shone w__th__ __t a single cloud.

Choose prepositions from the box to complete the sentences.

| past | after | against | since |

⑤ The awards were given out _____ the choir sang.

⑥ She was thrown _____ the rocks after the explosion.

⑦ In the _____, the athletes ran barefoot.

⑧ _____ the holidays, I have been ill.

Underline the adverbial phrases and circle the prepositions.

⑨ James ran quickly after dark as he was scared.

⑩ We all had to climb through the muddy tunnel.

⑪ Gemma won't go camping without her own tent.

⑫ There were massive crowds at the fairground.

Phonic Knowledge & Spelling

AC9E6LY09

Prefixes

> A **prefix** is attached to the beginning of a word to change its meaning.
> *Examples:* **semi**circle, **para**medic, **trans**port
>
> | Prefix | Meaning |
> |--------|---------|
> | in– | not |
> | super– | above/more than |
> | co– | with |
> | re– | again |
> | tri– | three |

Choose a prefix from the box to complete each word.

① The _____-pilot landed the plane during the storm.

② My dad is using lots of _____ foods in his cooking.

③ I'm training every day for the _____athlon next month.

④ We can't get to the next level because this level is _____complete.

⑤ He had to _____do the test because he got everything wrong.

Suffixes

> A **suffix** is attached to the end of a word, changing its meaning.
> *Example:* use, use**ful**, use**less**, us**able**
>
> | Suffix | Meaning |
> |--------|---------|
> | –ness | state of being |
> | –ship | position held |
> | –able | capable of being |
> | –ful | notable for |

Choose a suffix from the box to complete each word.

⑥ happi_____

⑦ truth_____

⑧ friend_____

⑨ like_____

Score 2 points for each correct answer! SCORE **/24** (0-10) (12-18) (20-24)

Score 2 points for each correct answer! SCORE **/18** (0-6) (8-14) (16-18)

Kindness Costs Nothing

Informative text – Personal recount
Author – Peter Alford

In school I was teased about the colour of my hair. People thought it was funny that I was the only person in my class with that shade of hair. Having that happen tore me up inside. It made me feel awful. Everything changed. I started to hate myself. Anything I did seemed totally wrong, even looking in the mirror was terrible. Kids didn't understand that their words cut me deeply. No, I didn't bleed on the outside, I bled on the inside. Words are like that, they can cause a wound that lasts your whole life. Tears and being ill were all because of my shattered feelings.

Then it happened – a new kid came to school. Being clever, great at sport and good-looking, he made friends quickly. When he heard me being teased one day, he 'stood up' for me. Everyone got to know he wouldn't see me being teased. He lifted me up and made life so much better. Kind words like: 'be proud of yourself', 'you are a good person' made me believe in myself. His kind words stopped me bleeding inside.

Write or circle the correct answer.

1 **What does 'he lifted me up' mean?**

   a He made me feel good about myself.

   b He lifted me up.

   c He made me feel taller.

2 **What was one bad part of the writer's life before the new kid came to school?**

_____

_____

3 **Why was the new kid so popular?**

_____

_____

4 **What is meant by 'tore me up inside'?**

   a made a mess of my insides

   b made me bleed

   c hurt me deeply

5 **When the new kid heard the teasing, what did he do?**

_____

_____

6 **Why didn't the writer like looking into the mirror?**

   a He hated seeing his hair.

   b He wanted to check his neatness.

   c He liked himself.

7 **What was one kind thing the new kid said?**

_____

_____

8 **What is the meaning of 'he stood up for me'?**

   a He would offer his chair.

   b He stopped people being nasty.

   c He loved to stand.

Score 2 points for each correct answer!

SCORE **/16** (0-6) (8-12) (14-16)

My Book Review

Title _____

Author _____

Rating ☆☆☆☆☆

Comment _____

_____

Number & Algebra

AC9M6N07

Calculating percentage discounts without digital technologies

Calculate the discounts offered on these toys.
Do not use a calculator.

ball
$1.00

wind-up
bird $2.50

elephant
$12.00

aeroplane
$6.00

① What is 10% discount on the aeroplane?
_____

② What is 25% discount on the elephant?
_____

③ What is 50% discount on the ball?
_____

④ What is 50% discount on the wind-up bird?
_____

⑤ What is 25% discount on the aeroplane?
_____

⑥ What will the price of the aeroplane be after a 25% discount has been subtracted?
_____

⑦ What will the price of the elephant be after a 50% discount has been subtracted?
_____

⑧ What will the price of the ball be after a 10% discount has been subtracted?
_____

⑨ What will the price of the wind-up bird be after a 10% discount has been subtracted?
_____

⑩ What will the price of the elephant be after a 25% discount has been subtracted?
_____

TERM 2 MATHS

Statistics & Probability

AC9M6P01

Conducting chance experiments

Experiments were conducted using these spinners:

• **Spinner #1** had 100 sections the pointer could point to. 24 sections were **1** and 16 sections were **2**.

• **Spinner #2** had 150 sections the pointer could point to. 18 sections were **8** and 60 sections were **9**.

Write your answers as decimal fractions.

① With Spinner #1, what chance did **1** have?
_____

② With Spinner #1, what chance did **2** have?
_____

③ With Spinner #2, what chance did **8** have?
_____

④ With Spinner #2, what chance did **9** have?
_____

⑤ With Spinner #1, what chance did either **1** or **2** have of coming up?
_____

⑥ With Spinner #2, what chance did either **8** or **9** have of coming up?
_____

⑦ If Spinner #2 had 36 sections for **50**, what chance did **50** have of coming up?
_____

⑧ If Spinner #2 had 30 sections for **100**, what chance did **100** have of coming up?
_____

⑨ If Spinner #2 had 90 sections of odd numbers, what chance did odd numbers have of coming up?
_____

Score 2 points for each correct answer! SCORE **/20** 0-8 10-14 16-20

Score 2 points for each correct answer! SCORE **/18** 0-6 8-14 16-18

TARGETING HOMEWORK 6 © PASCAL PRESS ISBN 9781925726480

Measurement & Space

AC9M6SP02, AC9M6SP03

Translations, rotations and reflections

The shape on this grid can be **translated** and **rotated** over the grid.
It can also be **reflected** about the three coloured lines of reflection.

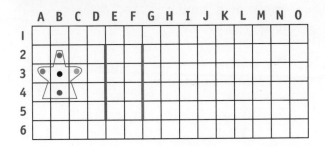

① If the shape is moved nine grid positions to the right and four down, what grid location would the blue circle be?

_____

② If the shape is rotated 90° clockwise with the purple circle as the axis, what grid location would the green circle end up?

_____

③ What grid location would the black circle end up if the shape was reflected along the red line?

_____

④ What grid location would the green circle end up if the shape was reflected along the blue line?

_____

⑤ What grid location would the blue circle end up if the shape was reflected along the red line and then translated 3 grid positions to the right and 2 down?

_____

⑥ What grid location would the black circle end up if the shape was reflected along the blue line and then translated 4 grid positions to the left and 2 up?

_____

⑦ What grid location would the purple circle end up if the shape was moved 11 grid locations to the right and then rotated 180° clockwise around the black circle?

_____

Problem Solving

AC9M6N07, AC9M6P01

Discount and chance spinner problems

Use the toys in **Number & Algebra** to answer the following questions. **Do not use a calculator.**

① If one of the toys was doubled in price and after a 25% discount its new sale price became $9, which toy was it?

_____

② If a toy was offered at a 50% discount if four of it were purchased and the discount came to $12, which toy was it?

_____

③ If Emilio used a $10 note to buy four wind-up birds at a 25% discount, how much change did he get?

_____

④ If the store offered a 25% discount on one toy and a 50% discount on another toy so that the combined saving came to $6.25, what were the two toys?

_____

You may use a calculator to answer the following questions.

⑤ If the number twenty had a 0.08 chance of turning up on a spinner that had 300 sections the pointer could point to, how many times would the number twenty appear on the spinner?

_____

⑥ On the same spinner as in the previous question, if the number thirty had a 0.15 chance of turning up, how many times did the number thirty appear on the spinner?

_____

⑦ On a spinner with 450 sections the pointer could point to, if the numbers seven and seventy had a combined chance of 0.32 that one of them would come up, how many times did seven appear on the spinner if it appeared one-third as many times as 70?

_____

⑧ On the same spinner as in the previous question, if there were eight numbers which had a combined chance of 0.32 that one of them would come up, how many times did each number appear if they each appeared the same number of times?

_____

Grammar & Punctuation

AC9E6LA06

Adverbials

> **Adverbials** are words and phrases that tell **how**, **when**, **where** and **why** things are happening in a sentence.
>
> *Examples:*
>
> The puppies slept **like babies** (how).
>
> **Every day** (when) we walk **to the beach** (where).
>
> Grandma made the cake **for my birthday** (why).

Circle the adverbial phrases in these sentences that tell you how.

① At the football they cheered loudly at the goal.

② Mr Shand spoke loudly over the noise.

③ Rabbits hopped quickly through the paddock during the night.

④ Pam swam poorly during lessons.

⑤ Lightning flashed brightly during the fierce storm.

⑥ She ran quickly to warn of the fire.

Choose an adverbial phrase from the box to complete each sentence.

inside our gym   amongst bamboo
over the deep gorge   in the deep dark ocean
around the streets of our town

⑦ Our school fete is always held _____ _____ .

⑧ Monstrous squid live _____ _____ .

⑨ Tigers hunt _____ which helps them to hide.

⑩ Men and women work _____ _____ with no safety harness.

⑪ Old cars drove _____ _____ .

Phonic Knowledge & Spelling

AC9E6LY09

Prefixes

> Remember! **Prefixes** are attached to the beginning of a word. They change the meaning of the word. Some words can be made to mean the **opposite** by adding the prefixes **un–**, **dis–**, **in–**.
>
> *Examples:* true, **un**true   obey, **dis**obey
> capable, **in**capable

Use the prefixes from the box to make these words mean the opposite.

un   dis   in

① _____appear

② _____likely

③ _____visible

④ _____complete

⑤ _____fortunate

⑥ _____courage

Match the meaning of these German words with their meanings.

hamster   noodle   waltz   spare ribs

⑦ a type of spaghetti: _____

⑧ a type of dance: _____

⑨ a small animal: _____

⑩ meat dish from cows or pigs: _____

Contractions

> Remember! A **contraction** is when two words are shortened and combined to become one word. An **apostrophe (')** is used to replace the missing letter/s.
>
> *Examples:* is not = isn't   I would = I'd

Join these words to make contractions by using an apostrophe.

⑪ are   not   = _____

⑫ you   will   = _____

⑬ there   has   = _____

⑭ what   is   = _____

⑮ they   are   = _____

Profile: City Life

Melbourne

Melbourne has the second largest population of any city in Australia (4.25 million) and will become the largest city as early as 2030. Melbourne is a large, sprawling city. There are only 440 people per square kilometre and most people live in houses. Melbourne has a fairly low density because there are development rules about buildings in the centre of the city. Melbourne's public transport system works best in the suburbs closest to the city centre. Therefore, most people own a car to allow them to travel further.

Informative text – Report
Author – Nicholas Brasch

Hong Kong

Most people in Hong Kong live in high-rise buildings. A population of more than 7 million in a very small, mountainous area makes Hong Kong one of the most densely populated places in the world. Population densities reach 90 000 people per square kilometre in some areas. Most people in Hong Kong do not own cars. There is so little space to park them.

Source: *Asia*, Go Facts, Blake Education.

Write or circle the correct answer.

① **Which city has the larger population?**

a Melbourne

b Hong Kong

② **If you lived in Hong Kong and owned a car, what would be difficult and why?**

_____

_____

_____

_____

③ **Would Melbourne or Hong Kong have more space for people to live and play?**

_____

④ **Would most people in Hong Kong have a house like those in Melbourne?**

a No, because there is so little space.

b No, most people live in high-rise apartments in Hong Kong.

c Yes, most people live in houses in Hong Kong.

⑤ **What does 'population density' mean?**

a There are a large number of people who are dense.

b How many people there are in a space.

c There are few people in a space.

⑥ **In what year will Melbourne become the largest city in Australia?**

_____

⑦ **What does 'Melbourne has a fairly low density' mean?**

a Melbourne has very high apartment buildings.

b Melbourne has lots of underground areas.

c People in Melbourne mainly live in houses.

My Book Review

Title _____

Author _____

Rating ☆☆☆☆☆

Comment _____

_____

Score 2 points for each correct answer!

SCORE **/14** (0-4) (6-10) (12-14)

Number & Algebra

AC9M6A03

Using mental strategies

Circle the adjoining **pairs** of numbers that add up to **20**. There could be more than one pair in each row.

①	15	3	12	4	5	13	7	8	14	3	19	10
②	9	10	6	4	12	1	5	11	4	17	3	8
③	1	19	5	12	3	18	2	7	16	5	2	13
④	3	17	2	11	6	5	0	16	4	12	9	6
⑤	9	11	7	9	0	14	12	4	18	14	3	8
⑥	18	1	12	8	2	8	7	13	8	15	4	12
⑦	7	6	14	5	9	10	13	5	15	9	13	8

Circle the adjoining sets of **three** numbers that add up to **20**. There could be more than one pair in each row.

⑧	10	3	1	4	15	13	7	8	12	7	2	14
⑨	17	10	6	4	19	1	3	12	5	12	3	8
⑩	4	12	5	18	3	1	2	17	16	5	8	11
⑪	11	16	7	8	9	3	0	11	4	12	7	5
⑫	6	11	4	9	13	16	12	4	2	9	7	4
⑬	8	3	9	13	7	19	10	16	8	1	11	13
⑭	1	2	3	13	17	6	7	7	9	19	13	8
⑮	9	10	3	7	19	2	7	3	11	6	4	8

Score 2 points for each correct answer!

SCORE **/30** (0-12) (14-24) (26-30)

Statistics & Probability

AC9M6ST01

Pie charts

These pie charts show the type and quantity of Australian snakes kept by three zoos.

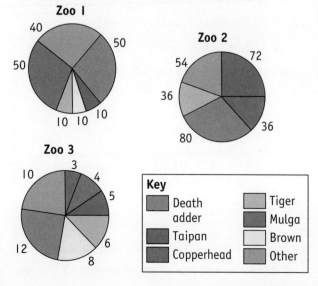

Zoo 1
40
50
50
10 10 10

Zoo 2
54 72
36
36
80

Zoo 3
10 3
4
5
6
12 8

Key
- Death adder
- Taipan
- Copperhead
- Tiger
- Mulga
- Brown
- Other

Use the pie charts to answer the following questions.

① How many snakes does Zoo 1 have?
_____

② How many snakes do Zoos 2 and 3 have, combined?
_____

③ In total, how many **taipans** are there?
_____

④ Which snakes do Zoos 1 and 3 have that Zoo 2 doesn't?
_____

⑤ Which snake do Zoos 2 and 3 have that Zoo 1 doesn't?
_____

⑥ Judging by the appearance of the pie chart, what fraction of Zoo 3's collection is made up of **death adders**? Estimate your answer.
_____

⑦ Judging by the appearance of the pie chart, do the **other** and the **death adder** make up **more**, **less** or **half** of Zoo 1's collection?
_____

⑧ Judging by the appearance of the pie chart, about what fraction of Zoo 2's collection do the **other**, **tiger**, **death adder** and **copperhead** make up?
_____

⑨ In Zoo 3's collection, the number of which three snakes combined equals the number of **death adders**?
_____

⑩ In Zoo 2's collection, the number of which two snakes combined is equal to the number of another of its snakes?
_____

_____

⑪ Is the combined number of **tiger**, **brown** and **taipan** snakes held by Zoo 1 equal to 25% of its collection? Answer **yes** or **no**.
_____

⑫ What percentage of Zoo 3's collection is the **death adder**?
_____

Score 2 points for each correct answer!

SCORE **/24** (0-10) (12-18) (20-24)

TARGETING HOMEWORK 6 © PASCAL PRESS ISBN 9781925726480

Measurement & Space

AC9M6M04

Missing angles

Complementary angles add to 90°.
Supplementary angles add to 180°.

What is the size of the missing angle?

① 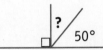   ? = _____

②   ? = _____

③   ? = _____

④   ? = _____

⑤   ? = _____

⑥   ? = _____

⑦   ? = _____

Score 2 points for each correct answer! **SCORE** **/14** (0-4) (6-10) (12-14)

Problem Solving

AC9M6A03, AC9M6M01

Number and capacity problems

Do not use a calculator to answer the following questions.

① If you subtract the secret number from 20 and from 14, the two answers added together will equal 8.
What is the secret number?

_____

② If you subtract the secret number from 8, 5 and 11, the three answers added together will equal 15.
What is the secret number?

_____

③ If you subtract the secret number from 17, 11 and 13, the three answers added together will equal 11.
What is the secret number?

_____

④ If you add the secret number to 4 and 12 and then add the answers together, you get 32.
What is the secret number?

_____

⑤ If you add the secret number to 15 and 30 and then add the answers together, you get 55.
What is the secret number?

_____

⑥ If you add the secret number to 20 and 40, then add the answers and then halve them, you get 40.
What is the secret number?

_____

You may use a calculator to work out these problems.

⑦ A man had 80 litres of fuel in his car at the start of his trip. At the end, he had only half left.
How much fuel did he have left?

_____

⑧ A woman had 92 litres of fuel in her car at the start of her trip. She used three quarters of it and then bought enough petrol to double what she had.
How much fuel did she have then?

_____

⑨ A driver had 45 litres of fuel in her car. She used half of it and then topped up to 45 litres again. If fuel is $1.98 per litre, how much did she pay to top up?

_____

⑩ A service station was down to one seventh of its fuel storage. Then there was a rush of motorists purchasing fuel and half of the remaining petrol was sold.
If there are 98 litres left now, how many litres can its fuel storage hold?

_____

Grammar & Punctuation

Add commas between the noun groups.

① Serina found glass floats cuttlefish bones and dead starfish on the beach.

② After the storm, they found broken trees swollen rivers and a tin roof in the paddock.

③ To make banana cake, you will need flour soft bananas a long tin and lots of butter.

Circle the verbs.

④ She laughed at the silly joke.

⑤ Finding the treasure, they rejoiced for hours.

⑥ Sheep farmers feared the wild dogs.

⑦ Kangaroos giggled at the spiny echidna.

Add commas between the verb groups.

⑧ Ethan scrubbed his car washed the dog and mowed the lawn on Saturday.

⑨ The wizard added snake powder said a spell and changed himself into a frog.

⑩ At the concert, she smiled took a deep breath and sang beautifully.

Add commas and speech marks.

⑪ Go over there said Kell.

⑫ Don't be late reminded Tom's mother.

⑬ Henry argued I think it's your turn to do the dishes.

⑭ She let the team down commented Coach Simpson.

Choose prepositions to complete the sentences.

without	through	until	across

⑮ The tired explorer slowly and painfully walked _____ the swamp.

⑯ _____ eating much food, people can survive for weeks.

⑰ _____ now, finding treasure was difficult but not impossible.

⑱ Walking _____ the desert was difficult for the explorers.

Phonic Knowledge & Spelling

Write the plurals by adding either –es or –s.

① piano _____

② mango _____

③ potato _____

④ stone _____

Choose words from the box to complete these compound words.

noon	ground	paste	cast

⑤ tooth_____

⑥ back_____

⑦ after_____

⑧ fore_____

Choose derivatives from the box to match with the words.

brunch	smog	telethon

⑨ television + marathon = _____

⑩ breakfast + lunch = _____

⑪ fog + smoke = _____

Choose the correct f sounds to complete the words.

ff	gh	ph

⑫ My grandmother never answers the tele____one.

⑬ Walking is di____icult for some older people.

⑭ I wanted to cou____ during the concert.

Choose antonyms from the box for the adjectives.

careful	safe	costly	weak

⑮ cheap _____

⑯ strong _____

⑰ dangerous _____

⑱ careless _____

Score 2 points for each correct answer! SCORE /36 (0-16) (18-30) (32-36)

Score 2 points for each correct answer! SCORE /36 (0-16) (18-30) (32-36)

TARGETING HOMEWORK 6 © PASCAL PRESS ISBN 9781925726480

Persuasive text – Discussion
Author – Peter Alford

Text 1

When you meet the Governor of the State you should just say, "Howdy". None of that bowing or scraping. What's the sense in that? People should all be equal and all that silly stuff about respecting people should be ignored. What a lot of rubbish that is!

So what if this bloke or lady is important! Doesn't mean they're more important than me. Doing all that formal stuff is just silly and old fashioned. My folks don't want me doing anything like showing respect for the position. If people get upset with kids not having manners, that's their problem. Who cares anyway? The governor probably doesn't. All dumb stuff.

Text 2

When meeting someone who is important, manners should always be **displayed**. A greeting should come first, followed by an introduction and greeting.

Firstly, you could say, "Good morning, Mr/Mrs/Ms/Miss/Sir/Lady ..."

Then, "My name is ... Welcome to our primary school."

Manners **demonstrate** respect and should always be used when welcoming visitors to your school. Most people believe that manners are important as this shows respect. Respecting your school, yourself, your parents, country, community and others is an important part of the way we live. Most families understand the importance of respect.

TERM 2 ENGLISH

Write or circle the correct answer.

① **What does displayed mean?**

   a outside   b worn   c shown

② **How are these texts different?**

   a Text 1 is about children and text 2 is about adults.

   b Text 1 says that respect is not important and text 2 says it is.

③ **What does demonstrate mean?**

   a show   b complain   c ignore

④ **What is the first thing you should do when meeting an important person?**

_____

_____

_____

⑤ **Why are manners important?**

_____

_____

_____

_____

Score 2 points for each correct answer!

SCORE **/10** 0-2 4-8 10

Number & Algebra

Circle the adjoining pairs of numbers that add up to **25**. There could be more than one pair in each row.

①	3	24	4	19	7	20	8	12	17	9	9	16
②	1	22	11	14	3	17	21	16	16	8	2	14
③	7	18	8	7	12	24	16	12	5	17	21	8
④	13	2	16	8	3	19	21	13	12	9	21	3
⑤	22	12	2	15	10	19	6	4	13	19	8	7

In this grid, the numbers in the rows and the columns add up to **50**, as do both diagonals. No number is repeated in the grid.

Write the missing numbers. You may use a calculator.

12	15	18	⑥
⑦	6	11	16
7	20	⑧	10
14	⑨	8	19

Work out the secret numbers. You may use a calculator.

⑩ I doubled my secret number. I halved my secret number. I added those two answers together and I ended up with forty-five. What was my secret number?

_____

⑪ I tripled my secret number. I multiplied my secret number by five. I added those two answers together and I ended up with eighty-eight. What was my secret number?

_____

⑫ I added fourteen to my secret number. I subtracted eight from my secret number. I added those two answers together and I ended up with thirty-eight. What was my secret number?

_____

⑬ I subtracted twenty-five from my secret number. I subtracted thirty-five from my secret number. I added those two answers together and I ended up with twenty. What was my secret number?

_____

Simplify these improper fractions and then convert them to mixed numbers.

Improper fraction		Simplified fraction		Mixed number
$\frac{30}{8}$	=	⑭	=	⑮
$\frac{24}{9}$	=	⑯	=	⑰
$\frac{105}{5}$	=	⑱	=	⑲
$\frac{49}{14}$	=	⑳	=	㉑
$\frac{28}{8}$	=	㉒	=	㉓

Score 2 points for each correct answer! **SCORE** **/46** (0-20) (22-40) (42-46)

Statistics & Probability

These are pie charts of the quantity of students attending two primary schools.

School #1   School #2

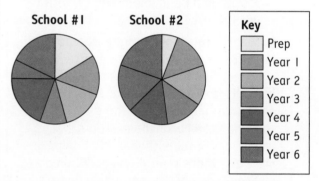

Key	
☐	Prep
☐	Year 1
☐	Year 2
☐	Year 3
☐	Year 4
☐	Year 5
☐	Year 6

Use the pie charts to answer the following questions.

① Can you tell from the pie charts if the schools have a similar number of students?

_____

② Which year level of School #1 has the most students?

_____

③ Which **consecutive** three year levels in School #1 have nearest to half the school's population?

_____

④ If School #1 had a total student population of 200, approximately how many students would be in Year 4?

_____

⑤ If School #2 had a total student population of 600, approximately how many students would be in Prep, Year 1 and Year 3 combined?

_____

Use the table below to answer the following questions.

Trips taken by the Hoppers family		
Year	Date	Distance (km)
2000	1/1	3010
	12/6	720
	3/9	860
2001	7/3	1500
	16/5	3115
2002	16/2	2000
	9/10	755
2003		
2004	23/4	500
	16/6	865
	23/12	3065

⑥ How many trips in total did the Hoppers take during the period of the chart?

_____

⑦ In which year or years did they take the most trips?

_____

⑧ In which year or years did they take the fewest trips?

_____

⑨ In which year did they take the longest trip?

_____

⑩ How far did they travel during 2000?

_____

⑪ In what years did they make trips that had a 5 km difference in distance?

_____

Score 2 points for each correct answer! **SCORE** **/22** (0-8) (10-16) (18-22)

Measurement & Space

Use the timetable to answer the following questions.

Bus timetable		
Stop	Pink Bus	Yellow Bus
Stop 1	8:00 am	11:05 am
Stop 2	8:20 am	11:30 am
Stop 3	9:10 am	12:20 pm
Stop 4	9:50 am	1:00 pm
Stop 5	10:25 am	1:35 pm
Stop 6	10:55 am	2:15 pm
Stop 7	11:40 am	2:55 pm

① In total, how long do both bus trips take?

_____

② Between which two places does Pink Bus take half an hour?

_____

③ Between which two places is Yellow Bus quicker than Pink Bus?

_____

④ Between which two pairs of places does Yellow Bus take forty minutes?

_____

⑤ If the Pink bus has a breakdown at 10:05 am and it had been travelling at an average of 80 km/h, how far out of Stop 5 is it?

_____

Both buses make the same trip in reverse, taking the same time between the stops.

Pink Bus begins its return trip at 12:00 pm. Yellow Bus begins its return trip at 3:30 pm.

⑥ What time does Pink Bus reach Stop 6 on its return trip?

_____

⑦ What time does Yellow Bus reach Stop 6 on its return trip?

_____

⑧ On its return trip, Pink Bus is at Stop 5 at 1:15 pm. How long before Yellow Bus arrives on its morning run is this?

_____

How has the first shape been transformed to get the second shape? Write translation, reflection or rotation.

⑨ _____

⑪ _____

⑩ _____

⑫ _____

Score 2 points for each correct answer! **SCORE** **/24** (0-10) (12-18) (20-24)

TARGETING HOMEWORK 6 © PASCAL PRESS ISBN 9781925726480

73

Grammar & Punctuation

AC9E6LA06

Adverbial phrases

> An **adverbial phrase** is a group of words that tells **how**, **when**, **where** and **why** something is happening in a sentence — just like an adverb. *Example:* I hung my wet robe **behind the door**.

Write whether the underlined adverbial phrases say how, when, where or why.

① Large waves smash on the rocks <u>along this coast</u>. _____

② <u>Between her two jobs</u>, Mum bakes cakes. _____

③ Riding a bike <u>without a helmet</u> can be dangerous. _____

④ <u>Before going to the play</u>, I didn't like drama. _____

⑤ We're going to Uluru <u>for a holiday</u>. _____

Prepositions in adverbial phrases

> Remember! **Adverbial phrases** usually begin with a **preposition**.
> *Example:* I walked home **during** the storm.
> (preposition)

Choose a preposition from the box to complete each sentence.

until	during	above	without	before

⑥ The balloon flew high _____ the smoke.

⑦ _____ warning, the waves crashed around our feet.

⑧ The storm raged _____ early the next morning.

⑨ The space ship landed _____ running out of fuel.

⑩ Huge leaves fell from the tree _____ the hail storm.

Unjumble the prepositions and write them correctly. The first two letters are correct.

⑪ Mum hid from Dad **bendih** (_____) the door.

⑫ The men made their way **toswrad** (_____) the mountain.

⑬ She couldn't leave the cake **witohtu** (_____) tasting the icing.

Phonic Knowledge & Spelling

AC9E6LY09

Homophones

> Remember! **Homophones** are words that have the same sound, but they are spelt differently and have different meanings.
> *Examples:* blue, blew   knew, new   meat, meet

Choose a word from the box to match with its homophone.

rose	cheque	eight	flower	rain	wring

① ate _____

② ring _____

③ check _____

④ reign _____

⑤ rows _____

⑥ flour _____

Choose words from the box to finish the sentences. These words come from the Dutch language.

cookies	waffles	snack	boss

⑦ When I get home from school, I like to have a _____.

⑧ _____ and cream is my favourite ice-cream.

⑨ For breakfast we sometimes have _____.

⑩ My mother's new _____ at work is Mrs Vincent.

Match the plural words in the box with their meaning.

dice	deer	aircraft	offspring

⑪ A number of aeroplanes: _____

⑫ More than one young of an animal: _____

⑬ English animals: _____

⑭ People often play games with these: _____

Cockroaches are Not the Bad Guys!

Persuasive text – Discussion
Author – Peter Alford

Cockroaches are amazingly important and beautiful little creatures. If there were to be a terrible war, cockroaches would be the only creatures to survive.

True, they may be a little unpleasant, but they have brilliant manners. Unlike flies, they do not interfere when families are having barbecues. Sure, they smell a little, but every creature has that teeny weeny problem.

Because they just love eating rubbish, we would all be worse off for them being eliminated. Rubbish is broken down by these wonder warriors of the insect world. Less rubbish means less disease.

Cockroaches may well become the pet of the future. Well behaved, they cause little noise at night. Unlike dogs, they do not bark, and unlike cats, they do not kill native creatures.

Write or circle the correct answer.

1. **What does 'much poorer for them being eliminated' mean?**

   a It would be great if cockroaches were to die out.

   b Losing cockroaches would mean that we have little money.

   c Cockroaches are useful and would be missed.

2. **What dirty insects are cockroaches compared with?**

   _____

3. **Why would cockroaches make better pets than dogs?**

   _____

   _____

4. **Why does the writer say 'they have brilliant manners'?**

   a Cockroaches don't eat with people.

   b Cockroaches don't interfere at barbecues.

   c Cockroaches don't cause disease.

5. **Which animals are troubled by cats?**

   _____

   _____

6. **What small problem do cockroaches have?**

   _____

   _____

7. **What type of text is this?**

   a a report from a scientist

   b a subjective text – opinion, thinking, feeling language

   c a report from a doctor

Score 2 points for each correct answer! SCORE **/14** (0-4) (6-10) (12-14)

My Book Review

Title _____

Author _____

Rating ☆☆☆☆☆

Comment _____

_____

TERM 3 ENGLISH

UNIT 17

Number & Algebra

AC9M6N07

Finding simple fractions of quantities

Complete the table.

	Equation	is the same as:
①	$\frac{1}{4}$ of 32	32 ÷ 4 =
②	$\frac{1}{8}$ of 64	÷ =
③	$\frac{1}{9}$ of 99	÷ =
④	$\frac{1}{5}$ of 225	÷ =
⑤	$\frac{1}{7}$ of 56	÷ =
⑥	$\frac{1}{3}$ of 123	÷ =
⑦	$\frac{1}{6}$ of 234	÷ =
⑧	$\frac{1}{2}$ of 500	÷ =
⑨	$\frac{1}{10}$ of 990	÷ =
⑩	$\frac{1}{3}$ of 758	÷ =
⑪	$\frac{1}{5}$ of 407	÷ =
⑫	$\frac{1}{9}$ of 874	÷ =
⑬	$\frac{1}{6}$ of 841	÷ =
⑭	$\frac{1}{4}$ of 1789	÷ =
⑮	$\frac{1}{8}$ of 9008	÷ =

Score 2 points for each correct answer!

SCORE /30 (0-12) (14-24) (26-30)

Statistics & Probability

AC9M6ST01

Using a table and a bar graph

This table and bar graph show new car sales in NSW each June over a ten year period.

They are incomplete and have some errors in them.

New car sales, NSW, June, 2006–14	
Year	Sales
2006	23 600
2007	B
2008	26 500
2009	24 300
2010	26 800
2011	24 400
A	28 300
2013	C
2014	29 300
2015	D

TERM 3 MATHS

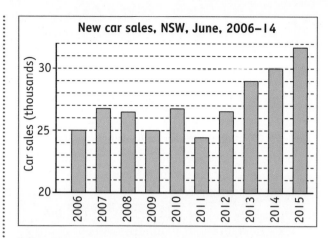

New car sales, NSW, June, 2006–14

What number should replace each of these labels in the data table? Refer to the graph for the values.

① A _____
② B _____
③ C _____
④ D _____

For the following questions, assume the data in the table is correct.

⑤ In the graph, is the 2006 bar **too high** or **too low**?

_____

⑥ Is the 2009 bar **too high** or **too low**?

_____

⑦ Is the 2012 bar **too high** or **too low**?

_____

⑧ Is the 2014 bar **too high** or **too low**?

_____

⑨ By how many is the 2006 bar incorrect?

_____

⑩ By how many is the 2009 bar incorrect?

_____

⑪ By how many is the 2012 bar incorrect?

_____

⑫ By how many is the 2014 bar incorrect?

_____

Score 2 points for each correct answer!

SCORE /24 (0-10) (12-18) (20-24)

TARGETING HOMEWORK 6 © PASCAL PRESS ISBN 9781925726480

Right angle, acute, obtuse and reflex angles

- A **right angle** measures exactly 90°.
- An **acute angle** measures less than 90°.
- An **obtuse angle** measures more than 90° and less than 180°.
- A **reflex angle** measures more than 180° and less than 360°.

What types of angles are these?
Write **right**, **acute**, **obtuse** or **reflex**.

Note: x marks each angle.

① _____

② _____

③ _____

④ _____

⑤ _____

⑥ _____

⑦ _____

⑧  _____

⑨ _____

⑩ _____

⑪ _____

⑫ _____

⑬ _____

⑭ _____

Fraction and angle problems

Solve these problems. Do not use a calculator.

① Phillis collected ants – I have no idea why. She had 232 ants but she left the back door open and an eighth of them marched away.
How many ants escaped?

_____

② Giorgio collected flies – don't ask why. He had 126 but half flew away and then the cat ate 50 of those that remained.
How many flies did Giorgio have left?

_____

③ Chunhua collected earwigs – she just liked them. She had 32 but a quarter of them wriggled away.
How many did she have left?

_____

④ Akihiro collected cockroaches, which is a rare hobby. He started with 25, then he increased that number by a fifth. Then he found seven more.
How many did Akihiro have then?

_____

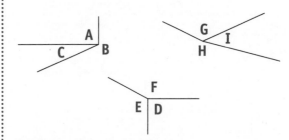

Use these line drawings to answer the following questions.

⑤ Which two angles are right angles?

_____

⑥ Which two angles are acute angles?

_____

⑦ Which three angles are obtuse angles?

_____

⑧ Which two angles are reflex angles?

_____

⑨ How many right angles make a straight line?

_____

Grammar & Punctuation

AC9E6LA06

Adverbial phrases

> Remember! An **adverbial phrase** is a group of words that tells how, when, where and why something is happening in a sentence — just like an adverb. *Example:* I hung my wet robe **behind the door**.

Write whether the underlined adverbial phrases say how, when, where or why.

1. Hundreds of butterflies were caught <u>after sunrise</u>. _____

2. Penny met her football coach <u>for extra coaching</u>. _____

3. Slaves were chained below deck <u>without food and water</u>. _____

4. <u>After choir practice</u>, I began to feel more confident. _____

5. Packs of wolves circled <u>beneath the tree</u>. _____

Prepositions in adverbial phrases

> Remember! **Adverbial phrases** usually begin with a **preposition**.
> *Example:* I walked home **during** the storm.
> ⌐ preposition

Choose a preposition from the box to complete each sentence.

until	before	above	without	beneath

6. The eagle soared high _____ the desert.

7. _____ a thank you, the girl snatched back her test papers.

8. Kangaroos gathered _____ the trees in fear of hunters.

9. The fighter pilot flew the jet _____ the safe landing zone.

10. _____ exploding violently, the volcano had only smoked.

Unjumble the prepositions and write them correctly. The first two letters are correct.

11. The surfers made their way **toswrad** (_____) the reef break.

12. They continued their march **thorhug** (_____) the lightning storm.

13. Marly couldn't leave her room **wiothtu** (_____) finishing her homework.

Phonic Knowledge & Spelling

AC9E6LY08, AC9E6LY09

Contractions

> Remember! A **contraction** is when two words are shortened and combined to become one word. An **apostrophe (')** is used to replace the missing letter/s.
> *Examples:* is not = isn't   I would = I'd

Write the contraction for each example.

1. they will _____

2. he is _____

3. it is _____

4. she will _____

5. I am _____

Add the suffix –ing to these words.
Example: hide, hiding

6. bake _____

7. like _____

8. hate _____

9. fake _____

10. require _____

Circle the 5 words that have been made opposites (antonyms) by adding a prefix.
Example: disprove

11.–15.

disappear	disrespect	impossible
terrified	umbrella	unhappy
rattle	unbelievable	

Make new words by adding word endings from the box to the base words.

–ly	–d	–ous	–er	–gish

16. order_____

17. teach_____

18. humour_____

19. slug_____

20. complicate_____

Score 2 points for each correct answer! SCORE **/26** (0-10) (12-20) (22-26)

Score 2 points for each correct answer! SCORE **/40** (0-18) (20-34) (36-40)

Ella's Chicken Coop

Imaginative text – Narrative
Author – Peter Alford

Ella's mother had finally agreed. She was able to keep chickens.

Problem was, she had nowhere to cage them. Ella thought hard. Her pop had all the tools and he could build things. Pop always had dinner with her family on a Thursday, so she planned to ask him then. Quickly, she planned out her 'chook mansion'. It needed a hutch and had to be covered in wire netting. Wood was the easiest material to build a strong frame.

Arriving one Sunday morning, Ella's pop brought his tools and he had bought all the wood and wire. Ella learnt how to drill and screw with the cordless drill. Jeremy, her neighbour, sat in his treehouse making fun of Ella.

"Girls don't do that!" he yelled, teasing Ella.

Her pop ignored Jeremy. Eventually Jeremy got tired of being silly and started to climb down from the tree. As he did, his hand slipped and the back of his pants caught on a piece of wood making him dangle in space. Jeremy wailed loudly, but his parents were out so they couldn't help. Ella climbed the fence with her electric screwdriver. When she removed the screw, Jeremy fell to the ground, with the piece of wood hitting him on the head.

Write or circle the correct answer.

1. **What did Ella plan to ask her pop at dinner?**

    _____
    _____

2. **What name did Ella think of for her chicken coop?**

    _____
    _____

3. **What material did Ella want to use for a frame? Why?**

    _____
    _____

4. **What was Ella going to use so the chickens didn't get loose?**

    a a timber frame

    b wire netting

    c a hutch

5. **Why did Jeremy stop teasing?**

    a Ella ignored him.

    b He needed a drink.

    c He got bored and tired.

6. **What did Ella use to attach the pieces of wood for the frame?**

    a nails   b rope   c wire   d screws

7. **What did Ella's pop do about Jeremy's teasing?**

    _____
    _____

8. **What did Ella do to free Jeremy?**

    _____
    _____

Score 2 points for each correct answer!

SCORE **/16** (0-6) (8-12) (14-16)

My Book Review

Title _____

Author _____

Rating ☆☆☆☆☆

Comment _____
_____

TERM 3 ENGLISH

Number & Algebra

AC9M6N07

Finding fractions of quantities

Solve these equations. Use a calculator if you need to.

	Equation	is the same as:					
①	$\frac{3}{4}$ of 32	32	÷	4	×	3	=
②	$\frac{3}{8}$ of 64	64	÷	8	×	3	=
③	$\frac{7}{9}$ of 99	99	÷	9	×	7	=
④	$\frac{4}{5}$ of 225		÷		×		=
⑤	$\frac{5}{7}$ of 56		÷		×		=
⑥	$\frac{2}{3}$ of 123		÷		×		=
⑦	$\frac{5}{6}$ of 234		÷		×		=
⑧	$\frac{7}{10}$ of 500		÷		×		=
⑨	$\frac{3}{8}$ of 760		÷		×		=
⑩	$\frac{2}{3}$ of 756		÷		×		=
⑪	$\frac{3}{5}$ of 405		÷		×		=
⑫	$\frac{6}{9}$ of 873		÷		×		=
⑬	$\frac{5}{6}$ of 840		÷		×		=
⑭	$\frac{7}{11}$ of 1782		÷		×		=
⑮	$\frac{5}{8}$ of 9000		÷		×		=

Score 2 points for each correct answer!   SCORE **/30** (0-12) (14-24) (26-30)

Statistics & Probability

AC9M6ST01

Using a table and a bar graph

This table and bar graph show road fatalities in Australia over a five year period. They are incomplete and have some errors in them.

Road Fatalities in Australia by age and year				
Age range (years)	2012	2013	A	2015
0–25	350	B	300	290
26–39	300	240	250	275
40–64	C	375	360	375
65+	260	275	240	D

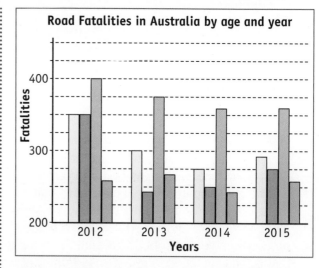

Road Fatalities in Australia by age and year

What number should replace each of these labels in the data table? Refer to the graph for the values.

① A _____

② B _____

③ C _____

④ D _____

For the following questions, assume the data in the table is correct.

⑤ Which age bar in the 2012 group is wrong?

_____

⑥ Which age bar in the 2013 group is wrong?

_____

⑦ Which age bar in the 2014 group is wrong?

_____

⑧ Which age bar in the 2015 group is wrong?

_____

⑨ By how many is the age bar in the 2012 group wrong?

_____

⑩ By how many is the age bar in the 2013 group wrong?

_____

⑪ By how many is the age bar in the 2014 group wrong?

_____

⑫ By how many is the age bar in the 2015 group wrong?

_____

Score 2 points for each correct answer!   SCORE **/24** (0-10) (12-18) (20-24)

TARGETING HOMEWORK 6 © PASCAL PRESS ISBN 9781925726480

Measurement & Space

AC9M6M04

Right, acute, obtuse and reflex angles

Write how many of each type of angle are inside and outside these shapes.

Square

	① Angles inside shape	② Angles outside shape
Acute		
Right		
Obtuse		
Reflex		

Rectangle

	③ Angles inside shape	④ Angles outside shape
Acute		
Right		
Obtuse		
Reflex		

Triangle

	⑤ Angles inside shape	⑥ Angles outside shape
Acute		
Right		
Obtuse		
Reflex		

Diamond

	⑦ Angles inside shape	⑧ Angles outside shape
Acute		
Right		
Obtuse		
Reflex		

Pentagon

	⑨ Angles inside shape	⑩ Angles outside shape
Acute		
Right		
Obtuse		
Reflex		

Score 2 points for each correct answer!

SCORE **/20** (0-8) (10-14) (16-20)

Problem Solving

AC9M6N09, AC9M6ST01

Fraction and data problems

① John divided a bag of Gummi Bears among his four best friends and himself. He gave each friend a sixth of the lollies and kept the rest for himself.

If John kept eight Gummi Bears, how many were in the bag at the start?

_____

② Kimiko shared her bag of jelly beans by giving the same number to her six friends and herself. Everyone got eight jelly beans but there were four left over.

How many jellybeans were in the bag at the start?

_____

③ Jessica had a bag of fifty-six peppermint humbugs. She gave $\frac{1}{8}$ to Kimiko, then she gave $\frac{1}{7}$ of what was left to Malika. Finally she gave $\frac{1}{6}$ of what was left to John.
Who got the most peppermint humbugs?

_____

④ Miguel gave three of his friends three-quarters of his Freddo Frogs. If he gave ten frogs to his first friend, eight to his second friend and nine to the third, how many Freddo Frogs did he have left?

_____

Use the bar graph in Statistics & Probability to answer these questions.

⑤ During one particular year, a very successful Road Safety campaign was held.

What year was it and what age group was it aimed at?

_____

⑥ If you take $\frac{3}{5}$ of the fatalities for one of the age groups of 2012, it would be very close to the number of fatalities for another age group in 2012.

What are the two age groups?

_____

⑦ Which age group is overall most in danger of being a victim of road fatality?

_____

UNIT 19

Grammar & Punctuation

AC9E6LA05

Conjunctions

Remember! **Conjunctions** are words that join ideas in sentences.

They can join words that are the same. *Example:* rain **or** shine

They can join phrases. *Example:* Emily ran down the bank **and** into the river.

They can also join simple sentences to make compound sentences. *Example:* It's starting to rain, **so** I'll go home now.

Other **conjunctions** can link a subordinate clause with the main clause in complex sentences. *Example:* I'll stay here **until** my parents pick me up.

Choose the correct ending for each sentence.

... Billy arrived at the party.
... it had come off the road.
... of her chicken pox.
... there are still accidents.

① We hid the presents before _____

_____

② Ships seem very safe, but _____

_____

③ We found the wrecked car after _____

_____

④ Gina couldn't go to the carnival because ____

_____

Choose a conjunction from the box to complete each sentence.

| but | because | after | until |

⑤ We were allowed to ride in the park _____ we were wearing helmets.

⑥ Tilly is allowed to play _____ she finishes her homework.

⑦ The game was fun, _____ we made a huge mess.

⑧ People couldn't get to space _____ rockets were invented.

Replace sausage with the correct conjunction from the box.

| and | because | after |

⑨ Mum was angry **sausage** the car wouldn't start. _____

⑩ The bird picked at the seed **sausage** it also drank the water. _____

⑪ Zookeepers put the snake back in its cage **sausage** capturing it. _____

Score 2 points for each correct answer! SCORE **/22** (0-8) (10-16) (18-22)

Phonic Knowledge & Spelling

AC9E6LY08, AC9E6LY09

Base words

Circle the word which does not come from the base word.

Base word   Derivative

① **please**   pleasant pleasure pleading

② **sure**   surely shore unsure

③ **skill**   sky skilful skilled

④ **eat**   edible uneaten feat

⑤ **print**   reprint interview printed

Find two words in the sentences that make compound words.

Example: In the morning I took a <u>fast</u> <u>break</u> before work. <u>breakfast</u>

⑥ In the game I had to keep my **eye** on the ball. eye_____

⑦ The sitter arrived late to look after the **baby**. baby_____

⑧ Who would think that **silk** came from a worm? silk_____

⑨ My brush fell to pieces when doing my **hair**. hair_____

Write –sion or –tion to complete the words.

⑩ mo_____   ⑬ confu_____

⑪ deci_____   ⑭ divi_____

⑫ atten_____

Homophones

Write the correct homophones into the spaces from the box.

| poor/pour plain/plane |
| male/mail brake/break |

⑮ He used his _____ heavily but didn't _____ a single egg.

⑯ The _____ landed on the edge of the _____.

⑰ Our postman, a _____, delivers the _____ daily.

⑱ We watched the _____ lady _____ out her tea.

Score 2 points for each correct answer! SCORE **/36** (0-16) (18-30) (32-36)

TERM 3 ENGLISH

82

TARGETING HOMEWORK 6 © PASCAL PRESS ISBN 9781925726480

Māori

Informative text – Report
Author – Caroline Tate

Māori arrived in New Zealand from East Polynesia in the thirteenth century.

The Māori were warrior hunter-gatherers. Tribes on the North Island also farmed vegetables. The population may have reached 100 000 before the British arrived.

British people colonised the country in the late eighteenth century.

Māori belong to iwi (tribes). Within each iwi are many hapū (clans or descent groups), each of which has one or more whānau (extended families). Māori are 15 percent of New Zealand's population.

Māori have a more positive experience of European colonisation than some first peoples, but they still experience disadvantage. On average they earn less and their life expectancy is shorter than for Pākehā (Māori word for white New Zealanders).

Source: *First Peoples*, Go Facts, Blake Education.

Write or circle the correct answer.

1. In what century did the Māori arrive in New Zealand?

   _____

2. Who arrived first in New Zealand, the British or the Māori?

   _____

3. What is the smallest group in Māori life?

   a iwi

   b whanau

   c hapu

4. What is one way in which Māori are disadvantaged in New Zealand?

   _____

   _____

5. What was the difference between Māori in the North Island and those in the South Island?

   _____

   _____

6. When did the British colonise New Zealand?

   _____

   _____

7. Where did Māori come from?

   a Europe

   b North Polynesia

   c East Polynesia

8. How big was the population before the British arrived?

   _____

9. What does **colonised** mean?

   a to settle

   b to look at

   c to come

   d to make

Score 2 points for each correct answer!

SCORE /18 0-6 8-14 16-18

My Book Review

Title _____

Author _____

Rating ⭐☆☆☆☆

Comment _____

_____

Number & Algebra

AC9M6N09

Multiplying decimals by whole numbers

Are these correct? Write **Y (yes)** or **N (no)**.
Do not use a calculator.

① $5.3 \times 7 = 35.21$ ☐

② $23.6 \times 3 = 70.8$ ☐

③ $200.01 \times 5 = 1000.05$ ☐

④ $18.6 \times 6 = 114.6$ ☐

⑤ $231.09 \times 2 = 462.08$ ☐

⑥ $0.36 \times 6 = 0.216$ ☐

⑦ $55.55 \times 3 = 16.665$ ☐

⑧ $90.09 \times 6 = 540.54$ ☐

⑨ $12.702 \times 5 = 63.51$ ☐

⑩ $1000.08 \times 2 = 2000.016$ ☐

⑪ $23.009 \times 9 = 207.081$ ☐

⑫ $9.73 \times 5 = 48.65$ ☐

⑬ $21.16 \times 4 = 94.64$ ☐

⑭ $25.5 \times 5 = 127.5$ ☐

⑮ $125.06 \times 3 = 375.18$ ☐

Score 2 points for each correct answer! SCORE **/30** (0-12) (14-24) (26-30)

Statistics & Probability

AC9M6ST01

Pie charts with %

This pie chart shows my sister's collection of Barbie dolls.

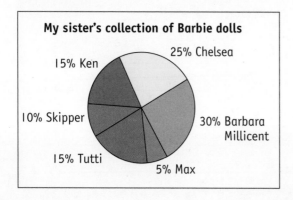

My sister's collection of Barbie dolls

25% Chelsea
15% Ken
10% Skipper
30% Barbara Millicent
15% Tutti
5% Max

Use the pie chart to answer the following questions.

① Of which doll does my sister have the most?

_____

② Which two dolls does my sister have in the same number?

_____

③ Of which doll does my sister have the fewest?

_____

④ My sister has a third as many of one doll as she has of Barbara. Which doll is that?

_____

⑤ Which doll does my sister have five times as many of as she has of Max?

_____

⑥ If my sister had a total of twenty dolls, how many of them were Chelsea?

_____

⑦ If my sister had a total of twenty dolls, how many of them were Max?

_____

⑧ If my sister had a total of 40 dolls, how many of them were Skipper?

_____

⑨ If my sister had six Skipper dolls, how many Barbara dolls did she have?

_____

⑩ If my sister had six Skipper dolls, how many Tutti dolls did she have?

_____

⑪ If my sister had ten Chelsea dolls, how many Ken dolls did she have?

_____

⑫ If my sister had eight Max dolls, how many Ken dolls did she have?

_____

⑬ If my sister had eight Max dolls, how many Skipper dolls did she have?

_____

⑭ Could my sister have a total of 50 dolls? Answer yes or no and give a reason.

_____

_____

Score 2 points for each correct answer! SCORE **/28** (0-12) (14-22) (24-28)

Measurement & Space

AC9M6M02

Perimeter and area

Use the shapes on the grid below to answer the following questions.

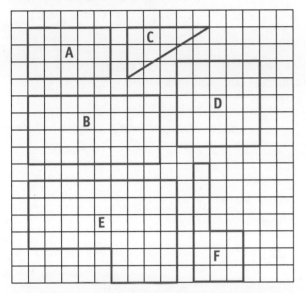

For the following questions, use **squares**, as shown on the grid, for units.

① What is the area of shape A? _____

② What is the area of shape B? _____

③ What is the area of shape C? _____

④ What is the area of shape D? _____

⑤ What is the area of shape E? _____

⑥ What is the area of shape F? _____

For the following questions, assume each square of the grid is 1 m².

⑦ What is the area of shape A in square metres?

_____

⑧ What is the perimeter of shape A in metres?

_____

Write the perimeter and area for each of these shapes. Assume each square of the grid is 1 m².

⑨ Area of shape D: _____

⑩ Perimeter of shape D: _____

⑪ Area of shape E: _____

⑫ Perimeter of shape E: _____

⑬ Area of shape F: _____

⑭ Perimeter of shape F: _____

⑮ Area of shape C: _____

Problem Solving

AC9M6N09, AC9M6M02

Decimal and shape problems

① 202.202 × 2 = 404.404 so
does 202.202 × 4 = 808.808? _____
Why? _____
_____

② 218.16 × 4 = 872.64 so
does 218.16 × 2 = 436.32? _____
Why? _____
_____

③ 32.026 × 8 = 256.208 so
does 16.026 × 6 = 128.104? _____
Why? _____
_____

Use the shapes in **Measurement & Space** to answer these questions. Use squares, as shown on the grid, for units.

④ If shape A's top right corner was kept in the position it is and the shape's Height (↕) was doubled, how many squares of shape B would it cover?

_____

⑤ If shape F was placed over shape D so that their bottom left corners aligned, how many squares of shape D would shape F cover?

_____

⑥ If shape C's width (↔) was doubled, what would be its area in squares?

_____

⑦ How many squares would need to be added to shape E to make it a square?

_____

⑧ What is the fewest number of squares that need to be taken from shape E to make it a rectangle?

_____

⑨ What is the fewest number of squares that need to be taken from shape E to make it a square?

_____

⑩ If both the height and width of shape B were doubled, how many times larger would it become?

_____

Grammar & Punctuation

AC9E6LA04, AC9E6LA06

Verbs

> Remember! **Verbs** tell what is 'going on' in a sentence. They tell us what people or things are doing, thinking and saying. *Example:* Billy **rode** his bike home.
>
> The same action can be described by many verbs. *Example*: run – sprint, plod, race, jog

Choose more interesting verbs from the box to replace the verbs in bold.
①–⑦

gathered	trap	sprinted	delivered
dragged	delighted	observe	

After Nick ate his lunch, he **ran**

(1)_____ to his best

friend's place. Amber had a telescope so that

they could **see** (2)_____

birds out at sea. Where birds **flocked**

(3)_____, there were fish.

They **pushed** (4)_____ their

canoe into the water. Amber and Nick would

paddle out to **get** (5)_____

fish in a net. They were **happy**

(6)_____ with their catch

and they **gave** (7)_____

their fish to the old people's home.

Circle the verb that does not fit the meaning of the bold verb.

⑧ **walk**   saunter   plod   amble   sprint

⑨ **talk**   babble   yell   giggle   comment

⑩ **think**   guess   look   consider   understand

⑪ **hear**   listen   get   heed   notice

Score 2 points for each correct answer!   SCORE **/22** (0-8) (10-16) (18-22)

Phonic Knowledge & Spelling

AC9E6LY09

Spelling confusion

> Some words look a little like another word but have a different spelling and meaning.
> *Example:* **Breath** (noun) and **breathe** (verb) are often confused.

Use one of the words from each pair to complete the sentence.

later/latter	device/devise	born/borne
	cause/course	father/farther

① My _____ was a soldier for many years.

② It is better to be a little _____ than coming too soon.

③ Our mare's foal was _____ during the night.

④ Investigators haven't found the _____ of the car accident.

⑤ Police took away the _____ because it looked dangerous.

Use the clues to choose a letter group from the box to complete each word.

er	sp	curr	pat	prev

⑥ to go into: ent_____

⑦ to stop something: _____ent

⑧ to use money: _____end

⑨ a dried grape: _____ant

⑩ a person in hospital: _____ient

Rearrange the letters of the bold word to make a new word. The first 2 letters are clues.

⑪ You will find the horses in the **bleats**.
st_____

⑫ Don't you **read** do that again!
da_____

⑬ Could you **pears** me some time?
sp_____

⑭ You'll need to **near** some money for that.
ea_____

Score 2 points for each correct answer!   SCORE **/28** (0-12) (14-22) (24-28)

TARGETING HOMEWORK 6 © PASCAL PRESS ISBN 9781925726480

Southern Brown Bandicoot

Informative text – Newspaper article
Author – Catherine Gordon

Town planners follow laws made by state and local governments. These laws have to balance the needs of people with those of the environment. This can be difficult, and often native animals like the endangered Southern Brown Bandicoot are the biggest losers. The newspaper article below is based on a true planning issue.

TOWN PLANNING PUTTING WILDLIFE AT RISK

Wildlife corridors crucial to the survival of the Southern Brown Bandicoot may not go ahead if new planned suburbs proceed.

Plans for a residential development near the Cranbourne Royal Botanic Gardens have been revealed. These gardens hold one of the last remaining communities of bandicoots. Originally, the government had planned to include wide, fenced wildlife corridors to run from the gardens, through the suburbs to other areas of bandicoot habitat. However, these plans are now in doubt as the government thinks they are not cost effective.

The Southern Brown Bandicoot is listed as nationally endangered. If its last remaining remnants of habitat aren't protected, it faces extinction.

The wildlife corridors originally planned to run through the residential development would allow the bandicoots to breed in the gardens behind predator-proof fences, then travel safely via the corridors to other habitat areas. If the corridors are not included within the suburbs, then the bandicoots will be restricted to the gardens. This threatens the bandicoots' survival. If a catastrophe like a bushfire goes through the gardens, then all the remaining bandicoots will be lost.

The government will decide whether to include the corridors or not, and will release their revised development plans later next week.

Source: *Australian Geography Centres*, Upper Primary, Blake Education.

Write or circle the correct answer.

Scan the text to find words that have these meanings:

① chance of injury or loss: ri_____

② a passage that connects different parts: co_____

③ very important: cr_____

④ where people live: res_____

⑤ to show or display: rev_____

⑥ to limit freedom of movement: res_____

⑦ **Cost effective** means:

  a not worth it.

  b very expensive.

  c good value for money.

⑧ **The government is not sure about the plans for wildlife corridors because:**

  a they may not be good value for money.

  b the bandicoots won't be safe.

  c they will upset too many people.

⑨ **The Southern Brown Bandicoot is only endangered near the Cranbourne Royal Botanic Gardens.**
  a True   b False

⑩ **Why are the corridors so important for the bandicoots?**

_____

_____

_____

_____

Score 2 points for each correct answer!

SCORE /20 (0-8) (10-14) (16-20)

My Book Review

Title _____

Author _____

Rating ☆☆☆☆☆

Comment _____

_____

TERM 3 ENGLISH

Number & Algebra

AC9M6A02

Multiplying decimals by whole numbers

Use a calculator to work out these equations.

	A	B	C	D	E
1	1.3	76	27.27	23	0.246
2	0.52	0.0046	82	406	16
3	48	2.9	71.3	0.707	13.31
4	18.052	0.84	43	0.8	64
5	38	0.202	0.9	28.8	0.68
6	12.4	37.82	208	0.925	55

The grid locations in the following equations refer to the numbers in the grid.

① (3B) × (4A) _____

② First do (2E) + (5B) and then × (1B)

_____

③ First do (6B) + (4D) and then × (2C)

_____

④ First do (4C) × (2A) and then × (5A)

_____

⑤ (5E) × (6E) _____

⑥ (6B) × (4D) _____

⑦ First do (3E) + (1B) and then × (4C)

_____

⑧ First do (3D) + (2C) and then × (1A)

_____

⑨ First do (6A) + (2A) and then × (4B)

_____

⑩ (3C) × (5A) _____

⑪ First do (1D) + (5E) and then × (3B)

_____

⑫ (3D) × (5A) _____

⑬ (3D) × (2C) _____

⑭ First do (1C) + (1E) and then × (6A)

_____

⑮ First do (6E) + (4B) and then × (2A)

_____

Statistics & Probability

AC9M6P01

Describing probabilities

This table shows different probabilities when one, two and three coins are tossed.

Some figures have been left out. Work out the answers for the spaces numbered 1–15.

Note: H = Head and **T** = Tail.
Target means 'the desired result'.

Toss	Target	Chance of getting the Target		
		Decimal	**Fraction**	**Percent**
1 coin	H	0.5		①
2 coins	H, T	0.5	②	
2 coins	T, T	③	$\frac{1}{4}$	25%
2 coins	at least 1 T	0.75	$\frac{3}{4}$	④
3 coins	H, T, T	0.375		⑤
3 coins	H, H, T	0.375	⑥	
3 coins	T, T, T	⑦		12.5%
3 coins	T, H, T	0.375	⑧	
3 coins	at least 1 H	⑨	$\frac{7}{8}$	
3 coins	at least 2 T		$\frac{1}{2}$	⑩
3 coins	T, H, H	0.375		⑪
3 coins	H, T, H	⑫	$\frac{3}{8}$	
3 coins	H, H. H		⑬	12.5%
3 coins	at least 1 T	0.875		⑭
3 coins	at least 2 H		$\frac{1}{2}$	⑮

Measurement & Space

AC9M6M02

Comparing lengths and areas

> **Perimeter** is the distance around the outside of a two-dimensional shape.
>
> **Area** is the amount of space inside a two-dimensional shape.

Write the missing values in the spaces below the table. Make sure you include the correct units in your answers.

Height	Width	Perimeter	Area
8 cm	6 cm	24 cm	①
②	12 m	32 m	48 m²
6 mm	③	30 mm	54 mm²
④	6 cm	36 cm	72 cm²
3 km	18 km	⑤	51 km²
9 m	7 m	32 m	⑥
⑦	14 km	48 km	140 km²
17 mm	2 mm	38 mm	⑧
2 m	21 m	⑨	42 m²
5 km	⑩	18 km	20 km²
6 cm	3 cm	18 cm	⑪
7 mm	7 mm	⑫	49 mm²

① _____   ⑦ _____
② _____   ⑧ _____
③ _____   ⑨ _____
④ _____   ⑩ _____
⑤ _____   ⑪ _____
⑥ _____   ⑫ _____

Score 2 points for each correct answer!

SCORE **/24** (0-10) (12-18) (20-24)

Problem Solving

AC9M6N08, AC9M6P01

Decimal and chance problems

Use a calculator to work out the answers.

① Lilly Hood walked 437.25 metres to her grandmother's cottage seventeen times. Then the incident with the wolf put an end to her grandmother and the walking.

How much walking was that, to the nearest kilometre? Don't forget she also walked home.

_____

② Mr B B Wolf, who still maintains his innocence in the incident at Lily Hood's grandmother's cottage, travelled to and from the courthouse thirty-nine times while he was on trial. The journey was 36.047 km, one way.

How much travel was that in total? Answer to the nearest kilometre.

_____

③ The three Piggy brothers, who were witnesses against Mr B B Wolf, said that once he scared them so much that they each ran 37.092 metres, which is a long way for a pig to run, to escape.

How far did the three brothers run altogether? Answer to the nearest metre.

_____

④ Wesley Weasel appeared in court as a character witness for Mr B B Wolf. He went to court seventeen times because he kept getting the date wrong. The court was 15.037 kilometres from Wesley's home.

To the nearest kilometre, how much did Wesley travel during those seventeen times?

_____

The following questions are about a game of coin toss, using four coins.

⑤ If the chance of getting four heads in the game is one out of sixteen, what is the chance of getting four tails?

_____

⑥ The coins were tossed seventy-two times and the combination of three heads and one tail came up eight times. That was exactly the probability for the number of times this combination would come up. What is that probability as a fraction?

_____

⑦ The coins were then tossed 144 times. If the probability of two heads and two tails coming up was a quarter, how many times would this combination have come up, according to probability?

_____

⑧ Since there is only one combination of coins that does not include at least one head (that is, four tails) and there are sixteen possible combinations, what is the chance of at least one head coming up, as a fraction?

_____

Grammar & Punctuation

AC9E6LA05, AC9E6LA06

Complex sentences and conjunctions

> Remember! A **complex sentence** has two (or more) clauses: a <u>main clause</u> which has the main idea, and a <u>subordinate clause</u> which gives more information about the main idea. A subordinate clause cannot stand on its own.
>
> *Example:* <u>The class was having a party</u> **because** <u>it was the end of the year</u>.
>
> **because** — conjunction   subordinate clause   main clause
>
> **Conjunctions** join clauses to make complex sentences. Some examples are: although, because, unless, when, while.

Circle the conjunctions in these complex sentences.

1. Shelly was really glad because she had been elected councillor.
2. Jed played alone as he was new to the school.
3. Although playing the drums is noisy, it's also fun.
4. While it was tiring climbing up, sliding down the sandhill was worth it.
5. We won't finish on time unless everyone pulls together.

Circle the best conjunction for each complex sentence.

6. We got to the cricket (after   before) the crowd got too large.
7. Seeing the art display was great (although   when) there was little room.
8. (As   Until) they are rare, rescuers battled the waves to save the whales.
9. (While   Until) building the boat was difficult, it was very rewarding.

Choose conjunctions from the box to complete the sentences.

because   until   after   once

10. Sunshine streamed through my window _____ it was morning.
11. _____ the terrible storm, we found a glass jar.
12. _____ the game started, I calmed down.
13. She rang the bell loudly _____ everyone was at assembly.

Phonic Knowledge & Spelling

AC9E6LY09

Palindromes

> **Palindromes** are spelt the same forwards as they are backwards. *Examples:* level, eye

Finish these palindromes.

1. mad_____
2. civ_____
3. de_____
4. ref_____
5. kay_____
6. rad_____

Word origin

> Some English words come from other languages, such as Italian.
> *Example:* cartoon, piano

Choose words from the box to complete these sentences. The words come from Italian.

granite   rocket   carpet   model

7. There's a large piece of _____ rock in the garden.
8. Wool is quite often used to make _____.
9. Scientists are preparing a _____ to go to Mars.
10. Sam likes to build _____ trains as a hobby.

Use one of the words from each pair to complete the sentence.

guerrilla/gorilla   capital/capitol creek/creak   cooperation/corporation lightening/lightning

11. When putting up a large tent you need to have _____.
12. You use a _____ letter to start a name.
13. My favourite animal in the zoo is the _____.
14. We paddled in the water down at the _____.
15. _____ flashed and thunder roared in the sky.

TARGETING HOMEWORK 6 © PASCAL PRESS ISBN 9781925726480

TERM 3 ENGLISH

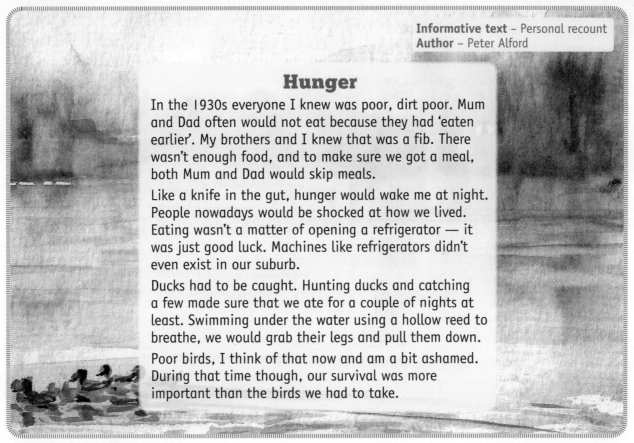

Informative text – Personal recount
Author – Peter Alford

Hunger

In the 1930s everyone I knew was poor, dirt poor. Mum and Dad often would not eat because they had 'eaten earlier'. My brothers and I knew that was a fib. There wasn't enough food, and to make sure we got a meal, both Mum and Dad would skip meals.

Like a knife in the gut, hunger would wake me at night. People nowadays would be shocked at how we lived. Eating wasn't a matter of opening a refrigerator — it was just good luck. Machines like refrigerators didn't even exist in our suburb.

Ducks had to be caught. Hunting ducks and catching a few made sure that we ate for a couple of nights at least. Swimming under the water using a hollow reed to breathe, we would grab their legs and pull them down.

Poor birds, I think of that now and am a bit ashamed. During that time though, our survival was more important than the birds we had to take.

Write or circle the correct answer.

① How did Mum and Dad make sure that their children had enough to eat?

_____

_____

② Hunger was 'like a knife in the gut'. What does that mean?

a Food was plentiful.

b Hunger was dangerous.

c Hunger was a stabbing pain.

③ When did this story take place?

_____

④ What does 'dirt poor' mean?

a People were extremely poor.

b People ate dirt.

c People didn't have a refrigerator.

⑤ How did these boys capture ducks?

_____

_____

⑥ How does the writer feel about taking the ducks?

_____

_____

⑦ How long would the ducks feed the family for?

_____

_____

⑧ How do you know the suburb didn't have a lot of money?

a They had to catch ducks.

b No-one could afford a fridge.

c There were many children.

Score 2 points for each correct answer! **SCORE** /16 (0-6) (8-12) (14-16)

My Book Review

Title _____

Author _____

Rating ☆☆☆☆☆

Comment _____

_____

TERM 3 ENGLISH

Number & Algebra

AC9M6N03

Equivalent fractions

These squares have been divided in equal parts. The parts of each square are **equal** so we call them **fractions of the whole**, or just **fractions.** Use them to answer the questions.

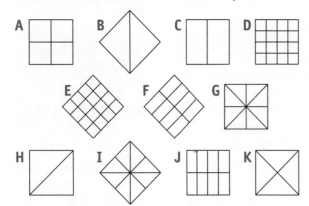

Note: Equivalent means things are equal in value, even if they are different in other ways.

① What is one part of square A as a fraction?

_____

② What is one part of square I as a fraction?

_____

③ What is one part of square E as a fraction?

_____

④ How many fractions of square D are equivalent to one fraction of square C?

_____

⑤ How many fractions of square G are equivalent to one fraction of square H?

_____

⑥ How many fractions of square B are equivalent to one fraction of square H?

_____

⑦ How many fractions of square J are equivalent to two fractions of square G?

_____

⑧ How many fractions of square F are equivalent to three fractions of square A?

_____

⑨ How many fractions of square I are equivalent to three fractions of square K?

_____

⑩ How many fractions of square F are equivalent to half the fractions of square E?

_____

⑪ As a fraction, what are three parts of square I?

_____

⑫ As a fraction, what are five parts of square J?

_____

⑬ As a fraction, what are eleven parts of square E?

_____

Score 2 points for each correct answer! SCORE **/26** (0-10) (12-20) (22-26)

Statistics & Probability

AC9M6P01

Describing probabilities

This table shows different probabilities when four and five coins are tossed.

Some figures have been left out. Work out the answers for the spaces numbered 1–12. Use a calculator if you need to.

Note: H = Head and **T** = Tail.
Target means 'the desired result'.

		Chance of getting the Target		
Toss	Target	Decimal	Fraction	Percent
4 coins	4 H	0.0625	$\frac{1}{16}$	①
4 coins	2 T	②	$\frac{3}{8}$	37.5%
4 coins	1 T	0.25	③	25%
4 coins	at least 1 H	④	$\frac{5}{16}$	31.25%
4 coins	at least 2 T	0.6875	$\frac{11}{16}$	⑤
4 coins	at least 3 H	0.3125	⑥	31.25%
5 coins	5 T	⑦	$\frac{1}{32}$	3.125%
5 coins	3 H	0.0625	⑧	6.25%
5 coins	1 H	⑨		6.25%
5 coins	at least 2 T		$\frac{26}{32}$	⑩
5 coins	at least 3 H	0.5	⑪	
5 coins	at least 4 T	0.1875	⑫	18.75%

Score 2 points for each correct answer! SCORE **/24** (0-10) (12-18) (20-24)

TARGETING HOMEWORK 6 © PASCAL PRESS ISBN 9781925726480

Converting units of volume

Each diagram shows one or more missing angles. What are the missing angles?

① a = _____

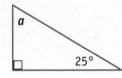

② a = _____
b = _____

③ a = _____
b = _____

④ a = _____
b = _____

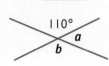

⑤ a = _____
b = _____
c = _____

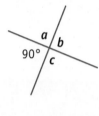

Write the name beside the correct angle. Choose from: acute, obtuse, reflex, right, straight line.

⑥ _____

⑦  _____

⑧ 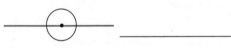 _____

⑨    _____

⑩    _____

Fractions and volume problems

① Jack had two-quarters of a cake and Jill had three-eighths of it.
Who had more cake?

_____

② Jack had three-sixteenths, Jill had a quarter and Humpty had an eighth of a cake.
Who had the most cake?

_____

③ Jack had two-quarters of a cake, Jill had half as much as Jack and Humpty had the rest.
Who had the most cake?

_____

④ Jack had three-sixteenths of a cake, Jill had two-eighths and Humpty had the rest.
Who had the most cake?

_____

⑤ Jack had three-eighths of a cake, Jill had half of it and Humpty had a sixteenth.
How much of the cake was left?

_____

⑥ In a game of chance, Meli had $\frac{1}{4}$ chance of winning and Malakai had 0.35 chance of winning.
Who had the better chance of winning?

_____

⑦ In a game of chance, Meli had the same chance of winning as Malakai but Pita had 40% chance of winning.
If one of them had to win the game, how much chance did Meli and Malakai each have?

_____

⑧ In a game of chance, the chances of winning were: $\frac{1}{4}$ to Meli, 0.125 to Malakai and 35% to Pita.
What was the chance that none of them would win?

_____

Grammar & Punctuation

AC9E6LA06

Verb tenses: simple present and past

> **Remember! Verb tenses** tell us **when** an action happened — present or past.
> **Simple present tense:** We **swim** at the creek.
> **Simple past tense:** Two weeks ago, we **swam** at the creek.

These film advertisements are in past tense. Change the verb to present tense.

Example: The heroes who **saved** the planet <u>save</u>

① The beast that ate Sydney _____

② She wasn't your usual hero _____

③ Mad Frank was so creepy _____

④ Felicia knelt for the king _____

These book titles are in present tense. Change the verb to past tense.

Example: She **Takes** the Cake   <u>Took</u>

⑤ How I Make Millions of Dollars
_____

⑥ Teddy Smith Comes to Town
_____

⑦ They Go to War
_____

⑧ She Speaks to Us from Space
_____

Write the verbs correctly and say if they are past or present.

Example: I really ekil <u>like</u> your hat. <u>past</u>

⑨ We emac _____ in peace.
_____

⑩ Our old car sevird _____ us safely.
_____

⑪ That meal semoc _____ with gravy.
_____

⑫ Jenna detiaw _____ for them for an hour. _____

Score 2 points for each correct answer!   SCORE **/24**   (0-10) (12-18) (20-24)

Phonic Knowledge & Spelling

AC9E6LY08, AC9E6LY09

Syllables

Choose a syllable from the box to complete each word.

| be | mur | son | site | ver |

① rea / _____ / a / ble

② op / po / _____

③ _____ / ne / fit

④ mur / _____ / ing

⑤ con / _____ / sa / tion

Silent letters

Each pair of words has a missing silent letter. Choose a silent letter from the box.

| w | k | b | w |

⑥ ___restle   ans___er

⑦ ___nobbly   ___nickers

⑧ ___rinkle   ___rong

⑨ su___tle   num___

Choose word parts from the box to fill the spaces.

| c | ty | red | s | ter | ch |

⑩ to strongly dislike: h a t ___ ___ ___

⑪ to smash or break glass: ___ h a t ___ ___ ___

⑫ to be talkative: ___ h a t ___ ___

⑬ when birds come out of their egg: h a t ___ ___

Suffixes

Match the sounds in the box with the underlined letters in the words.

| shon | shus | shall |

⑭ produc**tion** _____

⑮ electri**cian** _____

⑯ spe**cial** _____

⑰ spa**cious** _____

⑱ deli**cious** _____

⑲ educa**tion** _____

⑳ essen**tial** _____

㉑ exhibi**tion** _____

Score 2 points for each correct answer!   SCORE **/42**   (0-18) (20-36) (38-42)

Grandfather Clock

Imaginative text – Fantasy
Author – Peter Alford
Illustrator – Paul Lennon

Rory had always wondered what was inside the grandfather clock in the library. Mr Cromby, the librarian, told everyone that he bought it in a strange old shop in London. Falling in love with the old clock, Mr Cromby was surprised it had cost him so little. Forty pounds was the price asked by the strange little shopkeeper who wore an ancient pith helmet. Most explorers wore those hats in the past.

Mr Cromby was busy telling a lady about the large pot he'd purchased in Egypt. Rory took his chance and opened the door. Like dust being vacuumed up, he was sucked in, and the door slammed behind him. After a short struggle, he was able to force the door open.

Green trees and bushes surrounded the clock. A tyrannosaurus rex lifted its head and stared, before munching on the leg of a dead triceratops. Rory rubbed his eyes, his jaw dropped.

Write or circle the correct answer.

1. Which word is used which means **push**?

_____

2. Rory was amazed at what happened. Which **two** phrases tell you this?

   a rubbed his eyes   c short struggle

   b took his chance   d his jaw dropped

3. What was it that most explorers wore in the olden days?

_____

4. Compound words are made up of two complete words. Find **two** compound words.

   a _____

   b _____

5. Why was Mr Cromby surprised about the old clock?

   a It cost so little.

   b It was in London.

   c It was so large.

6. What words give the idea that Rory was sucked into the clock?

_____

_____

7. What gives the idea the clock may be a time machine?

   a ancient pith helmet

   b There were dinosaurs.

   c Rory rubbed his eyes.

8. Where was the grandfather clock bought?

_____

_____

9. Which words tell that the shopkeeper was a little different?

_____

_____

Score 2 points for each correct answer!

SCORE **/18**   0-6   8-14   16-18

My Book Review

Title _____

Author _____

Rating ☆☆☆☆☆

Comment _____

_____

TERM 3 ENGLISH

Number & Algebra

AC9M6N05

Adding and subtracting fractions

Simplify these improper fractions and write them as mixed numbers.

Improper fraction	Simplified fraction	Mixed number
$\frac{18}{4}$	$\frac{9}{2}$	①
$\frac{9}{6}$	②	$1\frac{1}{2}$
$\frac{38}{4}$	③	④
$\frac{100}{15}$	⑤	⑥
$\frac{78}{24}$	⑦	⑧
$\frac{126}{8}$	⑨	⑩

Work out these equations. Simplify the answers and write them as mixed numbers.

⑪ $\frac{4}{8} + \frac{3}{8} + \frac{3}{8}$

= _____

⑫ $\frac{1}{2} + \frac{1}{2} + \frac{1}{2} + \frac{1}{2}$

= _____

⑬ $\frac{2}{3} + \frac{1}{3} + \frac{1}{3} + \frac{2}{3} + \frac{1}{3}$

= _____

⑭ $\frac{5}{16} + \frac{3}{16} + \frac{10}{16}$

= _____

⑮ $\frac{3}{10} + \frac{7}{10} + \frac{6}{10} + \frac{4}{10}$

= _____

⑯ $\frac{3}{4} + \frac{1}{4} + \frac{2}{4} + \frac{3}{4} + \frac{3}{4} + \frac{2}{4}$

= _____

⑰ $\frac{8}{16} + \frac{5}{16} + \frac{12}{16} + \frac{7}{16} + \frac{2}{16}$

= _____

⑱ $\frac{3}{7} + \frac{3}{7} + \frac{5}{7} + \frac{5}{7} + \frac{4}{7}$

= _____

⑲ $\frac{1}{9} + \frac{2}{9} + \frac{3}{9} + \frac{4}{9} + \frac{5}{9} + \frac{6}{9}$

= _____

Score 2 points for each correct answer! **SCORE** **/38** (0-16) (18-32) (34-38)

Statistics & Probability

AC9M6ST01

Using a table and a line graph

This table and graph show Wesley Weasel's attempt to dig a tunnel to escape prison.

Tunnel to Freedom, by W Weasel										
Days	1	2	3	4	5	6	7	8	9	10
Digging (m)	5	0	5	5	$2\frac{1}{2}$	$2\frac{1}{2}$	0	5	0	5

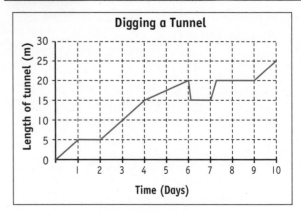

① In total, how long is the tunnel?

_____

② In total, how many metres did Wesley dig?

_____

③ What is the most likely explanation for the drop in the tunnel's length on day 6?
   a Wesley changed his mind and decided he quite liked being in prison.
   b There was a cave-in for 5 metres.
   c Wesley was digging in the wrong direction.

④ On how many days did Wesley do no digging at all?

_____

⑤ Describe Wesley's rate of digging on day 8.

_____

_____

⑥ On average, how many metres of tunnel length has Wesley added each day?

_____

⑦ If from day 11, Wesley could add an average of 5 metres of length to the tunnel every day, on what day would his tunnel get to 60 metres in length?

_____

Score 2 points for each correct answer! **SCORE** **/14**

TARGETING HOMEWORK 6 © PASCAL PRESS ISBN 9781925726480

Measurement & Space

AC9M6M04

Right, acute, obtuse and reflex angles

Write how many of each type of angle are inside and outside these shapes.

	Acute	Right	Obtuse	Reflex
① Angles inside shape				
② Angles outside shape				

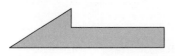

	Acute	Right	Obtuse	Reflex
③ Angles inside shape				
④ Angles outside shape				

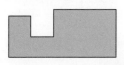

	Acute	Right	Obtuse	Reflex
⑤ Angles inside shape				
⑥ Angles outside shape				

	Acute	Right	Obtuse	Reflex
⑦ Angles inside shape				
⑧ Angles outside shape				

	Acute	Right	Obtuse	Reflex
⑨ Angles inside shape				
⑩ Angles outside shape				

Score 2 points for each correct answer!

SCORE **/20** (0-8) (10-14) (16-20)

Problem Solving

AC9M6N05, AC9M6N07

Fraction problems

① There was one cake and it was a very big cake. Aiysha took $\frac{3}{16}$ of it and spread Vegemite over it. Mosiya took $\frac{1}{8}$ of it and dribbled tomato sauce over it. Kamili took $\frac{3}{8}$ of it and sprinkled pepper all over it.

How much of the cake altogether did the three friends take?

_____

② After the friends ate the cake they felt pretty sick. Kamili said if there was a worst bellyache in the world, he had $\frac{7}{12}$ of it. But Aiysha said she had $\frac{3}{4}$ of the worst bellyache in the world and Mosiya said she had $\frac{5}{6}$ of it.

How much of the worst bellyache in the world did the three friends claim to have?

_____

③ Three friends found some money which they decided to share. Mosiya claimed $\frac{4}{5}$ of the money because she saw it first. Aiysha grumbled and claimed $\frac{7}{10}$ of the money because she had picked it up. Kamili turned purple and said that as he was the first one to lick it, which he did right then, he claimed $\frac{18}{20}$ of it.

How much of the money did they claim altogether?

_____

④ Aiysha said she would fly a kite $\frac{11}{12}$ of the way up to the sky.

Kamili bragged that he would fly his kite as high as Aiysha and another $\frac{5}{6}$ of the way up to the sky higher.

Mosiya scoffed and said that she would fly her kite as high as Aiysha and another $\frac{2}{3}$ of the way up to the sky higher.

What mixed number do you get when you add Kimili's, Mosiya's and Aiysha's claims?

_____

Grammar & Punctuation

AC9E6LA06

Auxiliary verbs

> **Auxiliary verbs** are helping verbs. They help the main verb express meaning and they show the tense of a sentence. These verbs are: **be**, **do**, **have**.
>
> **Be:** am, is, are, was, were, be, being, been
>
> **Do:** do, does, did
>
> **Have:** has, have, had
>
> *Example:*
>   We **are** <u>travelling</u> to see the new dam.
>   <small>auxiliary verb   main verb</small>

Underline the auxiliary verbs and the main verbs.

1. During winter we didn't use our pool.
2. My sister is learning to knit with needles.
3. We have paddled to the island for fun.
4. Old gum trees were cut for their wood.
5. I am sleeping over at my friend's house tonight.

Use the auxiliary verbs to form verbs in the past tense. Some will be used more than once.

6. – 11.

had	was	were

Scientists (6)_____ discovered life on Mars. They (7)_____ looking through powerful telescopes. The army (8)_____ scared that people would panic. That sort of news (9)_____ worried the public in the past. Governments (10)_____ seen what happened when news like that reached the newspapers. People (11)_____ frightened and they tried to escape into the forest.

Phonic Knowledge & Spelling

AC9E6LY08, AC9E6LY09

Plurals – words ending in –y

> If the letter before the **y** is a **vowel**, just add **s**. *Examples:* toy, toy**s**   key, key**s**
>
> If the letter before the **y** is a **consonant**, change the **y** to **i** and add **es**. *Example:* fairy, fair**ies**

Change these words to plurals.

1. memory _____
2. territory _____
3. donkey _____
4. lobby _____
5. holiday _____
6. ferry _____

The bold word in each of these compound words is jumbled. Write the correct spelling.

7. partner **spih**   partner_____
8. back **roudng**   back_____
9. sea **hsero**   sea_____
10. **dhsi** washer   _____washer
11. **bkoo** case   _____case

Choose a word from the box that makes the derivative.

element	information	tiger

12. liger   lion + _____
13. pixel   pict + _____
14. infomercial   _____ + commercial

Choose words from the box to complete these sentences about hobbies or pastimes.

shovel	camera	anchor	parachute

15. The photographer had an expensive _____.
16. When gardening, Mr Bib used a _____ to dig.
17. Jumping from an aeroplane requires a _____.
18. Fishing boats need to have a heavy _____.

TARGETING HOMEWORK 6 © PASCAL PRESS ISBN 9781925726480

Text 1
Finders Are Keepers

Persuasive text – Argument
Author – Peter Alford

Have you found anything recently? If you didn't hand it to the police or a teacher and kept it for yourself, you broke the law. Yes, you are a criminal! How silly is that?

Finders are keepers **must** become **the law**. People who lose things are **stupid**, with a capital **S**. I say **too bad too sad!!** You lose something, it should be gone forever. You didn't deserve it in the first place. Only silly people lose their valuables. Having to hand something to police or teachers is ridiculous! What's to say they don't keep it for themselves?

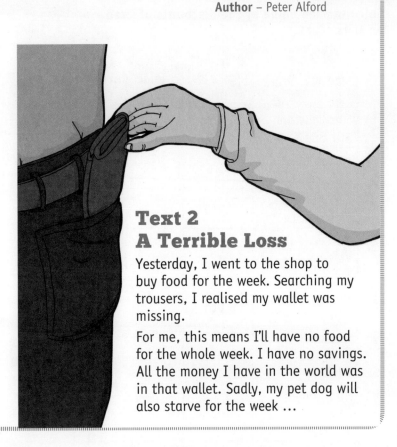

Text 2
A Terrible Loss

Yesterday, I went to the shop to buy food for the week. Searching my trousers, I realised my wallet was missing.

For me, this means I'll have no food for the whole week. I have no savings. All the money I have in the world was in that wallet. Sadly, my pet dog will also starve for the week …

Write or circle the correct answer.

① **Which two words are used that mean the same as silly.**

a criminal   d stupid

b ridiculous   e means

c searching   f savings

② **Which phrase tells that the writer of the first text is uncaring?**

a is ridiculous

b too bad too sad

c broke the law

③ **Who will starve if the person in text 2 doesn't have money?**

_____   _____

④ **In text 1 the writer says that police or teachers may do something. What may they do?**

_____

_____

⑤ **What is the reason the person in text 2 has no money at all?**

_____

_____

⑥ **What question in text 1 does the writer ask to suggest that people are not clever.**

_____

_____

Score 2 points for each correct answer!

SCORE /12   0-4   6-8   10-12

My Book Review

Title _____

Author _____

Rating ☆☆☆☆☆

Comment _____

_____

Number & Algebra

AC9M6N07, AC9M6N09

Calculating percentage discounts

Calculate the value of the discounts offered on these cars.

	Car Marked price	Discount (as a % of price)	Value of discount (nearest $)
①	Ford Mustang $61 394	9.6%	
②	Mazda MX-5 $37 351	11.15%	
③	Fiat Abarth 124 $43 500	7.25%	
④	Mercedes-Benz Valente $65 149	12.125%	
⑤	Honda Civic $24 990	3.05%	
⑥	Holden Colorado $39 990	5.25%	
⑦	Alfa Romeo Giulia $59 900	6.66%	
⑧	Lexus IS $66 535	6.57%	
⑨	Hyundai i40 $43 187	13.35%	
⑩	Suzuki APV $18 990	0.75%	

Score 2 points for each correct answer! **SCORE** /20 (0-8) (10-14) (16-20)

Statistics & Probability

AC9M6P02

Conducting chance experiments

The following data shows the number of tries and the results for different tests of chance.

Notes:

- **Target** means a specific result. For example, the number of times that three sixes were thrown by three dice.
- **Reliability** is the assessment of how reliable or dependable the test was. When deciding how reliable a test was, consider the number of times a test was repeated, and any difference between the probability and the actual results.

Decide how reliable each test was. Rank the reliability from **A** (**Not reliable at all**) to **E** (**Very reliable**).

No. tries	No. times Target hit	Probability as % of No. tries	Reliability
2000	200	10%	①
6750	1013	15%	②
11 800	1180	10%	③
100	25	25%	④
5250	40	0.75%	⑤
500	250	50%	⑥
7500	1125	15%	⑦
50	3	5%	⑧
10 000	7500	75%	⑨
2250	450	20%	⑩
10	1	10%	⑪
12 050	1800	15%	⑫

Score 2 points for each correct answer! **SCORE** /24 (0-10) (12-18) (20-24)

Measurement & Space

AC9M6M03

Interpreting timetables

This timetable shows Qantas and Jetstar flights from Adelaide to Brisbane.

Flights Out: Adelaide to Brisbane, August 2018									
Depart (Adelaide Time)	Arrive (Brisbane Time)	18	19	20	21	22	23	24	Flight No.
06:00	07:50	◣	◣	◣	◣	◣	-	-	QF660
07:10	09:00	-	-	-	-	-	-	◣	QF1590
07:20	09:05	-	◣	◣	-	-	◣	-	QF6606
09:50	11:40	◣	-	◣	◣	◣	-	-	QF1592
13:00	14:50	◣	◣	◣	◣	◣	-	◣	QF662
13:40	15:30	-	-	-	-	-	◣	◣	QF662
16:20	18:10	◣	◣	◣	◣	◣	-	-	QF1598
16:20	18:20	-	-	-	◣	◣	◣	◣	QF664
17:05	19:00	★	★	★	★	★	★	★	JQ783
19:25	21:15	◣	◣	◣	◣	◣	-	-	QF656

Key: ◣ Qantas/QantasLink, ★ Jetstar

Source: Qantas, https://www.qantas.com/au/en.html.
The timetable was modified for the purpose of this exercise.

Use the timetable to answer the following questions.

① How many flights are there in total?

_____

② Why are the departure times clarified with 'Adelaide Time' and 'Brisbane Time'?

_____

_____

③ What flight number is the earliest Qantas flight departure?

_____

④ How long is Flight QF662 scheduled to take on 19 August?

_____

⑤ What flight numbers have only two departures out of Adelaide?

_____

⑥ How many Qantas flights are there?

_____

⑦ Which Qantas flight is scheduled to be the quickest?

_____

⑧ Which Qantas flight is scheduled to take the longest?

_____

⑨ What is the most common time a Qantas flight is scheduled to take?

_____

⑩ How long are the Jetstar flights scheduled to take?

_____

⑪ On which date are there the fewest flights scheduled?

_____

⑫ On which date are there the most Qantas flights scheduled?

_____

Decimal problems with discounts and chance

You may use a calculator for these questions. Round decimals to the nearest three decimal places.

① Chi bought a house for $800 000 which was at a discount of $2000 off the asking price.
What is that discount as a percentage of the asking price?

_____

② Dinh got a 12% discount on a bicycle that was marked at $250. He gave a quarter of the money he saved to his sister and spent the rest on a helmet.
How much did the helmet cost?

_____

③ Linh had a $600 budget for a new TV, but the TV cost $800.
What's the smallest percentage discount Linh needs to get to afford the TV?

_____

④ Dinh got 20% off a computer game that was marked at $80. Linh got a 15% discount on a board game that was marked at $60.
Who saved more and by how much?

_____

⑤ Linh had $55.00, Chi had $46.50 and Dinh had $63.50. They put their money together to buy a radio priced at $160.00, but they got it at a 12% discount.
How much money did they have left after buying the radio?

_____

⑥ Dinh had a 40% chance of winning a game. This was twice as good as Linh's chance of winning.
What was Linh's chance of winning, as a decimal?

_____

⑦ Chi and Linh had an equal chance of winning a game while Dinh had a $\frac{2}{5}$ chance of winning. There was a 20% chance that no one would win.
What was Linh's chance of winning, as a decimal?

_____

Score 2 points for each correct answer!   SCORE   /24   0-10   12-18   20-24

TARGETING HOMEWORK 6 © PASCAL PRESS ISBN 9781925726480

TERM 3 MATHS

101

Grammar & Punctuation

AC9E6LA06

Verb tenses

> **Verbs** say **when** something happens in a sentence: **present, past, future.**
>
> **Present tenses:** I **do** my homework every day. I **am doing** my homework now.
>
> **Past tenses:** I **did** my homework. I **was doing** my homework.
>
> **Future tenses:** I **will do** my homework. I **am going to do** my homework.

Underline the verbs and say if they are present, past or future tense.

① We were playing in the pool after school on Tuesday. _____

② My class took a look at the swamp down the road. _____

③ I am going to visit Asia on the next school holidays. _____

④ I'm eating my favourite meal of stir-fry veges. _____

⑤ Jai trains for football three times a week. _____

⑥ I'll finish off my project on the weekend. _____

Change the bold present tense verbs to past tense.

⑦ Jess **loves** her netball club. _____

⑧ Mum **drinks** heaps of water after her jog. _____

⑨ Bella **is training** with her swimming coach. _____

⑩ The train **leaves** at 10:00 pm. _____

Change the tense of this story to past by changing the verbs.

⑪–⑰

Tom **walks** (11)_____ to school along the river. He **jumps** (12)_____ the fence and **sees** (13)_____ a large brown snake on the track. He **knows** (14)_____ about snakes but **is** (15)_____ still nervous. Tom **picks** (16)_____ up a stick and **lifts** (17)_____ the snake carefully.

Phonic Knowledge & Spelling

AC9E6LY08, AC9E6LY09

Irregular plural nouns

> To make the **plural** of most common nouns add **s** or **es**. *Example:* car, cars   bus, bus**es**
>
> Some **plural nouns** are **irregular** and the spelling has to be changed.
> *Examples:* goose, **geese**   man, **men**

Write the plural for these singular nouns.

① mouse _____

② woman _____

③ child _____

④ tooth _____

⑤ foot _____

⑥ person _____

Choose a syllable from the box to complete each word.

ter	cov	tion	py	het

⑦ spag / _____ / ti

⑧ com / pu / _____

⑨ dis / _____ / er

⑩ in / for / ma / _____

⑪ un / hap / _____

Add suffixes –er or –ing to these words. (Hint: Some words will need a double consonant.)

⑫ develop

_____ _____

⑬ begin

_____ _____

⑭ travel

_____ _____

Circle one word in each group that is the antonym (opposite) to the bold word.

⑮ **villain** hero woman

⑯ **clever** smart stupid

⑰ **cheap** expensive inexpensive

⑱ **dawdle** sprint walk

⑲ **guardian** enemy companion

⑳ **awesome** spectacular unimpressive

㉑ **argument** agreement discussion

㉒ **confident** shy mean

102

TARGETING HOMEWORK 6 © PASCAL PRESS ISBN 9781925726480

TERM 3 ENGLISH

Building Blocks

Imaginative text – Narrative
Author – Peter Alford

Clancy had one talent — building things out of Lego. 'Superstar' was one word that could describe his amazing talent. In year twelve his hobby was definitely not cool. Other 17-year-olds wouldn't be seen dead using Lego.

Mr Lawrence found Clancy designing a Lego building for the eighth time during his History class. Furious at this, the teacher took his design and crumpled it in Clancy's face before throwing it in the bin.

Mr Lawrence leant in and whispered, "You really are a waste of space!"

Clancy was hurt. Comments like that do one of two things, crush you or motivate you.

Sometime in the future …

Entering the lift of the brand new skyscraper, Mr Lawrence's back was tired. At eighty everything made him feel that way. Standing in the lift, a young man smiled. He held rolls of paper plans under his arm. Figuring he was the architect of this amazing glass-covered building, the old teacher smiled back.

"You designed this?" he asked.

"Yes," the architect replied. "I made sure that there wasn't a waste of space, or that anybody felt that way," the young man commented.

Offering his hand, he introduced himself. "Hi, I'm Clancy."

Write or circle the correct answer.

1. **What do architects do?**

   a They paint buildings.

   b They ride in lifts of new buildings.

   c They plan buildings.

2. **Why was Mr Lawrence angry with Clancy in class?**

   _____

   _____

3. **What does motivate you mean in this story?**

   a You try harder.

   b You give up.

   c You feel sad.

4. **What does design mean?**

   a build   c plan

   b construct   d develop

5. **What would most 17-year-olds think about Clancy's hobby?**

   _____

   _____

6. **What words tell you that Mr Lawrence taught in a school in the second part of the story?**

   _____

   _____

7. **Which sentence tells you that the young man is Clancy from school?**

   _____

   _____

   _____

Score 2 points for each correct answer!

SCORE **/14** (0-4) (6-10) (12-14)

My Book Review

Title _____

Author _____

Rating ☆☆☆☆☆

Comment _____

_____

Number & Algebra

AC9M6N06

Multiplying and dividing decimals

Calculate these equations.
Do not use a calculator.

① 4.032 × 10 = _____

② 4.032 × 100 = _____

③ 403.26 ÷ 1000 = _____

④ 4.32 × 10 = _____

⑤ 403.232 ÷ 100 = _____

⑥ 4.032 × 1000 = _____

⑦ 403.26 × 10 = _____

⑧ 4.32 ÷ 100 = _____

⑨ 403.032 ÷ 10 = _____

⑩ 0.403 × 100 = _____

⑪ 403.2 × 10 = _____

⑫ 4.2 ÷ 100 = _____

⑬ 0.04 × 100 = _____

⑭ 0.4 ÷ 1000 = _____

⑮ 403 × 10 = _____

Score 2 points for
each correct answer! **SCORE** **/30** (0-12) (14-24) (26-30)

Statistics & Probability

AC9M6ST01, AC9M6P01

Predicting likely outcomes

What points along the probability scale would these events be? Write the matching letters in the boxes.

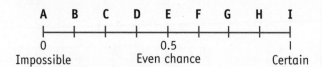

A   B   C   D   E   F   G   H   I

0   0.5   1
Impossible   Even chance   Certain

① ☐ An ant will knock over a power pylon.

② ☐ A kangaroo will jump.

③ ☐ The next time you flip a coin, it will come up head.

④ ☐ The next time you roll a die, it will come up 6.

⑤ ☐ The next time you are on your way to school, you will see a dog.

⑥ ☐ The next time you are on your way to school, you will see a parrot.

⑦ ☐ You will sneeze within the next quarter of an hour.

⑧ ☐ You will sneeze within the next two hours.

⑨ ☐ You will sneeze at least once tomorrow.

⑩ ☐ There will be a major car accident somewhere in Australia in the next five minutes.

⑪ ☐ There will be a major car accident in your neighbourhood in the next five hours.

⑫ ☐ An animal from an Australian zoo will be mentioned in the news today.

⑬ ☐ An animal will escape from a zoo somewhere in the world today.

⑭ ☐ An animal from a zoo somewhere in the world will die today.

⑮ **Are events that are either impossible or certain to happen chance events? Answer yes or no.**

_____

Range and mode

> **Range:** the difference between the highest and lowest values
>
> **Mode:** the value that occurs most often

Bean Bag Toss is a game where players throw 3 bean bags onto a grid like this:

6	5	9
1	4	2
3	8	7

Players add the scores the bean bags land on.

Sometimes bean bags miss the grid, and sometimes more than one bean bag lands on a square.

Here are the scores of 5 games.
What is the range and mode of each game?

⑯ 9, 10, 15, 9, 22, 9

range = _____

mode = _____

⑰ 11, 15, 24, 12, 15, 6, 15, 24

range = _____

mode = _____

⑱ 12, 10, 7, 16, 19, 14, 16, 6

range = _____

mode = _____

⑲ 16, 15, 24, 12, 15, 16, 15, 24

range = _____

mode = _____

⑳ 4, 36, 9, 9, 7, 12, 7, 9

range = _____

mode = _____

Use the range and the mode to work out the missing scores in each set.

㉑ 5, 7, ?, 9, 8, ?, 7, 9

range = 12, mode = 9

missing scores: _____, _____

㉒ 13, 12, 3, ?, ?, 6, 12, 6

range = 18, mode = 12

missing scores: _____, _____

㉓ ?, 5, 7, ?, 5, 6, 7

range = 18, mode = 7

missing scores: _____, _____

Score 2 points for each correct answer!

SCORE /46 (0–20) (22–40) (42–46)

Measurement & Space

There are no measurement & space activities in this unit.

Problem Solving

AC9M6N06, AC9M6P02

Number and chance problems

① There were 24.05 gizmos that were multiplied by 10 and painted purple, one fine inventive day.

So how many gizmos was that, would you say?

_____

② There were 0.35 gadgets that were multiplied a hundred times and then halved just for fun, one fine inventive day.

So how many gadgets was that, would you say?

_____

③ There were 42.8 thingamajigs that were divided by a hundred before a quarter of them were made into judges, one fine inventive day.

So how many gadgets were now judges, would you say?

_____

④ There were 33.33 doohickeys that were divided by a thousand before a third were made kings and queens, one fine inventive day. So how many doohickeys became royalty, would you say?

_____

⑤ If I rolled two ordinary dice, would it be an even chance that an even number would come up? _____

Why? _____

_____

⑥ If I rolled an ordinary die ten times and added the number rolled each time, is the total likely to be an odd or an even or either?

_____

⑦ If I rolled two ordinary dice ten times, would it be impossible to roll a double six each time?

_____

⑧ I rolled two ordinary dice ten times and rolled double one every time. Why might that have happened? Give two reasons.

_____

_____

⑨ If I rolled two ordinary dice ten times, is six certain to be rolled at least once by either of the dice?

_____

Grammar & Punctuation

Choose prepositions from the box to complete the sentences.

above	during	around	without

① The rocket flew high _____ the earth.

② _____ warning, the waves crashed around our feet.

③ _____ feeding time, the tigers wowed the audience.

④ The boys jogged _____ the school oval.

Circle the best conjunctions in these complex sentences.

⑤ (Before After) the concert started, the singers warmed up their voices.

⑥ (When Although) they don't move, we are still in awe of the plastic dinosaurs.

⑦ Rescuers battled to save the skiers (unless until) it became dark.

⑧ We had fun sailing the boat (before unless) the race started.

Change the past tense verbs to present tense in these film advertisements.

⑨ The dragon **crushed** Sydney

_____

⑩ She **wasn't** a galaxy soldier

_____

⑪ Crazy Horse **was** a real leader

_____

Underline the auxiliary verbs and the main verbs.

⑫ Our friends are coming to stay with us during Christmas.

⑬ During the trek we had run out of water.

⑭ My brother didn't train with his team this week.

Underline the verbs and say if they are present, past or future tense.

⑮ Bonny is going to have surf lessons this summer. _____

⑯ Harry was allowed to watch the game after his chores. _____

⑰ More people live in cities than in the country. _____

⑱ My parents will take me to Europe to visit our family. _____

Score 2 points for each correct answer! **SCORE** **/36** (0-16) (18-30) (32-36)

Phonic Knowledge & Spelling

Write either –sion or –tion to complete the words.

① mo_____

② divi_____

③ atten_____

④ deci_____

Use prefixes un–, dis–, in– to make these words mean the opposite.

⑤ _____appoint

⑥ _____loved

⑦ _____happy

⑧ _____accurate

Circle the 5 words that have been made opposites (antonyms) by adding a prefix.

Example: disprove

⑨–⑬

disappear	disrespect	impossible
terrified	umbrella	unhappy
rattle	unbelievable	

Use one of the words from each pair to complete the sentences.

later/latter	device/devise	father/farther

⑭ Their _____ was very upset when he found out about the bullying.

⑮ You have to come _____ as you are too early.

⑯ In hospital there is a _____ to help people breathe.

Add suffixes –er or –ing to these words.

⑰ develop

_____ _____

⑱ begin

_____ _____

⑲ travel

_____ _____

Circle one word in each group that is the antonym (opposite) to the bold word.

⑳ **villain**   hero   man

㉑ **clever**   smart   stupid

㉒ **cheap**   expensive   inexpensive

㉓ **dawdle**   sprint   walk

Score 2 points for each correct answer! **SCORE** **/46** (0-20) (22-40) (42-46)

TARGETING HOMEWORK 6 © PASCAL PRESS ISBN 9781925726480

TERM 3 ENGLISH

Wave Rider

Imaginative text – Narrative
Author – Peter Alford

Surfing, forget that! You need to have legs to be able to stand on a board, Steph thought. Steph's legs had been stolen from her. Limp bits of flesh couldn't be called legs. They just dangled uselessly.

Horseriding was what she loved, almost as much as she did the sea. Racing her brother to wrangle a calf on their cattle station, the angry snake had reared. Clarrie, her horse, saw the reptile. Steph flew over his neck. Landing heavily, Steph broke her back.

Nurse April flew in with the Flying Doctor each month. Exercising those useless lumps helped blood flow to her toes. Steph was angry at everyone and everything. Nurse April was on holiday and replaced by Merrie.

Steph didn't like new — everything was new. She certainly hated the 'new' of a broken back. Merrie saw Steph's pain in every sharp answer. Finally, Merrie had had enough.

"Right, young lady, you need a surf!" Merrie insisted.

"Surf, oh sure, with these legs," Steph spat back angrily.

"Bodyboards don't need legs," Merrie insisted. "Currently I am ranked number two in the country as a bodyboarder," she explained. "You, me, we surf, kid, no arguments!" Merrie exclaimed.

Three weeks later Steph's legs trailed as she flew down a wave on her new bodyboard.

Write or circle the correct answer.

1. **Which word is used instead of snake?**

   _____

2. **What does it mean that Steph's legs had been 'stolen from her'?**

   a Her legs had been cut off.

   b Her legs were useless.

   c Someone stole her legs.

3. **How did the doctor and nurse travel to the station?**

   a They drove in a car.

   b They came by boat.

   c They flew in a plane.

4. **What did nurse Merrie do in her spare time?**

   _____

5. **Which words best tell that this story didn't take place in the city?**

   a on their cattle station

   b a calf

   c horseriding was what she loved

6. **What part of the body is not used in Merrie's sport?**

   _____

7. **What caused Clarrie to stop suddenly?**

   _____

8. **Why did nurse April exercise Steph's legs?**

   _____

9. **What word is used instead of 'said' after Merrie told Steph that she needed a surf?**

   _____

10. **How long did it take for Steph to be in the waves?**

    _____

11. **What word was used to tell about rounding up the calves in the story?**

    _____

12. **Which sentence tells you that Merrie was a very good bodyboard surfer?**

    _____

    _____

Score 2 points for each correct answer!

SCORE /24   0-10   12-18   20-24

Number & Algebra

You may use a calculator if you need to.

① $\frac{1}{8}$ of 248 = _____

② $\frac{1}{7}$ of 210 = _____

③ $4\frac{1}{5}$ of 75 = _____

④ $24\frac{1}{3}$ of 81 = _____

⑤ $16\frac{1}{10}$ of 730 = _____

⑥ $16\frac{1}{6}$ of 726 = _____

⑦ $52\frac{1}{2}$ of 91 = _____

⑧ $\frac{3}{8}$ of 89 = _____

⑨ $35\frac{2}{3}$ of 26 = _____

⑩ $2\frac{3}{4}$ of 9 = _____

Complete the table.

Improper fraction	Simplified fraction	Mixed number
$\frac{14}{4}$	⑪	⑫
$\frac{18}{24}$	⑬	⑭
$\frac{26}{8}$	⑮	⑯
$\frac{14}{12}$	⑰	⑱
$\frac{32}{6}$	⑲	⑳

Calculate the value of the discounts offered on these prices. You can use a calculator.

	Marked price	Discount (as a % of price)	Value of discount (nearest $)
㉑	$450.00	3.6%	
㉒	$315.00	5%	
㉓	$280.00	12.5%	
㉔	$1200	2.25%	
㉕	$78	4.4%	

SCORE /50 0-22 24-44 46-50

Statistics & Probability

Use this data table and bar graph to answer the following questions. There are some differences between their representations of the data.

Teddy Bears at Picnic					
Year	1930	1940	1950	1960	1970
Teddy Bears	140	200	275	63	55
Year	1980	1990	2000	2010	
Teddy Bears	60	60	220	225	

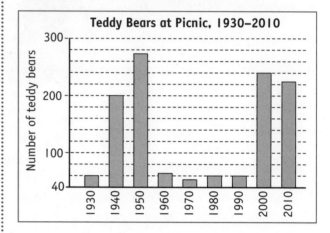

① How many years does the data cover?

_____

② In what year were there the most teddy bears at the picnic?

_____

③ In what year were there the fewest teddy bears at the picnic?

_____

④ How many graph bars are clearly wrong, according to the table?

_____

⑤ According to the graph, which two years have a difference of 120 teddy bears?

_____

⑥ According to the graph, is the value of the 2010 bar four times as large as the 1980 bar?

_____

⑦ At one time, there was a great conflict between the bears, which terribly spoilt their friendships. According to this data, during what decade did that conflict most likely happen?

_____

⑧ According to this data, during what decade did that conflict get resolved?

_____

SCORE /16 0-6 8-12 14-16

Measurement & Space

What types of angles are these?
Write **right, acute, obtuse** or **reflex**.

Note: **x** marks each angle.

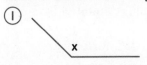

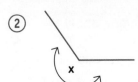

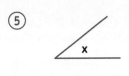

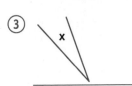

Write the missing values in the table.

Height	Width	Perimeter	Area
16 mm	⑦	40 mm	64 mm²
8 cm	8 cm	32 cm	⑧
⑨	2 km	7 km	3 km²
2.25 m	4 m	⑩	9 m²
1.75 km	2 km	7.5 km	⑪

Use the partial timetable of a teddy bear's planner in the next column to answer the following questions.

⑫ What does Teddy spend most time on?

_____

⑬ What does Teddy spend least time on?

_____

⑭ What time will Teddy need his reading glasses?

_____

⑮ If it takes Teddy 12 minutes to prepare his lunch, what time can he start to eat?

_____

⑯ If it takes Teddy 16 minutes to get dressed, how long does he have to wash himself?

_____

Event	Comment
9:00 am: Wake up and get out of bed	Good morning to myself
9:10 am: Morning wash and getting dressed	Wear yellow bow tie, pink shirt and blue suit
9:35 am: Breakfast	Honey on toast and glass of milk
10:00 am: Do some gardening	Be careful not to get clothes dirty.
11:30 am: Morning tea	Just a cup of tea, no biscuits
11:45 am: Read book	Reading glasses are in the desk drawer.
1:00 pm: Lunch	Honey with berries and salad
1:40 pm: Visit Lilly	It takes nine minutes to get to Lilly's cottage and I intend to spend 2 hours visiting her. Remember to take her flowers.

⑰ Teddy will have to wash his hands before he starts preparing his lunch. Assume it takes him an extra three minutes to wash his hands, and he didn't consider this time in his planning.

If everything else remains the same, what time will he arrive at Lilly's cottage?

_____

⑱ If Teddy spent 50% more time gardening than the time he'd allowed, what time will he have morning tea?

_____

⑲ If Teddy gardens for only $\frac{2}{3}$ of the time he planned, what time will he have morning tea?

_____

Score 2 points for each correct answer! **SCORE** **/38** (0-16) (18-32) (34-38)

Grammar & Punctuation

AC9E6LA06

Modal verbs

> Remember! Auxiliary verbs are helping verbs. **Modal (auxiliary) verbs** are a special type of helping verb that work with the main verb to show ability, possibility, obligation, intention and permission. These verbs are: **can, could, may, might, should, must, will, would.**
>
> *Examples:*   modal verb   main verb
> I **can** <u>play</u> guitar.
> Mum **may** <u>let</u> me go to the movies.
>   modal verb   main verb
> You **should** <u>have</u> a shower.

Underline the modal verbs and auxiliary verbs.

1. She will wait for the actor to arrive.

2. Aden must be freezing at the ice rink.

3. Rene could swim but didn't like getting wet.

4. Mum said, "I should listen to you read more often."

5. Zac may go to the match next week.

Modal verbs for persuasion

> **Modal verbs** are often used in persuasive texts to make arguments stronger or softer.
> *Examples:*
> You **could** recycle.
> You **should** recycle. (stronger)
>
> Everyone **can** clean up.
> Everyone **must** clean up. (stronger)
>
> I **might** visit the dentist next week.
> I **will** visit the dentist next week. (stronger)

Circle modal verbs that make the arguments stronger.

6. The doctor said I (should   could) take this medicine.

7. Dad said I (must   can) do well on my exams.

8. Jenna (might   will) go to choir practice tonight.

9. Luke (will   may) heat up the soup because it's cold.

10. People (can   must) not use so many plastic bags!

Phonic Knowledge & Spelling

AC9E6LY08, AC9E6LY09

Doubling consonants

> In words with a **short vowel** and **one consonant**, the consonant is **doubled** before the ending is added.
> *Examples:* run, run**n**ing   fat, fat**t**er
> BUT NOT lick, li**ck**ing strong, stro**ng**er

Add endings to these words and apply the doubling rule where needed.

	add –ing	add –ed
1. drag	_____	_____
2. hiss	_____	_____
3. shop	_____	_____

	add –er	add –est
4. long	_____	_____
5. hot	_____	_____
6. thin	_____	_____

Underline the American English words and write the matching Australian English words.

jam   full stop   holiday   cot

7. The baby looked so small in the crib.

_____

8. Toast and jelly are a popular breakfast food.

_____

9. She ended the sentence with a period.

_____

10. Our vacation was ruined by rain.

_____

Use the clues to finish the 'man' words.

11. a female person: __ __ man

12. being polite: man __ __ __ __

13. wanting something: __ __ man __

14. a type of fruit: man __ __

15. a person who is a boss: man __ __ __ __

Evelyn Sampson

Informative text – Report
Author – Peter Alford

Evelyn Sampson was never good at sport because she didn't have time to play. Reporters didn't want her picture for the nightly TV news or the newspapers as she was not famous.

As soon as she was old enough, Evelyn had to care for her three younger brothers and two sisters. Often she would be left alone with her siblings for a whole week while her mother and father had to 'go bush', hunting kangaroos and donkeys. Kangaroo hide was worth money and the meat fed the family.

Evelyn dreamed of becoming a school teacher but that could never happen because she had to leave school at year six. As a young lady she became known as a strong leader in her community. Evelyn became a role model for younger people as she obeyed the law and cared for the older folk in her small town. Her kindness and understanding meant that she earnt respect by helping others to better their lives.

To her people, she was a hero. TV and newspaper stories weren't needed. Everyone in that small town knew her value.

Write or circle the correct answer.

① **What did Evelyn want to become?**

_____

② **What does the phrase 'go bush' mean?**
  a find the bush
  b travel into the bush
  c find things in the bush

③ **How many siblings did Evelyn have?**

_____

④ **Apart from their meat, what else were kangaroos used for?**

_____

⑤ **What was Evelyn known as in her community?**

_____

⑥ **What did Evelyn's father and mother hunt?**

_____

⑦ **What earnt Evelyn respect?**

_____

⑧ **When did Evelyn have to leave school?**

_____

_____

⑨ **What does 'role model' mean?**
  a She was a fashion model.
  b She liked ham rolls.
  c People looked up to her.

Score 2 points for each correct answer!

SCORE /18   (0-6) (8-14) (16-18)

My Book Review

Title _____

Author _____

Rating ☆☆☆☆☆

Comment _____

_____

TERM 4 ENGLISH

Number & Algebra

AC9M6N06

Dividing decimals by whole numbers

Calculate these equations without the use of calculators.

① 28.45 ÷ 5 = _____

② 74.2 ÷ 2 = _____

③ 21.21 ÷ 7 = _____

④ 21.021 ÷ 3 = _____

⑤ 26.04 ÷ 6 = _____

⑥ 88.32 ÷ 4 = _____

⑦ 120.06 ÷ 6 = _____

⑧ 23.0 ÷ 2 = _____

⑨ 73.5 ÷ 5 = _____

⑩ 302.8 ÷ 2 = _____

⑪ 17.5 ÷ 7 = _____

⑫ 14.22 ÷ 3 = _____

⑬ 28.04 ÷ 8 = _____

⑭ 74.07 ÷ 9 = _____

⑮ 608.407 ÷ 1 = _____

Score 2 points for each correct answer! **SCORE** /30 (0-12) (14-24) (26-30)

Statistics & Probability

AC9M6ST01

Using a table and a line graph

Use this line graph to answer the following questions.

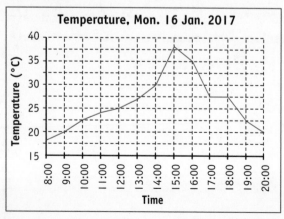

Temperature, Mon. 16 Jan. 2017

① What time was the highest temperature reached?

_____

② During which hour was there the largest single increase in temperature?

_____

③ How much was the largest single hour increase in temperature?

_____

④ When did the cool change begin?

_____

⑤ During which hour was there the largest drop in temperature?

_____

⑥ During which hour was the temperature constant?

_____

⑦ At what other time was the temperature the same as it was at 9:00?

_____

⑧ At what approximate time was the temperature the same as it was at 11:00?

_____

⑨ Use the graph to complete the table.

Temperature, 16 Jan. 2018	
Time	**Temp. (°C)**
8:00	
9:00	
10:00	
11:00	
12:00	
13:00	
14:00	
15:00	
16:00	
17:00	
18:00	
19:00	
20:00	

Score 2 points for each correct answer! **SCORE** /18 (0-6) (8-14) (16-18)

TARGETING HOMEWORK 6 © PASCAL PRESS ISBN 9781925726480

Measurement & Space

AC9M6M04

Investigating angles on a straight line

A straight line is 180° on both sides.

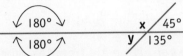

Two angles that make up a straight line must equal 180°. So angle **x** = 180 – 45 = 135°.
Angle **y** = 180 – 135 = 45°

The diagrams below show angles on a straight line. Use them to answer the following questions.

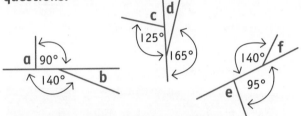

Write the values of these angles.

① a = _____   ④ d = _____
② b = _____   ⑤ e = _____
③ c = _____   ⑥ f = _____

Use this diagram to answer the following questions.

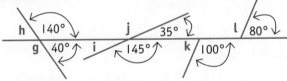

Write the values of these angles.

⑦ g = _____   ⑩ j = _____
⑧ h = _____   ⑪ k = _____
⑨ i = _____   ⑫ l = _____

Score 2 points for each correct answer!   SCORE **/24** (0-10) (12-18) (20-24)

Problem Solving

AC9M6N09, AC9M6M04

Number and angle problems

① What would you get if you divided a lolly snake that was fifteen centimetres long into five equal parts, then you glued three of the parts back together and threw away the leftover bits?
Answer in centimetres.

_____

② What would you get if you divided a lolly snake that was 1.6 metres long into four equal parts, then you superglued two of the parts back together and threw away the leftover bits?
Answer in metres.

_____

③ What would you get if you divided a lolly snake that was 40.8 millimetres long into eight equal parts, then you superglued five of the parts back together and threw away the leftover bits?
Answer in centimetres.

_____

④ What would you get if you divided a lolly snake that was 42.6 centimetres long into six equal parts, then you superglued five of the parts back together and threw away the leftover bits?
Answer in metres.

_____

Use the clock diagrams to answer the following questions. Estimate your answers to the nearest 10 degrees.

⑤ What is the smaller angle made by the hands on the first clock?

_____

⑥ What is the larger angle made by the hands on the second clock?

_____

⑦ What is the smaller angle made by the hands on the third clock?

_____

⑧ What would be the smaller angle made by the hands of a clock showing 5:32?

_____

⑨ What would be the two angles made by the hands of a clock showing 6 o'clock?

_____

TERM 4 MATHS

Grammar & Punctuation

AC9E6LA06

Verb tenses: simple present and past

Remember! **Verb tenses** tell us **when** an action happened — present or past.

Simple present tense: We **swim** at the creek.

Simple past tense: Two weeks ago, we **swam** at the creek.

To change **regular verbs** from present to past tense, add **–ed**.

Examples: jump, jump**ed**   cook, cook**ed**

Some words only need **–d**.

Example: pace, pace**d**

Irregular verbs are spelt differently in the past tense. *Examples:* run, **ran**   drink, **drank**

Write these present tense verbs in the past tense.

① play _____
② trick _____
③ find _____
④ wear _____
⑤ tell _____
⑥ sit _____
⑦ race _____
⑧ stand _____

Circle the verbs and write their present tense form.

⑨ We flew for the first time today. _____

⑩ Who broke the chair? _____

⑪ Coach yelled at the kids during the game.

_____

⑫ The stockman tied the rope.

_____

⑬ He answered very gruffly. _____

Write the verbs in brackets in past tense.

⑭ The officials _____ us that our team was best overall. (tell)

⑮ Our parents _____ in the rain watching the assembly. (stand)

⑯ Before the race my stomach _____ with nerves. (churn)

⑰ Many people _____ the bad news. (hear)

⑱ Birds _____ deeply from the water trough. (drink)

Score 2 points for each correct answer! | SCORE | **/36** | 0-16 | 18-30 | 32-36

Phonic Knowledge & Spelling

AC9E6LY09

Prefixes

Remember! **Prefixes** are attached to the beginning of words and they change the meaning of words.

Examples: **after**noon, **semi**circle

Choose the correct prefix from the box to complete the words.

Prefix	Meaning	Prefix	Meaning
para	beside	ultra	beyond
counter	against	therm	heat
ob	block	mid	middle

① The policewoman was in the _____ terrorist group.

② Cars parking over there may _____ struct traffic.

③ She is playing _____ field in the football side.

④ Doctor Su used the _____ ometer to check Isla's temperature.

⑤ You rely on your _____ chute for a safe landing.

⑥ The wings of any aeroplane need to be _____ -strong.

Circle the synonyms that best fit these sentences.

⑦ Trying to find a way out of the maze was (puzzling   mysterious).

⑧ His house was clearly too (brief   small) for family to stay.

⑨ Getting over the river required a (plan   plot).

⑩ When trying to stand for the first time, the foal took a (tumble   fall).

Make these words plural by adding –s if needed. (*Hint:* Some words are already plural.)

⑪ geese___
⑫ salmon___
⑬ plant___
⑭ space___
⑮ cod___
⑯ fish___

Score 2 points for each correct answer! | SCORE | **/32** | 0-14 | 16-26 | 28-32

114

TARGETING HOMEWORK 6 © PASCAL PRESS ISBN 9781925726480

Text 1
Child Labour

Persuasive text – Argument
Author – Peter Alford

Parents are harsh! Children are being put to work by uncaring adults. Take out the rubbish, clean your room, set the table, blah, blah, blah. Child labour was banned in the 1800s, yet we still see innocent children being **exploited** by their parents. Unkind adults forcing their helpless children to do chores. Sometimes children are bribed with pocket money.

No! I say NO, enough! Children **should** be able to do what they want, when they want. Given too little time on important things like games and iPads, kids are becoming stressed. Parents **must** do those chores. They have no right to use children any longer.

Text 2
Chores for Children

Giving children jobs is a great way for them to learn that they are part of a team. When kids earn money for chores, they learn that nothing in life is free. Earning their own money teaches them how to spend wisely. Scientists in the 1990s looked at families in which children did jobs and in which they did nothing. Children who had jobs were happier than those doing little. They also ended up in better paid jobs as adults.

Write or circle the correct answer.

1. When was child labour banned?

    _____

2. Write two of the jobs that children are asked to do.

    _____

    _____

3. What is another word for **jobs** in the text?

    _____

4. Which sentence from text 1 tells how parents get their children to do chores?

    _____

    _____

5. Who observed families in the 1990s?

    _____

6. Which phrase says that jobs are important for children?

    a a team

    b way for them to learn

    c earn money for

7. What is a lesson learnt by children who did chores?

    _____

    _____

8. What does **exploited** mean in this text?

    a used   b have   c could

9. Which text uses subjective (opinion, thinking, feeling) language and would be less believable?

    _____

Score 2 points for each correct answer!   SCORE **/18**   0-6   8-14   16-18

My Book Review

Title _____

Author _____

Rating ☆ ☆ ☆ ☆ ☆

Comment _____

TERM 4 ENGLISH

Number & Algebra

AC9M6N07

Equivalent fractions, decimals and percentages

Complete the tables.

	Percentage	Common fraction, hundredths	Common fraction, simplified
①	15%	$\frac{15}{100}$	
②	75%		
③	25%		
④	90%		
⑤	20%		

	Decimal	Common fraction, hundredths	Common fraction, simplified
⑥	0.75		
⑦	0.20		
⑧	0.4		
⑨	0.05		
⑩	0.95		

Simplify the fractions to complete these equations.

⑪ $\frac{25}{75} \times 24 = $ ____ $\times 24 = 8$

⑫ $\frac{25}{30} \times 2 = $ ____ $\times 2 = 1\frac{2}{3}$

⑬ $\frac{7}{14} \times 8 = $ ____ $\times 8 = 4$

Write the answers.

⑭ $\frac{18}{24} \times 4 = \frac{3}{4} \times 4 = $ _____

⑮ $\frac{8}{12} \times 6 = \frac{2}{3} \times 6 = $ _____

Score 2 points for each correct answer! SCORE /30 (0-12) (14-24) (26-30)

Statistics & Probability

AC9M6P02

Pie charts

These pie charts have not had the values added but they have been labelled a to k. Use them to answer the following questions.

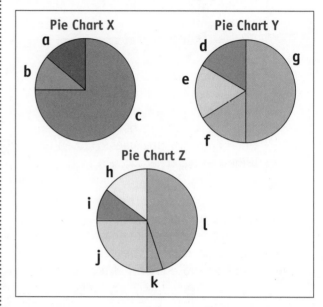

Pie Chart X, Pie Chart Y, Pie Chart Z

① Which value is 50% of the total?

_____

② Which pie chart is most likely to be referring to the seasons of the year?

_____

③ Which value is 5%? _____

④ Which value is 45%? _____

⑤ Which value is approximately 150, if the total of that pie chart is 200?

_____

⑥ Which pie chart is most likely related to the weekdays, Monday to Friday?

_____

⑦ If **j** is 30, what is the total of **Pie Chart Z**?

_____

⑧ If **f** is 5, what is **g**? _____

⑨ If **c** is 120, what is **a** and **b** combined?

_____

⑩ Which pie chart has the most equal parts?

_____

⑪ If **k** is 75, what is **i**? _____

⑫ Which of all the values is 75%? _____

Score 2 points for each correct answer! SCORE /24 (0-10) (12-18) (20-24)

Measurement & Space

AC9M6SP02

Using the Cartesian coordinate system

> The Cartesian coordinate system is used to plot points, as shown on the grid below.
>
> First you read along the horizontal axis, then you read along the vertical axis. So to plot point **X** at (2, 1), start at 2 on the horizontal axis and move up 1.

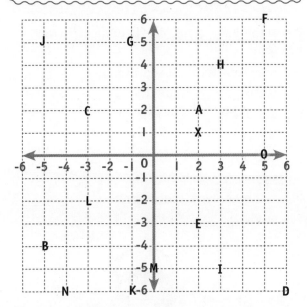

① What letter is at coordinates (2, 2)?

_____

② What letter is at coordinates (3, 4)?

_____

③ What letter is at coordinates (-3, 2)?

_____

④ What letter is at coordinates (-4, -6)?

_____

⑤ What letter is at coordinates (2, -3)?

_____

⑥ What letter is at coordinates (5, 0)?

_____

⑦ What letter is at coordinates (-5, -4)?

_____

Write the coordinates of these letters.

⑧ J _____ ⑫ M _____
⑨ D _____ ⑬ G _____
⑩ L _____ ⑭ F _____
⑪ K _____ ⑮ I _____

Problem Solving

AC9M6ST01, AC9M6SP02

Pie chart and Cartesian plane problems

A pie chart had 20% coloured yellow, 30% coloured blue and 15% coloured red.

① If the pie chart represented a total of 200 roses, how many roses did the blue section show?

_____

If the last colour in the pie chart was green, how many roses did green represent?

_____

② If the pie chart represented a total of 500 daffodils, how many daffodils did the red and yellow sections combined represent?

_____

③ If the pie chart was about a total of 150 daisies, which colour represented 45 daisies?

_____

Use the Cartesian grid in Measurement & Space to answer the following questions.

For these questions, each grid square represents 1 cm².

④ If you drew a straight line between coordinates (3, 3) and coordinates (3, -4), how long would it be?

_____

⑤ If you drew a straight horizontal line 7 cm long from coordinates (5, -4), at what coordinates would it end?

_____

⑥ If you drew a straight vertical line 11 cm long from coordinates (-6, 5), at what coordinates would it end?

_____

⑦ How many centimetres apart are the letters C and L?

_____

⑧ What is the smallest number of straight lines you need to get from letter E to letter C, without crossing over another letter?

_____

Grammar & Punctuation

AC9E6LA06

Auxiliary verbs

Remember! **Auxiliary verbs** are helping verbs. They help the main verb express meaning and they show the tense of a sentence. These verbs are: **be, do, have**.

Be: am, is, are, was, were, be, being, been

Do: do, does, did

Have: has, have, had

present tense auxiliary verb   main verb

Example: We **are** <u>travelling</u> to see the dam.
   We **were** <u>travelling</u> to see the dam.

past tense auxiliary verb   main verb

Underline the past tense auxiliary verbs and main verbs in these sentences.

① We were eating dinner when the huge storm broke.

② Lucy was trapped in the cave because of the rockfall.

③ Both horses had galloped away during the night.

④ Harry had played the trumpet solo bravely.

⑤ Some poor people had eaten only leaves in the past few weeks.

Underline the 7 past tense auxiliary verbs in this paragraph.

⑥–⑫

Our class visited the zoo. We were watching the elephant as she was bathing, while other animals were feeding happily. The lions, antelopes and crocodiles didn't notice us. We had walked for hours, it seemed, to reach the hyenas. They were laughing loudly. Most students were standing on the grass listening. The hyenas seemed to excite and disturb all the other animals.

Add vowels to these present tense auxiliary verbs.

⑬ We __r__ eating our dinner in front of the television.

⑭ My sister __s studying in the spare room again.

⑮ Jake h__s bought a special fish to help clean the tank water.

⑯ Despite being blind, Bree c__n play the piano beautifully.

⑰ Georgia __s counting her money while she waits in line.

Score 2 points for each correct answer! **SCORE** /34 (0-14) (16-28) (30-34)

Phonic Knowledge & Spelling

AC9E6LY08, AC9E6LY09

Prefixes and suffixes

Remember! We add **prefixes** to the beginning of base words to change their meaning.
Examples: possible (base word), **im**possible
 obey (base word), **dis**obey

We add **suffixes** to the end of base words to change how the word is used.
Examples: use (base word), use**ful**
 care (base word), care**less**

Write the base word, prefix and suffix as needed.

① **unacceptable**   base word: _____
  prefix: _____   suffix: _____

② **murdered**   base word: _____
  suffix: _____

③ **delivery**   base word: _____
  suffix: _____

④ **disagreement**   base word: _____
  prefix: _____   suffix: _____

Contractions

Remember! A **contraction** is when two words are shortened and combined to make one word. An **apostrophe** is used in place of the missing letter/s.
Examples: do not – **don't**, I am – **I'm**

Write the contractions for these words.

⑤ should have: _____

⑥ should not: _____

⑦ are not: _____

⑧ that will: _____

⑨ you have: _____

⑩ they are: _____

Write how many syllables are in these words.

⑪ signature _____

⑫ silence _____

⑬ horizon _____

⑭ remarkable _____

Score 2 points for each correct answer! **SCORE** /28 (0-12) (14-22) (24-28)

TARGETING HOMEWORK 6 © PASCAL PRESS ISBN 9781925726480

Bubblo Gal

Imaginative text – Narrative
Author – Peter Alford

Her tenth birthday was when it all started. Katrin had been given a bubble machine as a gift. She spent hours blowing bubbles as large as beach balls. Catching them, she could control them like pets. Bubbles seemed to want to follow her and do as she wished. University didn't even stop her love of bubbles.

Working alone in her lab one night, she produced an amazing bubble. This bubble read her mind and did everything she was thinking. This was no ordinary bubble — it was super strong. Katrin suggested to herself that the bubble should surround the pot plant on the windowsill. Within seconds the plant was inside a shiny sphere. But trying to force her way into the bubble proved totally impossible. The shiny, bright walls of the bubble refused to release what it had surrounded. Thinking about the bubble, Katrin whistled out loud. Immediately the bubble disappeared.

She lay awake in bed that night, imagining how the bubble she invented might be used.

Write or circle the correct answer.

① What did Katrin imagine about the bubble before going to sleep?

_____

_____

② When did Katrin fall in love with bubbles?

_____

_____

③ What does 'Katrin suggested to herself' mean?

   a Katrin spoke to herself.

   b Katrin thought to herself.

   c Katrin imagined.

④ Where was Katrin when she invented the bubble?

_____

_____

⑤ What does 'the bubble refused to release the pot plant' mean?

   a The bubble spoke to Katrin.

   b The bubble had a soft wall.

   c The bubble would not let Katrin get the pot plant.

⑥ What was Katrin given for her tenth birthday?

_____

⑦ How big were the bubbles Katrin could make as a child?

_____

⑧ What seemed to break the bubble in the lab?

_____

_____

Score 2 points for each correct answer! SCORE **/16**

My Book Review

Title _____

Author _____

Rating ☆☆☆☆☆

Comment _____

_____

TERM 4 ENGLISH

Number & Algebra

AC9M6A01

Number sequences

Write the missing numbers in these sequences.

① 3, 8, 13, 18, 23, 28, 33, ____

② 32, 39, ____, 53, 60, 67, 74

③ 36, 33, 30, 27, 24, 21, ____

④ 16, 17, 19, 22, 26, 31, ____, 44, 52, 61

⑤ 500, 480, 461, 443, 426, _____, 395, 381

⑥ 1, 2, 4, 8, 16, 32, ____, 128, 256, 512

⑦ 10 000, 5000, 2500, _____, 625

⑧ 3, 9, 27, 81, _____, 729, 2187

⑨ 0, 1, 1, 2, 3, 5, 8, 13, ____, 34, 55

⑩ 367, 350, 333, 316, _____, 282, 265

What would be the third number in the sequence when you follow the given instructions? Complete the calculations mentally and write the answers.

⑪ Start at 4. Subtract 2 and multiply by 3.

4, -- , -- , _____

⑫ Start at 5. Multiply by 2 and subtract 3.

5, -- , -- , _____

⑬ Start at 8. Subtract 6, multiply by 3 and then add 2.

8, -- , -- , _____

⑭ Start at 30. Add even consecutive numbers from 4.

30, -- , -- , _____

Score 2 points for each correct answer! SCORE **/28** (0-12) (14-22) (24-28)

Statistics & Probability

AC9M6P02

Investigating games of chance

In this game of chance, a regular deck of cards is used, without the jokers. Two cards are turned up. If the next card turned up is equivalent in value to one of those cards, or in between them, the player wins.

Aces are valued at 1, Jacks at 11, Queens at 12 and Kings at 13. The suit or colour of the cards does not matter.

For example, if the two cards turned up are an eight and a Queen, the player wins if the next card turned up is an 8, 9, 10, Jack or Queen.

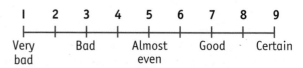

1	2	3	4	5	6	7	8	9
Very bad		Bad		Almost even		Good		Certain

Work out what the chance of winning is. Write the matching number from the probability scale above.

① The two cards turned up are a **6** and a **jack**.

_____

② The two cards turned up are a **9** and a **10**.

_____

③ The two cards turned up are a **7** and a **4**.

_____

④ The two cards turned up are a **queen** and a **9**.

_____

⑤ The two cards turned up are a **3** and a **4**.

_____

⑥ The two cards turned up are an **8** and an **8**.

_____

Answer these questions as simplfied fractions.

Hint: Two cards have been taken out, so your fractions will be fiftieths.

For the cards turned up, the probability of turning up the same value is $\frac{3}{50}$. For all the other cards, the probability is $\frac{4}{50}$.

⑦ The two cards turned up are a **2** and a **7**.

_____

⑧ The two cards turned up are a **King** and an **8**.

_____

⑨ The two cards turned up are a **5** and a **5**.

_____

⑩ The two cards turned up are a **Jack** and a **Queen**.

_____

⑪ The two cards turned up are a **9** and a **7**.

_____

Score 2 points for each correct answer! SCORE **/22** (0-8) (10-16) (18-22)

Measurement & Space

AC9M6SP02

Describing locations

Use this map of Australia on a Cartesian plane to answer the following questions.

Round the coordinates to the nearest 0.5.

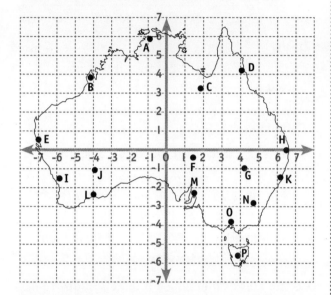

① What point is at coordinates (2, 3)? ☐

② What point is at coordinates (4, 4)? ☐

③ What point is at coordinates (-4, -1)? ☐

④ What point is at coordinates (-4, 4)? ☐

⑤ What point is at coordinates (4, -5.5)? ☐

⑥ What point is at coordinates (-1, 6)? ☐

⑦ What are the coordinates of L? _____

⑧ What are the coordinates of E? _____

⑨ What are the coordinates of G? _____

⑩ What are the coordinates of K? _____

Score 2 points for each correct answer! **SCORE** | /20 | (0-8) (10-14) (16-20)

Problem Solving

AC9M6A01, AC9M6P02, AC9M6SP01

Number, chance and Cartesian plane problems

Break the code. The letters of the alphabet have been given this sequence: **multiply** the letter's place in the alphabet **by 8, subtract 4** and then **multiply by 3.**

For example:

A = 12   B = 36   C = 60

You may use a calculator.

① 180, 348, 540, 84, 588

_____

② 180, 348, 276, 12

_____

③ 444, 12, 276, 12, 12, 300

_____

④ 324, 12, 300, 12, 444, 468, 108

_____

The following questions are based on the card game in **Statistics & Probability.**

⑤ A player had $\frac{14}{50}$ chance of winning. One of the turned-up cards was 6. What are the two possibilities for the other turned-up card?

_____

⑥ A player had $\frac{26}{50}$ chance of winning. One of the turned-up cards was 7. What are the two possibilities for the other turned-up card?

_____

⑦ A player had $\frac{18}{50}$ chance of winning.

For the player to win, a Queen is the highest card that can be turned up next.

What two cards did the player already have?

_____

Use the map of Australia in **Measurement & Space** to answer these questions.

Assume the grid lines are **150 km apart** from north to south and from east to west and **180 km apart diagonally.** Round the coordinates to the nearest **0.5.** You may use a calculator.

⑧ How far apart are I and K?

_____

⑨ What is the shortest distance between L and E?

_____

⑩ Without travelling diagonally, how far apart are E and D?

_____

⑪ What is the shortest distance between B and O?

_____

TERM 4 MATHS

Grammar & Punctuation

AC9E6LA06, AC9E6LA09

Commas in lists of verbs

> When verbs are written in a list, they need to be separated by commas.
> *Example:* Mum **peels, chops, slices** and cooks the vegetables.

Place commas between the verbs.

1. During the race, competitors had to run swim crawl and ride kilometres.

2. Trying to get to school on time, she rode walked and sprinted through the bush.

3. Whilst painting, the artist sketched shaded viewed and selected colours.

4. As we cooked, we separated beat and whisked eggs for the dish.

5. Waiting for the birth of his son, he strode walked and examined the floor.

Choose more interesting verbs from the box to complete the sentences.

| gazed | bound | chattered | gather | scaled |

6. They had to (get) _____ their own fruit from the orchard.

7. We (looked) _____ out at the spectacular view.

8. Brendon (climbed) _____ the red gum tree.

9. She (talked) _____ nervously before the exam.

10. King Kangaroo used his strong forelegs to (jump) _____ through the bush.

Write the present tense verbs.

11. swam _____

12. flew _____

13. drank _____

14. stood _____

15. wrote _____

16. listened _____

17. drew _____

18. walked _____

Phonic Knowledge & Spelling

AC9E6LY08, AC9E6LY09

Antonyms

Match the words in the box with their antonyms (opposites) so the sentences make sense.

| kind | untidy | exciting | coward | serious |

1. Jill's desk was very (clean) _____ because it was never cleaned.

2. We found the movie to be too long and (humorous) _____.

3. Watching bulls at a rodeo can be quite (boring) _____.

4. No one could accuse him of being a (hero) _____ in the battle.

5. The (cruel) _____ woman looked after orphaned kittens.

Use the clues and choose a letter group from the box to complete the words.

| unia | com | ition | rol | pup | al |

6. a flower: pet_____

7. part of a flower: pet_____

8. goes in a car: pet_____

9. has a winner and loser: _____pet_____

10. may look like a doll: _____pet

Homophones

Use one of the words from each pair to complete the sentence.

| desert/dessert | formally/formerly | led/lead |
| current/currant | envelop/envelope | |

11. A place that is very dry: _____

12. A small dried grape: _____

13. A paper pouch: _____

14. A very heavy metal: _____

15. Being properly introduced: _____

TERM 4 ENGLISH

Storm Warnings

Informative text – Report
Author – Janette Ellis

Storm warnings save lives and minimise damage during extreme weather events. Unfortunately, some storms develop in less than an hour, so warnings are not always possible.

When a storm approaches, the closest meteorological agency relays information to the local police, emergency services and radio and television stations. The extent of the threat is determined using radar, satellite imaging, computer modelling systems and observations from the ground.

Despite the technology available, the power of the human eye is still valuable. Volunteer storm spotters on the ground provide information about the strength of the storm and its direction of travel.

Source: *Forecasting*, Go Facts, Blake Education.

Write or circle the correct answer.

1. How quickly can storms develop?

_____

_____

2. Name two organisations who are told about storms as they form.

_____

_____

3. Why are television and radio stations told of storms coming?

   a to make money off advertisements

   b lots of people can be warned

   c for fun and entertainment

4. What does **the threat is determined** mean?

   a deciding that sport should be cancelled

   b deciding how safe the storm is

   c deciding how dangerous the storm is

5. What does **observations from the ground** mean?

   a People look at the weather.

   b People dig in the ground.

   c People watch television.

6. Who are the people that watch storms but are not paid?

_____

7. Name two things forecasters use to check for storms.

_____

_____

8. What does **determined** mean in this text?

   a trying hard

   b making a decision

   c being sure

9. What are two things volunteer storm spotters do?

_____

_____

Score 2 points for each correct answer!

SCORE /18   0-6   8-14 16-18

My Book Review

Title _____

Author _____

Rating ☆☆☆☆☆

Comment _____

_____

TERM 4 ENGLISH

Number & Algebra

AC9M6A01

Number sequences with fractions and decimals

Write the missing numbers in these sequences. You may use a calculator.

① 37.5, 69.5, 101.5, 133.5, 165.5, _____

② $43\frac{3}{8}$, $49\frac{4}{8}$, $55\frac{5}{8}$, _____, $67\frac{7}{8}$, 74, $80\frac{1}{8}$

③ 10, 25, 62.5, 156.25, 390.625,

_____

④ $256\frac{2}{16}$, $260\frac{3}{16}$, $264\frac{4}{16}$, _____, $272\frac{6}{16}$, $276\frac{7}{16}$

⑤ 0.751, _____, 2.251, 3.001, 3.751, 4.501, 5.251

⑥ $82\frac{5}{8}$, $93\frac{2}{8}$, $103\frac{7}{8}$, $114\frac{4}{8}$, _____, $135\frac{6}{8}$, $146\frac{3}{8}$, 157

⑦ 24, 40, 72, 136, 264, _____, 1032, 2056

These sequences involve two steps. The first is doubling and the second step is subtracting a number. Write the missing numbers.

⑧ 16, 22, 34, 58, 106, 202, 394, _____

⑨ 200, 300, 500, 1700, 3300, _____, 12 900, 25 700

⑩ 20, 27.5, 42.5, 72.5, 132.5, 252.5, _____, 972.5

⑪ 1, 1.25, 1.75, 2.75, 4.75, 8.75, 16.75, _____, 64.75, 125.75

⑫ 12.75, 17.5, 27, 46, 84, _____, 312, 616

What would be the third number in the sequence when you follow the given instructions?

⑬ Add $6\frac{3}{7}$

15, -- , -- , _____

⑭ Add 0.009

0.003, -- , -- , _____

⑮ Subtract 0.085

100, -- , -- , _____

Statistics & Probability

AC9M6P01, AC9M6N08

Investigating games of chance

Pachinko is a game of chance popular in Japan. In this game, balls fall down an obstacle track. With luck, some balls come out. The chance of a ball coming out depends on which zone it is dropped into.

This version of pachinko has three zones. Here are the probabilities for balls coming out when they are dropped into each of the three zones.

- Zone 1: Chance of a ball coming out = $\frac{1}{6}$
- Zone 2: Chance of a ball coming out = $\frac{5}{6}$
- Zone 3: Chance of a ball coming out = $\frac{1}{6}$

Example:

12 balls were dropped into Zone 1.
36 balls were dropped into Zone 2.
19 balls were dropped into Zone 3.
How many balls probably came out?

$12 \times \frac{1}{6} + 36 \times \frac{5}{6} + 19 \times \frac{1}{6}$

$= 2 + 30 + 3\frac{1}{6}$ (Round $3\frac{1}{6}$ to 3, as you can't have fractions of balls in real life.)

2 + 30 + 3 = 35 balls

How many balls probably came out in these games of pachinko?

① 26 balls were dropped into Zone 1.
9 balls were dropped into Zone 2.
24 balls were dropped into Zone 3.

_____

② 32 balls were dropped into Zone 1.
13 balls were dropped into Zone 2.
20 balls were dropped into Zone 3.

_____

③ 8 balls were dropped into Zone 1.
56 balls were dropped into Zone 2.
21 balls were dropped into Zone 3.

_____

This version of pachinko has **five zones**. Here are the probabilities for balls coming out when they are dropped into each zone.

- Zone 1: Chance of a ball coming out = $\frac{1}{9}$
- Zone 2: Chance of a ball coming out = $\frac{3}{8}$
- Zone 3: Chance of a ball coming out = $\frac{1}{2}$
- Zone 4: Chance of a ball coming out = $\frac{3}{8}$
- Zone 5: Chance of a ball coming out = $\frac{1}{9}$

How many balls probably came out in these games of pachinko?

④ Zone 1: 18 balls   Zone 2: 8 balls
Zone 3: 21 balls   Zone 4: 8 balls
Zone 5: 14 balls

_____

⑤ Zone 1: 6 balls   Zone 2: 0 balls
Zone 3: 20 balls   Zone 4: 13 balls
Zone 5: 4 balls

_____

⑥ Zone 1: 25 balls   Zone 2: 13 balls
Zone 3: 41 balls   Zone 4: 5 balls
Zone 5: 1 ball

_____

⑦ Zone 1: 36 balls   Zone 2: 19 balls
Zone 3: 32 balls   Zone 4: 18 balls
Zone 5: 35 balls

_____

Score 2 points for each correct answer!   SCORE **/14**   (0-4)   (6-10)   (12-14)

Measurement & Space

AC9M6M04

Investigating angles on straight lines

Write the values of these angles along the straight lines in the diagram.

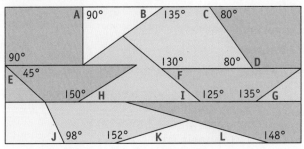

① Angle **A** = _____   ⑦ Angle **G** = _____
② Angle **B** = _____   ⑧ Angle **H** = _____
③ Angle **C** = _____   ⑨ Angle **I** = _____
④ Angle **D** = _____   ⑩ Angle **J** = _____
⑤ Angle **E** = _____   ⑪ Angle **K** = _____
⑥ Angle **F** = _____   ⑫ Angle **L** = _____

Score 2 points for each correct answer!   SCORE **/24**   (0-10)   (12-18)   (20-24)

Problem Solving

AC9M6A01, AC9M6M04

Number and angle problems

Break the code. The letters of the alphabet have been given this sequence: the letter's place in the alphabet + 19, × 5 and then − 7.
For example:
• **A = 93**
• **B = 98**
• **C = 103**

You may use a calculator.

① 93, 108, 133, 113, 193

_____

② 188, 163, 188, 183, 133, 113, 158, 183

_____

③ 93, 178, 178, 133, 198, 113, 108, 113, 178, 103, 133

_____

④ 183, 93, 213, 163, 158, 93, 178, 93

_____

Use the protractor diagram to answer the following questions.

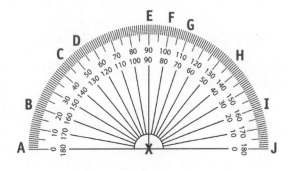

⑤ Start at **X**, facing directly at **I**.
Turn anticlockwise 60°.
What letter are you facing now?

_____

⑥ Start at **X**, facing directly at **B**.
Turn a right angle clockwise.
What letter are you facing now?

_____

⑦ Start at **X**, facing directly at **H**.
Turn half a right angle anticlockwise.
What letter are you facing now?

_____

⑧ Start at **X**, facing directly at **I**.
Turn anticlockwise 105°.
What letter are you facing now?

_____

TERM 4 MATHS

Grammar & Punctuation

AC9E6LA05

Complex sentences and conjunctions

Remember! A **complex sentence** has two (or more) clauses: a <u>main clause</u> which has the main idea, and a <u>subordinate clause</u> which gives more information about the main idea. A subordinate clause cannot stand on its own.

Example: <u>The class was having a party</u> **because** it was the end of the year.

conjunction • subordinate clause • main clause

Conjunctions join clauses to make complex sentences. Some examples are: after, although, because, before, unless, when, while.

Circle the best conjunctions to complete these complex sentences.

① (Before   While) we went to the party, we had some dinner.

② Having to do gym was a pain (although   before) most people did enjoy it.

③ He swam against the tide (unless   until) he could see the mainland.

④ Helping Dad build was easy (because   before) he did most of the heavy lifting.

Underline the subordinate clauses in these complex sentences.

⑤ Before they knew the whole story, people began to judge him.

⑥ The police officer searched the crime scene while the thief hid in the bushes.

⑦ Although it was expensive, Tran decided to hire the tools he needed.

⑧ Emma didn't want to go ice-skating because she was so tired.

Commas in complex sentences

Remember! Add a **comma (,)** when the subordinate clause is first in a complex sentence.

Example: <u>While we watch the fireworks display</u>, we'll eat our dinner.

subordinate clause • comma • main clause

Write the missing commas where needed to separate the clauses in these complex sentences.

⑨ After we move the furniture we can clean the carpets properly.

⑩ Saving the trapped horse was hard as water kept flooding in.

⑪ Because of the accident drivers were suing the government.

Score 2 points for each correct answer! **SCORE** **/22** 0-8 10-16 18-22

Phonic Knowledge & Spelling

AC9E6LY09

Synonyms

Synonyms are words that have a similar or the same meaning.
Example: cold – freezing, chilly, fresh

Match the bold words with a synonym from the box.

achieve	remove	seize	gather	adhere

① Eggs are sometimes hard to **get** amongst all of the birds. _____

② Water made it hard to **stick** the sticker on the bin. _____

③ After falling, the climber had to **grab** his friend's hand. _____

④ Do not **take** the glass from the window.
_____

⑤ People found it hard to **reach** the target.
_____

Circle the synonym for the bold words.

⑥ **party:**   solve   gathering   reply

⑦ **sound:**   noise   sneeze   loud

⑧ **shine:**   sausage   trophy   sparkle

⑨ **shout:**   whisper   yell   laugh

⑩ **right:**   wrong   different   correct

Match the words in the box with their antonyms (opposites).

calm	cheerful	cruel	arrive
absent	cheap	combine	bent

⑪ sad _____

⑫ kind _____

⑬ windy _____

⑭ depart _____

⑮ expensive _____

⑯ straight _____

⑰ present _____

⑱ separate _____

Score 2 points for each correct answer! **SCORE** **/36** 0-16 18-30 32-36

AC9E6LA03, AC9E6LA08, AC9E6LY03, AC9E6LY05

Dentists – why bother?

Persuasive text – Argument
Author – Peter Alford

I feel strongly that forcing children to go to the dentist is silly. Facing the drill and that pain can make children go bonkers through worry before even arriving at the dentist.

Most kids clean their teeth at least once a week and that should be enough! It's not as though children eat lollies every day or have cool drinks all the time. Sugar isn't a worry. Kids don't have breath like fire-breathing dragons. No-one is going to melt because they were breathed on by a child.

I'm sure that I read somewhere that thick, yellow coating on teeth stops tooth decay. Think of the money saved by parents allowing that coating to grow. Poking and prodding by a dentist should not be needed. The money that's saved could be better used to feed the poor people of the world.

So, in conclusion, it is not necessary for kids to go to dentists.

Write or circle the correct answer.

① What are the two things that children don't want to face?

_____

_____

② What could parents do with the money they saved by not sending children to dentists?

_____

_____

③ Write the sentence where the writer compares bad breath to something.

_____

_____

_____

④ What is not a worry for dentists and parents?

_____

_____

⑤ The writer says that children may go **bonkers**. What does that mean?

a happy   b fearful   c mad

⑥ What does the writer think may help stop tooth decay?

_____

⑦ The writer says that 'sugar isn't a worry'. What two things contain sugar in the text?

_____

_____

⑧ What would dentists not have to do if children didn't visit them?

_____

Score 2 points for each correct answer!

SCORE **/16**

My Book Review

Title _____

Author _____

Rating ☆☆☆☆☆

Comment _____

TERM 4 ENGLISH

Number & Algebra

AC9M6A02

Using the order of operations

Write the answers.

Remember the correct order of operations:
- brackets
- orders
- division and multiplication
- addition and subtraction

(1) $6 + 3 \times 7$

= _____

(2) $15 \div (19 - 16) \times 2$

= _____

(3) $(13 - 9) \times (2 + 5)$

= _____

(4) $24 \div (12 - 8 + 6 - 7)$

= _____

(5) $(35 \div 7 + 23) \div (16 \div 4)$

= _____

(6) $13 + 6 \times 2 - 16$

= _____

(7) $45 \div 9 + 6 \times 6 - 28$

= _____

(8) $(3 + 9 - 7 + 14 - 9) \times (120 - 40 + 8 + 6 - 15)$

= _____

(9) $18 \div 3 + 21 \div 3 + 24 \div 3 + 27 \div 3$

= _____

(10) $246 \div (9 \times 4 - 30)$

= _____

(11) $(5 + 3) \times (26 - 11 - 9) \times (17 - 12 + 5)$

= _____

(12) $17 + \frac{1}{3}$ of $24 - 9$

= _____

(13) $\frac{3}{4}$ of $(23 - 11) + 8$

= _____

(14) $15 - 120 \div \frac{1}{2}$ of $24 + 1$

= _____

(15) $\frac{3}{8}$ of $32 + \frac{2}{5}$ of $25 - \frac{3}{7}$ of 21

= _____

Statistics & Probability

AC9M6P01

Predicting likely outcomes

The following questions involve using a regular deck of playing cards, without jokers. There are **four suits** in a deck:
- **hearts** and **diamonds** (the red cards)
- **spades** and **clubs** (the black cards).

There are **13 cards** in each suit: ace, 2 to 10, Jack, Queen and King.
That means **52 cards** altogether.
In this exercise, the ace has a value of 1.

What is the probability of drawing these cards? Circle the correct answer.

(1) drawing a red card

  a $\frac{1}{52}$ **b** $\frac{1}{26}$ **c** $\frac{1}{13}$ **d** $\frac{1}{2}$

(2) drawing a spade

  a $\frac{1}{52}$ **b** $\frac{1}{26}$ **c** $\frac{1}{13}$ **d** $\frac{1}{4}$

(3) drawing the jack of spades

  a $\frac{1}{52}$ **b** $\frac{1}{26}$ **c** $\frac{1}{13}$ **d** $\frac{1}{2}$

(4) drawing a jack

  a $\frac{1}{52}$ **b** $\frac{1}{26}$ **c** $\frac{1}{13}$ **d** $\frac{1}{2}$

(5) drawing an ace or a two

  a $\frac{2}{52}$ **b** $\frac{2}{26}$ **c** $\frac{2}{13}$ **d** $\frac{2}{2}$

(6) drawing a jack, queen or king

  a $\frac{1}{13}$ **b** $\frac{2}{13}$ **c** $\frac{3}{13}$ **d** $\frac{4}{13}$

(7) drawing a black 4 or a red jack

  a $\frac{1}{52}$ **b** $\frac{2}{52}$ **c** $\frac{4}{52}$ **d** $\frac{13}{52}$

(8) drawing a card equal to or higher than seven

  a $\frac{1}{7}$ **b** $\frac{7}{13}$ **c** $\frac{7}{26}$ **d** $\frac{7}{52}$

(9) drawing a card lower than seven

  a $\frac{6}{52}$ **b** $\frac{1}{6}$ **c** $\frac{3}{13}$ **d** $\frac{6}{13}$

(10) drawing a black card that is an even number

  a $\frac{1}{2}$ **b** $\frac{10}{13}$ **c** $\frac{6}{52}$ **d** $\frac{5}{26}$

Score 2 points for each correct answer!

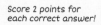 

SCORE **/30** (0–12) (14–24) (26–30)

TARGETING HOMEWORK 6 © PASCAL PRESS ISBN 9781925726480

⑪ The first card you drew was a king. You put the king back in the deck. What is your chance of drawing a king on your next try?

a $\frac{1}{11}$ b $\frac{1}{13}$ c $\frac{1}{15}$ d $\frac{1}{26}$

Score 2 points for each correct answer! SCORE **/22** (0-8) (10-16) (18-22)

Measurement & Space

AC9M6M04, AC9M6N08

Estimating and classifying angles

Circle the best estimate for the size of each angle.

① s
a 30°
b 60°
c 90°

② t
a 45°
b 160°
c 95°

③ u
a 90°
b 45°
c 110°

④ v
a 180°
b 160°
c 205°

⑤ w
a 35°
b 200°
c 320°

⑥ x
a 175°
b 180°
c 185°

⑦ y
a 360°
b 270°
c 335°

⑧ z
a 80°
b 45°
c 15°

Write the letters of the angles from the diagrams above to answer the following questions.

⑨ Which angles are acute angles? _____

⑩ Which angle is a right angle? _____

⑪ Which angles are obtuse angles? _____

⑫ Which angles are reflex angles? _____

Score 2 points for each correct answer! SCORE **/24** (0-10) (12-18) (20-24)

Problem Solving

AC9M6M04, AC9M6P01

Probability and angle problems

Circle the correct answers.

① If all the kings, all the queens and two of the jacks were taken out of a deck of cards, what is the chance of turning up a Jack on the next try?

a $\frac{1}{17}$ b $\frac{1}{19}$ c $\frac{1}{21}$ d $\frac{1}{23}$

② You picked 16 cards and none of them was an ace. You kept these 16 cards out of the deck. What is the chance that the next card you pick will be a red ace?

a $\frac{1}{17}$ b $\frac{1}{18}$ c $\frac{1}{19}$ d $\frac{1}{20}$

③ If you picked 50 cards, without putting them back, and none of them was the queen of diamonds, what is the chance that it will be the next card turned up?

a $\frac{1}{4}$ b $\frac{1}{13}$ c $\frac{1}{2}$ d $\frac{2}{1}$

Write the correct answers.

④ If you turned 45° clockwise, then 60° clockwise and then 110° clockwise, would you be facing in exactly the opposite direction from which you started?

_____

⑤ If you turned 90° anticlockwise, then a right angle anticlockwise, then 60° anticlockwise and finally 120° anticlockwise, in which direction would you be facing, compared to the direction from which you started?

_____

⑥ If you turned 180° clockwise, then 50° anticlockwise, then 40° anticlockwise then 180° clockwise again, then a right angle clockwise, in which direction would you be facing, compared to the direction from which you started?

_____

Grammar & Punctuation

AC9E6LA05, AC9E6LA06, AC9E6LA09

Adjectival clauses

> **Adjectival clauses** follow the nouns they describe. They are part of a noun group. The clauses can begin with **who**, **that** or **which**.
> *Example:* It was a plane **that** roared through the sky.
>
> Use **who** to describe people. *Example:* The woman, **who** is wearing the big hat, is crying.
>
> Use **which** to describe things. *Example:* I want to read the book **which** was just released.
>
> Also use **which** for any information which is not important in the sentence. *Example:* The chips, **which** I don't like, are stale.
>
> Use **that** to describe things when adding important information in sentences. *Example:* We picked all the apples **that** were red.

Underline the adjectival clauses.

1. Curry, which is very spicy, is enjoyed all over the world.
2. Ships that were wrecked in the storm had to be repaired.
3. The teacher who marked the exams is away today.

Add who, which or that to complete the adjectival clauses.

4. People _____ donated money received a receipt.
5. The school bus _____ comes at 8 am is the quickest.
6. The illness _____ my dog had was caused by ticks.

Adjectival clauses and commas

> Use commas around adjectival clauses that are not adding important information to a sentence. *Example:* The woman, **who is wearing the big hat**, is crying.
>
> Clauses that begin with **that** never need commas because they always add important information. *Example:* We picked all the apples **that** were red.

Add commas around these adjectival clauses where necessary.

7. The show that I watch every night has just been cancelled.
8. The fire which had been raging all night damaged many homes.

9. A biologist is a scientist who studies life.
10. The jockey who is my uncle won the horse race.

Score 2 points for each correct answer! **SCORE** /20 (0-8) (10-14) (16-20)

Phonic Knowledge & Spelling

AC9E6LY08, AC9E6LY09

Homophones

> Remember! **Homophones** are words that sound the same but have different spelling and meanings.
> *Example:* **waist** and **waste** are homophones. **Waist** is the area around the centre of the body and **waste** means rubbish.

Underline the two homophones in each question.

1. their   they're   thair
2. toad   tode   towed
3. moad   mowed   mode
4. prophet   profit   proffit

Use the clues and choose a letter group from the box to complete the cat words.

fish	ch	astrophe	dupli	e	walk

5. to grasp: cat_____
6. a disaster: cat_____
7. type of fish: cat_____
8. models walk on this: cat_____
9. copy: _____cat_____

Circle the base words in the words below.

10. sausages
11. unusual
12. unemployed
13. wonderful
14. hauling
15. opening

Write the suffix –or or –our to spell these words.

16. a taste: flav_____
17. a fine mist: vap_____
18. a person who gives: don_____
19. to eat hungrily: dev_____
20. a male singer: ten_____

Score 2 points for each correct answer! **SCORE** /40 (0-18) (20-34) (36-40)

AC9E6LY05

Derec and the Dugong

Imaginative text – Narrative
Author – Peter Alford

Covered in seaweed, the old wreck was hard to find if you didn't know where to look. Meadows of seagrass surrounded what was left of the ship that went down before the beginning of the 20th century. Dugongs (sea cows) were always found grazing lazily on the rich grass. Free diving off this part of the coast was made better by the clear water.

Derec was hovering over the barnacle-covered rusting pile when he looked away for a moment. Rolling over and over on the seabed was a dugong trapped in a fishing net. Derec swam to the animal. Using his razor-sharp diving knife, he slashed at the netting until the animal broke free. Instead of swimming away the dugong paddled towards the boy. Stopping at Derec's chest, the sea cow nuzzled him in thanks.

Months later, Derec was at the wreck. **Excruciating** cramps in his legs pulled him down to the seabed. He struggled to reach the surface. Then it happened, a huge whiskered nose pushed him upwards. Gasping for air, the frightened boy turned to see a dugong staring at him.

Write or circle the correct answer.

① **Which word gives the idea that the dugong is a sea cow?**

a barnacle   b netting   c meadows

② **When did the ship sink?**

_____

③ **What did Derec use to free the snared dugong?**

_____

_____

④ **Which phrase helps you to picture how the wreck looked?**

a barnacle-covered rusting pile

b beginning of the 20th century

c meadows of seagrass

⑤ **Why was free diving so good in this place?**

_____

_____

⑥ **Which word is a synonym (same meaning) for painful?**

a excruciating

b frightened

c struggled

⑦ **Why was the dugong in danger?**

_____

_____

⑧ **How did the dugong thank Derec for being saved?**

_____

_____

⑨ **Why was the wreck hard to find?**

_____

_____

Score 2 points for each correct answer!

SCORE | /18

My Book Review

Title _____

Author _____

Rating ☆☆☆☆☆

Comment _____

TERM 4 ENGLISH

Number & Algebra

AC9M6A02

Properties of whole numbers

What number do you end up with when you follow these instructions? Write the correct answers.

These abbreviations are used for place values:

M = millions, HT = hundreds of thousands,
Tt = tens of thousands, T = thousands,
h = hundreds, tens = tens, ones = ones.

① **307 237** Swap the Tt digit with the ones digit, double the Ht digit and add 6 to the tens digit.

_____

② **4 048 361** Halve the even digits then double the odd digits. Next, swap the M digit with the h digit and subtract 3 from the tens.

_____

③ **32 688** Halve the digit that appears twice. Then move the T digit into the ones place and put a 7 in the T place.

_____

④ **250 000** This number is a quarter of a million. Rearrange the digits to make the number comes as close as possible to half a million.

_____

⑤ **2 679 801** Change the M digit to the largest odd number. Swap the tens digit with the Ht digit and then swap the h digit with the Tt digit.

_____

⑥ **8 322 467:** Make this number the smallest it can be, using the same digits.

_____

⑦ **94 132** First subtract 1 from each digit. Then halve the even digits and double the odd digits. Finally, rearrange the digits in order with the largest digit in the Tt place and the smallest digit in the ones place.

_____

⑧ **3 589 025** Make this number the largest it can be, using the same digits.

_____

⑨ **4 305 126** Swap the Ht digit with the T digit, subtract 1 from the tens digit and add 3 to the Tt digit. Finally, change the M digit to the largest single-digit prime number.

_____

⑩ **246 517:** Add 2 to every digit that is a prime number. Then swap the Tt digit with the tens digit and swap the ones digit with the Ht digit.

_____

Score 2 points for each correct answer! SCORE **/20** (0-8) (10-14) (16-20)

Statistics & Probability

AC9M6ST02

Misleading data representations

These graphs and descriptions are deliberately incorrect or misleading. Write the letter of the correct explanation beside each graph.

①	This pie chart shows how snakes are responsible for so many deaths!	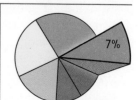
②	This pie chart shows how snakes **kill** more people than you think!	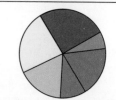
③	This pie chart shows how snakes killed more people over time than any other animal!	
④	This bar graph shows how the pay of rat catchers has increased over time.	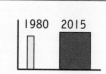
⑤	This bar graph shows how the pay of rat catchers has improved over time.	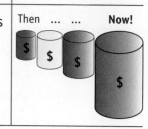

Explanations

A The increasing 3-D perspective makes the column heights difficult to compare.

B The use of the red 'kill' suggests that the largest red section of the graphs is for snakes. But there is no key and no labels to identify the different categories.

C Enlarging the wedge exaggerates its value and importance. Other sections of the pie chart are actually larger.

D The chart has no categories or values for other animals, except for the total which is much lower for snakes than it is for 'others'.

E The greater width of the second bar and it's bright colour make it difficult to see the actual difference over time.

Score 2 points for each correct answer! SCORE **/10** (0-2) (4-8) (10)

Measurement & Space

AC9M6M03

Using timetables

This timeline shows Hanna watching a TV show. It is not drawn to scale.

Points B and J are marked with an arrow. The other letters indicate periods of time.

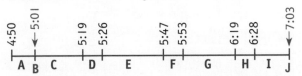

① During which time period was Hanna most likely waiting for the show to start?
_____

② Which point probably marks the end of the show?
_____

Periods D, F and H are commercial breaks.

③ How long was the longest commercial break?
_____

④ How long was the shortest commercial break?
_____

⑤ Which time period marks the longest uninterrupted time that the show was on?
_____

⑥ Which time period marks the shortest uninterrupted period that the show was on?
_____

⑦ How long was the show, including the commercial breaks?
_____

⑧ How long was the show, excluding the commercial breaks?
_____

⑨ How long was period A? _____

Score 2 points for each correct answer! SCORE **/18** (0-6) (8-14) (16-18)

Problem Solving

AC9M6M03

Timetable problems

Use this information from a TV Guide to answer the following questions.

3:10 am Movie: The Hat	4:55 am The Smiths	5:15 am Fishing Show
6:00 am Breakfast Serial	7:00 am Cartoon Time	8:30 am Baby School
9:00 am Shopping Time	9:50 am The Detectives	11:05 am Jack's Show
11:55 am Jill's Show	1:00 pm Good Cooking	1:40 pm The Doctors

① Which two shows are the same length?
_____
_____

② Which show runs for half an hour?
_____

③ Which show were you watching if the time was eight o'clock in the morning?
_____

④ Which is the last show of the morning?
_____

⑤ If you wanted to watch exactly 1 hour and 25 minutes of TV, which two shows would you watch?
_____
_____

⑥ Which two shows combined are as long as the *Breakfast Serial* and *Cartoon Time*, combined?
_____
_____

⑦ Which is the shortest show?
_____

⑧ Which show is half as long as *Cartoon Time*?
_____

⑨ Which two shows combined are as long as *The Breakfast Serial* and *Good Cooking* combined?
_____

Grammar & Punctuation

AC9E6LA06

Adverbial phrases

> Remember! An **adverbial phrase** says **how**, **when**, **where** and **why** something happened.
> *Examples:* I usually go to football training **at 7 pm**. (when)
> Kate walked **through lots of cobwebs**. (where)
> **Adverbial phrases** usually start with a **preposition**. Prepositions are words like: about, above, after, before, behind, for, on, through, until, with, within, without, etc.

Complete these adverbial phrases with the prepositions in the box.

into	between	without	through	under

① Always make sure that you swim _____ the flags at the beach.

② Our plane flew _____ Perth late at night.

③ Jed's bull broke _____ the fence railings.

④ Swimming _____ the water, the guards did not see him enter.

⑤ _____ trying, she passed the leader on the line.

Commas with adverbial phrases

> Remember! **Commas** are used to separate **adverbial phrases** when they are at the beginning of a sentence.
> *Examples:* **Over the weekend,** my sister found fool's gold.
> **From our porch,** I could see the school.

Complete these adverbial phrases with the prepositions in the box. Add commas where necessary.

on	beneath	within	through	for

⑥ _____ minutes the entire house was in flames.

⑦ I'm waiting _____ my parents.

⑧ _____ my window I could see the sun come up.

⑨ _____ Sunday morning I have my gymnastics competition.

⑩ Lifeguards dived _____ the waves to grab the drowning man.

Score 2 points for each correct answer!

SCORE **/20** (0-8) (10-14) (16-20)

Phonic Knowledge & Spelling

AC9E6LY09

Suffixes

Match word endings from the box to these base words.

–ly	–y	–ous	–er

① order_____

② teach_____

③ humour_____

④ health_____

Word origins

Choose a meaning from the box for each root word. The example words will help.

life	water	one	eight	world	tooth

Root word	Example word	Meaning
⑤ denti	dentist	_____
⑥ mono	monorail	_____
⑦ hydro	hydroelectricity	_____
⑧ geo	geography	_____
⑨ octo	octopus	_____
⑩ bio	biology	_____

Choose a suffix or two from the box to add to each word. Write the new words.

–ish	–ent	–ment	–ness

⑪ short _____

⑫ depend _____

⑬ sick _____

⑭ retire _____

⑮ resent _____

⑯ mean _____

⑰ discern _____

⑱ self _____

Score 2 points for each correct answer!

SCORE **/36** (0-16) (18-30) (32-36)

TARGETING HOMEWORK 6 © PASCAL PRESS ISBN 9781925726480

Reading & Comprehension

AC9E6LA03, AC9E6LA08, AC9E6LY03, AC9E6LY05

UNIT 31

ALL NEW FLABBO

Persuasive text – Advertorial
Author – Peter Alford

Ever wanted to smash down something that will give you a million times more energy than you have now? NEW FLABBO is that product.

Made from white sugar, pure butter, peanuts, olive oil, flavouring, white chocolate with added lard (pig fat), it is the energy seeker's dream. Spread thickly on fresh white bread, it'll make your breakfast an amazing adventure every day.

Our company doctor has written 'FLABBO is a wonderful, healthy snack to liven up every morning'. FLABBO promises your ugly morning feeling will fly out the window after breakfast. Grumpy feelings suffered by some will be no more just by enjoying FLABBO. Mint flavoured FLABBO also fights 'death breath', putting your toothbrush out of business.

Write or circle the correct answer.

① **What does 'smash down' mean in this advertisement?**

   a Throw FLABBO in the bin.

   b Eat FLABBO.

   c Love FLABBO.

② **What are three ingredients FLABBO is made from?**

   _____

   _____

   _____

③ **Which ingredient is from an animal?**

   _____

④ **What is one thing FLABBO promises to do about energy?**

   _____

   _____

⑤ **What does 'will fly out the window after breakfast' mean?**

   a FLABBO is thrown out the window.

   b You will grow wings.

   c You will be less unhappy.

⑥ **Who does the advertiser use to persuade us that FLABBO is healthy?**

   _____

⑦ **What should people spread FLABBO on?**

   _____

   _____

⑧ **What will no longer be needed in the morning?**

   a cleaning teeth

   b eating breakfast

   c eating mint

⑨ **What oil is used to make FLABBO?**

   _____

⑩ **What words does the writer use in the last line to make the advertisement humorous?**

   _____

Score 2 points for each correct answer!

SCORE **/20** (0-8) (10-14) (16-20)

TERM 4 ENGLISH

My Book Review

Title _____

Author _____

Rating ☆☆☆☆☆

Comment _____

Number & Algebra

AC9M6N05

Adding and subtracting fractions

Rewrite the fractions so that they have common denominators. Then work out the answers. Change your answers to mixed numbers if you need to.

① $\frac{1}{4} + \frac{3}{8} + \frac{6}{8} =$ _____

= _____

② $\frac{3}{5} - \frac{3}{10} =$ _____

= _____

③ $\frac{6}{7} + \frac{5}{14} + \frac{1}{7} =$ _____

= _____

④ $\frac{4}{9} + \frac{2}{3} + \frac{5}{9} =$ _____

= _____

⑤ $\frac{3}{4} - \frac{11}{16} =$ _____

= _____

⑥ $\frac{3}{10} + \frac{2}{5} + \frac{7}{20} =$ _____

= _____

⑦ $\frac{65}{100} - \frac{31}{50} =$ _____

= _____

⑧ $\frac{4}{6} - \frac{11}{24} =$ _____

= _____

⑨ $\frac{1}{2} + \frac{3}{4} + \frac{1}{4} + \frac{1}{2} =$ _____

= _____

⑩ $\frac{1}{3} + \frac{3}{4} + \frac{2}{6} + \frac{3}{6} =$ _____

= _____

⑪ $\frac{1}{2} + \frac{3}{5} =$ _____

= _____

⑫ $\frac{1}{4} + \frac{2}{3} + \frac{3}{4} + \frac{4}{6} =$ _____

= _____

⑬ $\frac{5}{8} - \frac{3}{5} =$ _____

= _____

Score 2 points for each correct answer!

SCORE **/26** (0-10) (12-20) (22-26)

Statistics & Probability

AC9M6ST03

Interpreting bar graphs

These bar graphs show the statistics of top cricket batsmen.

- **W** is the number of centuries scored.
- **X** is total number of runs, in thousands.
- **Y** is their highest innings.
- **Z** is their career average.

The letters **A** to **F** represent the same batsmen in each of the graphs.

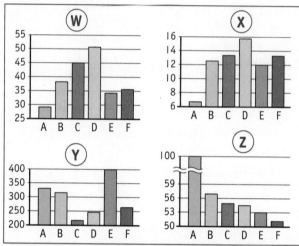

Source: http://www.espncricinfo.com, Viewed 15 Aug 2018

Use the information below to work out which letter, A to F, represents which batsman. Write the correct letters in the boxes.

① ☐ R Dravid's highest innings score was 270.

② ☐ K Sangakkara made 12 400 runs during his career.

③ ☐ J Kallis made 45 centuries during his career.

④ ☐ D Bradman made a total of 6996 runs in his career.

⑤ ☐ B Lara has a career average of 52.88.

⑥ ☐ S Tendulkar has two 'highest' values.

Write the correct answers.

⑦ Why was graph Z broken?

_____

⑧ Does the combined highest innings of batters D and F come close to that of B?

_____

TARGETING HOMEWORK 6 © PASCAL PRESS ISBN 9781925726480

TERM 4 MATHS

Write the letters A to F to answer the following questions.

⑨ Which batsman has close to 15 more centuries than the batsman with fewest runs?

_____

⑩ Which batsman's highest innings was close to eight times higher than his career average?

_____

⑪ Which batsman's total number of runs is close to 70 times his career average?

_____

⑫ Overall, which two batsmen have the most similar statistics?

_____

Measurement & Space

AC9M6SP01

Symmetry and angles

Which lines of symmetry do the letters have? Write the matching letters, a to d. Some letters have more than one.

Example:	Lines of symmetry
 **K** ─ d The letter **K** has the line of symmetry marked **d**.	b a ╳ c d

① _____   ③ _____   ⑤ _____

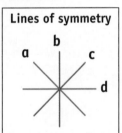

A H X

② _____   ④ _____   ⑥ _____

B W E

Use the letter shapes in questions 1 to 6 to answer the following questions.

How many internal acute angles are there in these letter shapes?

⑦ **A** _____   ⑨ **W** _____

⑧ **H** _____   ⑩ **E** _____

How many internal right angles are there in these letter shapes?

⑪ **W** _____   ⑬ **X** _____

⑫ **E** _____   ⑭ **H** _____

How many external reflex angles are there in these letter shapes?

⑮ **X** _____   ⑰ **E** _____

⑯ **H** _____   ⑱ **W** _____

Problem Solving

AC9M6N05, AC9M6M04

Fraction and symmetry problems

① Francis is a fraction. If you add Francis to $\frac{1}{6}$, the answer will be $\frac{1}{2}$. What fraction is Francis, simplified?

_____

② Freya is a fraction. If you add Freya to $\frac{3}{8}$, the answer will be $\frac{10}{16}$. What fraction is Freya, simplified?

_____

③ Fred is a fraction. The answer will be $\frac{3}{4}$ if you add Fred to $\frac{3}{12}$. What fraction is Fred, simplified?

_____

④ Frankie is a fraction. The answer will be $1\frac{2}{5}$ if you add Frankie to $\frac{8}{10}$. What fraction is Frankie, simplified?

_____

⑤ Freda is a fraction. If you add Freda to $\frac{2}{8}$, the answer will be 1. What fraction is Freda, simplified?

_____

⑥ Two snails, Flash and Speedy, sat back to back.

They each slid 0.15 metres forwards then Flash made a 90° turn to its left and Speedy made a 90° turn to its right.

They each slid another 0.15 metres forwards and Flash turned 90° to its right and Speedy turned 90° to its left.

Then they slid 0.15 metres forwards.

Can a line of symmetry be drawn between the trails they left?

_____

TERM 4 MATHS

Grammar & Punctuation

AC9E6LA05, AC9E6LA09

Embedded clauses and complex sentences

> Remember! A **complex sentence** has two (or more) clauses: a main clause which has the main idea, and a subordinate clause that gives more information about the main idea. A subordinate clause does not stand on its own.
>
> An **embedded clause** is a clause placed in the middle of another clause.
>
> *Example:* **My dinner,** which has gone cold, **does not taste good.**
>
> The clause My dinner does not taste good is a main clause. It makes sense on its own.
>
> The embedded clause which has gone cold does not stand on its own. It is a type of subordinate clause.

Underline the embedded clauses in these sentences.

① The nurse, who was very kind, took my temperature.

② My bag, which is old, has a frayed strap.

③ The cat, which was hiding, pounced at the mouse.

④ Sue, who had a headache, went home early.

⑤ Abul, who loves the rain, went for a walk.

> **Commas** are placed on either side of an embedded clause.
>
> *Example:* My dog, who is friendly, likes to go for walks.

Place the commas in the correct places.

⑥ The girl who was only 12 could play the piano.

⑦ The sun which was too bright gave me a headache.

⑧ My cousin who went overseas came back last week.

⑨ The bananas which are too ripe are covered in black spots.

⑩ My father who loves to cook is making dinner.

Phonic Knowledge & Spelling

AC9E6LY09

Word origin

> Remember! Some English words come from other languages. Where they come from is their **origin**.

Match words from the box with their meanings. The words come from Spanish.

cockroach   guerrilla   cargo mosquito   patio

① little fly: _____

② cucaracha: _____

③ small war: _____

④ inner courtyard: _____

⑤ to load: _____

Choose words from the box to complete these sentences. The words come from Aboriginal languages.

drongo (silly)	yakka (work)
yabber (talk)	galah (bird/silly)
gidgee (barbed spear)	mulga (scrubby) bush

⑥ After working in the sun all day, everyone agreed it had been hard _____.

⑦ There was lots of _____ in the classroom and no work got done.

⑧ Nanja trapped the fish and used his _____ to spear them.

⑨ In the comedy he was an absolute _____.

⑩ While he waited, he acted like a _____ without its feathers.

⑪ Gold prospectors often lived out in the _____ for months on end.

Match the words in the box with those that have the same sound.

bri**dge**   stu**ff**   ho**se**   **c**ity

⑫ tele**ph**one _____

⑬ **g**iant _____

⑭ mi**ss** _____

⑮ fu**zz**y _____

Score 2 points for each correct answer! SCORE **/20** (0-8) (10-14) (16-20)

Score 2 points for each correct answer! SCORE **/30** (0-12) (14-24) (26-30)

TARGETING HOMEWORK 6 © PASCAL PRESS ISBN 9781925726480

Lizard Dinner

Imaginative text – Recount
Author – Peter Alford

Rattling along the dusty, red dirt road, the old school bus limped towards the billabong. School was just too hot for the kids and Mr Sheridan. A cooling dip in the cold, deep waters of Python Pool was needed before they could do more work. At forty-seven degrees, the heat outside was searing. The windows on the bus were closed. With nothing to keep them cool, it was best that the fiery blast of the wind be kept out of the bus.

Aboriginal people had lived in the desert for thousands of years and the heat was part of their lives. Low, grey-green spinifex clumps with scraggy, spindly leaves hardly growing out of the red soil were everywhere.

Shouting loudly, a boy yelled for the bus to stop. Mr Sheridan thought a toilet break was needed. Nathan, one of the older boys, leapt off the bus and picked up a stone. Nathan's

hand was a blur as he threw the rock. His throw was fast, straight and accurate. No-one saw where the rock was going. The huge racehorse goanna hadn't either as he lay stunned on the red dust.

Write or circle the correct answer.

1. **Which words tell what was going to happen to the big goanna?**

_____

2. **Which words tell about the heat of the wind?**
   a too hot   b fiery blast   c the heat

3. **Which plant is mentioned?**

_____
_____

4. **Which words tell you that the children were going swimming?**

_____

5. **'Nathan's hand was a blur.' What does this mean?**
   a It was in slow motion.
   b It was fast.
   c It became invisible.

6. **Which words tell you that Mr Sheridan was probably a teacher?**

_____

7. **What sort of goanna is mentioned?**

_____

8. **Which group of people did the boys probably belong to?**
   a a school group
   b a swimming club
   c a group of Aboriginal students

9. **Which words tell you that Aboriginal people were used to the heat?**
   a too hot for the kids
   b the heat outside was searing
   c the heat was part of their lives

10. **What does the Aboriginal word billabong mean?**
    a animal   b lizard   c waterhole

Score 2 points for each correct answer!   **SCORE** /20   0-8   10-14   16-20

My Book Review

Title _____

Author _____

Rating ☆☆☆☆☆

Comment _____
_____

Number & Algebra

AC9M6A02

Using the order of operations

Write the answers. You can use a calculator.

> Remember the correct order of operations:
> • brackets
> • orders
> • division and multiplication
> • addition and subtraction

① $(8 + 9) \times 24 \div 8$

= _____

② $15 \div (279 + 146 - 405) \times 2$

= _____

③ $(306 - 72) \times (8 + 16)$

= _____

④ $180 \div (8 \times 9 - 54) - 10$

= _____

⑤ $35 \div 7 + 2.08 + 36 \div 6$

= _____

⑥ $(29 - 13) \times 8.6 \times 9 - 238$

= _____

⑦ $6.6 \times 6.6 - 43.5$

= _____

⑧ $(13 + 25.8 - 6.05 + 12.8 - 32.65) \times (12.05 - 30.4 + 21.65)$

= _____

⑨ $\frac{4}{5}$ of $42 + 24 \div 6 + 24 \div 3$

= _____

⑩ $255 \div (19 \times 3 - 32)$

= _____

⑪ $(6.5 + 3.75) \times (2.4 - 3 + 5.8)$

= _____

⑫ $20.8 + \frac{5}{6}$ of $243 - 129$

= _____

⑬ $\frac{7}{8}$ of $(239 - 187) + 54.5$

= _____

⑭ $6 - 132 \div \frac{3}{8}$ of 64

= _____

Score 2 points for each correct answer! SCORE **/28** (0-12) (14-22) (24-28)

Statistics & Probability

AC9M6ST01

Interpreting a line graph

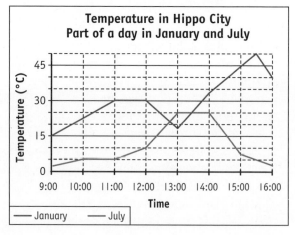

Temperature in Hippo City
Part of a day in January and July

— January   — July

① What was the highest temperature reached?

_____

② What is the lowest temperature reached?

_____

③ How many times do the months have the same temperature at the same time of day?

_____

④ What is the temperature difference between the months at 11:00?

_____

⑤ What is the temperature difference between the months at the latest time recorded?

_____

⑥ What is the temperature difference between the months when January is at its maximum temperature?

_____

⑦ What is the temperature difference between the months when July is at its lowest temperature during the afternoon?

_____

⑧ During which hour did the temperature rise most sharply in January?

_____

⑨ During which hour did the temperature fall most sharply in July?

_____

⑩ During which time did the temperature fall most sharply in January?

_____

Score 2 points for each correct answer! SCORE **/20** (0-8) (10-14) (16-20)

TARGETING HOMEWORK 6 © PASCAL PRESS ISBN 9781925726480

Measurement & Space

AC9M6SP02

Rotation and angles

Use the Cartesian plane, compass and protractor to answer the questions.

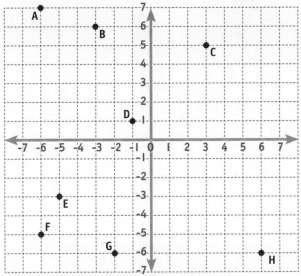

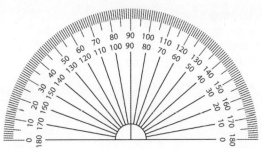

① You stand at (0, 0) on the Cartesian plane, facing north. Then you turn 30° clockwise. Which point on the Cartesian plane are you facing now?

_____

② You stand at (0, 0) facing north and you turn 175° anticlockwise. Which point are you facing now?

_____

③ You stand at (4, -5) facing north west and you turn 45° W. Which point are you facing now?

_____

④ You stand at (-4, 4) facing E and you turn 45° S. Which point are you facing now?

_____

⑤ You stand at (0, 0) facing W and you turn 120° N. Which point are you facing now?

_____

⑥ You stand at (0, 0) facing SE and you turn 180° W. Which point are you facing now?

_____

⑦ You stand at (-8, 0) facing E and you turn 80° N. Which point are you facing now?

_____

⑧ You stand at (8, -3) facing SW and you turn 45° W, Which point are you facing now?

_____

⑨ You stand at point D facing W and you turn 47.5° N. Which point are you facing now?

_____

Score 2 points for each correct answer!

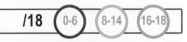

SCORE /18 (0-6) (8-14) (16-18)

Problem Solving

AC9M6N09

Decimal money problems

① A man started with $428.00. He multiplied this amount by the number of days in a week less the number of seasons in a year. Then he lost three quarters of his money. How much money did he lose?

_____

② A woman had $894.00 in a shoebox. She had promised to give her daughter three-eighths of it, which she did. Then she took two-thirds of $273.00 she had hidden in a sock and added it to her shoebox money. She gave the rest of the sock money to her son. How much money did she have in her shoebox then?

_____

③ A man saved $215.25 every week for an entire year but he had to give a quarter of it to his dentist. How much money did he have left?

_____

④ A woman earned $7.75 every day for an entire year (by the way, it was a leap year). She also earned $132.55 every month for that same year. When she combined her earnings, she found that she only had two-thirds of the money she needed for treatment to stop her chronic hiccupping. How much money did she need for her treatment?

_____

Grammar & Punctuation

Underline the verbs and say if they are present, past or future tense.

① We stayed at the game after school on Wednesday. _____

② I'm competing in the swimming trials today. _____

③ My sister took a look at the bush near the river. _____

④ We are going to France next summer. _____

Underline the auxiliary verbs and main verbs in these sentences.

⑤ He had waited for the principal to leave.

⑥ Pam was laughing at her spelling mistakes.

⑦ Zach has rowed all the way down to the river mouth.

⑧ Aunty Jan is watching the gymnastics competition.

Underline the adjectival clauses.

⑨ Lamingtons, which I love, are often eaten on Australia Day.

⑩ Books that were damaged in the flood had to be replaced.

⑪ The teacher who takes the athletics training is not here.

Underline the modal verbs and main verbs.

⑫ Our music teacher will be late this afternoon.

⑬ The train to the city should come on time.

⑭ Emma might take her homework to Grandma's house.

⑮ Can I give the dog its food?

Underline the subordinate clauses in these complex sentences.

⑯ When the snake found the chook run, it ate the eggs.

⑰ After Ryan came home from school, he relaxed and then made dinner.

⑱ Because the soup was hot, I put it on the table and waited for it to cool.

Place commas between the verbs.

⑲ Whilst building, the lady hammered sawed nailed and screwed the wood.

⑳ As we waited, we played jumped skipped and hopped in the playground.

Score 2 points for each correct answer!

SCORE **/40**

Phonic Knowledge & Spelling

Write the contractions for these words.

① should have _____

② should not _____

③ are not _____

④ that will _____

⑤ you have _____

⑥ they are _____

Match the words in the box with their antonyms (opposites).

| windy | clean | cruel | depart | hero | boring |

⑦ kind _____

⑧ untidy _____

⑨ arrive _____

⑩ calm _____

⑪ exciting _____

⑫ coward _____

Add endings to these words and apply the doubling rule where needed.

	add –ing	**add –ed**
⑬ hiss	_____	_____
⑭ shop	_____	_____

	add –er	**add –est**
⑮ long	_____	_____
⑯ thin	_____	_____

Make these words plural by adding –s if needed. (*Hint:* Some words are already plural.)

⑰ geese___

⑱ plant___

⑲ space___

⑳ fish__

Write how many syllables are in these words.

㉑ signature _____

㉒ silence _____

㉓ horizon _____

㉔ remarkable_____

Score 2 points for each correct answer!

SCORE **/48**

TARGETING HOMEWORK 6 © PASCAL PRESS ISBN 9781925726480

TERM 4 ENGLISH

Surviving in the Outback

Informative text – Report
Author – Peter Alford

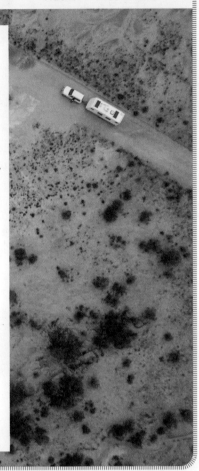

Every year people **perish** in the outback of Australia. Many people have no idea of the size of this **vast** place. Lives are put at risk when people are not fully prepared for their journey and an accident or breakdown happens.

Heat and lack of water are the real killers in this **environment**. Temperatures can reach as high as 50 degrees and there is often very little shade. Very few trees are able to live in this cruel and unforgiving place. Those that can grow are spindly with few leaves.

When it is that hot, a body cannot survive without water for more than 5–7 hours. People who do get into trouble make the mistake of not taking enough water. Thirty to fifty litres or more of water should be part of any trip into the desert.

Visitors to Australia often think there will be service — a town or petrol station — every one hundred kilometres. Places giving service are often many hundreds of kilometres apart. When they become bogged or have a breakdown, visitors to the outback make the deadly mistake of leaving their vehicle. The first rule for survival is to stay with the car. Cars are far easier to spot when people begin a search.

Making sure that people know when you depart and when you think you may arrive at your destination is also **vital**. Spare tyres and parts are also very important. Rocks and bushes can puncture even the toughest of tyres.

Write or circle the correct answer.

1. **What does perish mean?**

   a survive   b die   c get lost

2. **How long are you able to last without water in the desert during summer?**

   _____

3. **What does vast mean?**

   a small   b dangerous   c large

4. **What would you never do if you broke down in the outback?**

   _____
   _____

5. **How much water should you take with you when driving in the outback?**

   _____
   _____

6. **What does vital mean?**

   a unimportant   b important   c usable

7. **Aside from water, what two things should people take when driving in the outback?**

   _____
   _____

8. **Why is there not much shade in the outback?**

   _____
   _____

Score 2 points for each correct answer! SCORE **/16** (0-6) (8-12) (14-16)

My Book Review

Title _____

Author _____

Rating ☆☆☆☆☆

Comment _____
_____

TERM 4 ENGLISH

Number & Algebra

Simplify these fractions.

① $\frac{12}{32}$ = _____

② $\frac{4}{20}$ = _____

③ $\frac{15}{45}$ = _____

④ $\frac{14}{36}$ = _____

⑤ $\frac{16}{42}$ = _____

Calculate these equations. Convert the answers to simplified mixed numbers.

⑥ $\frac{3}{8} + \frac{2}{8} + \frac{4}{8} - \frac{3}{8}$

= _____

⑦ $\frac{3}{4} + \frac{2}{12} + \frac{4}{6} - \frac{1}{6} + \frac{8}{12}$

= _____

⑧ $\frac{8}{10} - \frac{2}{5} + \frac{7}{10} - \frac{3}{10} - \frac{1}{5} + \frac{6}{10}$

= _____

⑨ $\frac{3}{6} - \frac{2}{9} + \frac{4}{6} - \frac{1}{18} + \frac{2}{9}$

= _____

⑩ $\frac{12}{15} + \frac{2}{5} - \frac{6}{15} - \frac{1}{5} + \frac{2}{3} - \frac{1}{15}$

= _____

Use calculators to work out these equations. Remember the correct order of mathematical operations.

⑪ $8 \times (14 - 7 + 23) \times (57 - 19 + 4)$

= _____

⑫ $28 + \frac{1}{3}$ of $84 - 168 \div 4$

= _____

⑬ $\frac{3}{4}$ of $(1366 - 994) + 21$

= _____

⑭ $68.75 - 225.6 \div \frac{1}{2}$ of $94 + 45 - 18$

= _____

⑮ $\frac{3}{8}$ of $72 + \frac{3}{5}$ of $125 - \frac{3}{7}$ of 84

= _____

Score 2 points for each correct answer!

SCORE /30 (0-12) (14-24) (26-30)

144

Statistics & Probability

Use this temperature graph to answer the ten questions.

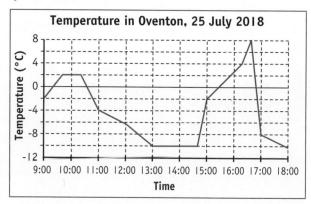

Temperature in Oventon, 25 July 2018

① What was the lowest temperature recorded?

_____

② During which four hours was the temperature 0 °C?

_____

③ What was the difference between the highest and lowest temperatures?

_____

④ What was the temperature halfway between the highest and lowest points?

_____

⑤ How much did the temperature rise between 14:30 and 16:30?

_____

⑥ How long was the longest period of the temperature constantly dropping?

_____

⑦ What was the difference in temperature between 16:30 and 17:30?

_____

⑧ Approximately how long in total was the temperature below zero?

_____

There are 20 balls numbered 1 to 20 in a box. They are pulled out at random.
Write your answers as percentages.

⑨ What is the chance of an even numbered ball being picked?

_____

⑩ What is the chance of ball 1 being picked?

_____

⑪ If five balls have been picked, what is the chance that ball 6 is one of them?

_____

Write your answers as decimals.

⑫ If 15 balls have been picked, what is the chance that ball 6 is one of them?

_____

⑬ If two balls are picked at once, what is the chance of ball 20 being one of them?

_____

Write your answers as simplified fractions.

⑭ What is the chance of a ball with a prime number being picked?

_____

⑮ If balls 8, 9, 10, 11 and 12 have already been picked, what is the chance of ball 13 being picked next?

_____

In another box there are 100 balls.
Five of them are numbered 1, ten balls are numbered 2 and fifteen balls are numbered 3.
The remaining balls are numbered from 4 to 73.

⑯ What is the chance of a 1 being picked?
Write your answer as a percentage, a decimal and a simplified common fraction.

_____

⑰ Which two numbers have a combined chance of being picked of a quarter?

_____

⑱ Twenty balls have been picked and kept aside instead of being put back in the box. None of these 20 balls was 4. What is the chance that 4 will be picked next?
Write your answer as a percentage, a decimal and a simplified common fraction.

_____

Score 2 points for each correct answer! SCORE **/36** (0-16) (18-30) (32-36)

Measurement & Space

Use this diagram to answer the following questions.

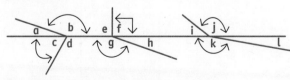

① Which angles are acute angles?

_____

Write the missing angles to make these statements correct.

② Angle **a** + angle ___ = 180°

③ Angle **d** + angle ___ = 180°

④ Angle **e** + angle ___ = 180°

⑤ Angle **g** + angle ___ = 180°

⑥ Angle **l** + angle ___ = 180°

⑦ Angle **j** + angle ___ = 180°

Follow the instructions over this Cartesian plane. Assume the grid lines are 1 km apart from north to south and from east to west and 1.4 km apart diagonally.

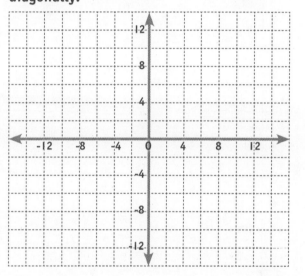

⑧ You start at (0, 0), go 3 km north, 4 km west and then 8 km south. At what coordinates are you now?

_____

⑨ You start at (-14, -8), go 4.2 km NE, 4 km N and then 9 km E. At what coordinates are you now?

_____

⑩ You start at (4, -6), go 6 km N, 2 km E and then 9 km S. At what coordinates are you now?

_____

⑪ You start at (-10, 9), go 7 km E, 5 km S, 3 km E, 4 km S. At what coordinates are you now?

_____

⑫ You start at (9, 12), go 4.2 km SW and then 8 km S. At what coordinates are you now?

_____

Score 2 points for each correct answer! SCORE **/24** (0-10) (12-18) (20-24)

MY READING LIST

Name: _____

_____

	Title	Author	Rating	Date
1			☆☆☆☆☆	
2			☆☆☆☆☆	
3			☆☆☆☆☆	
4			☆☆☆☆☆	
5			☆☆☆☆☆	
6			☆☆☆☆☆	
7			☆☆☆☆☆	
8			☆☆☆☆☆	
9			☆☆☆☆☆	
10			☆☆☆☆☆	
11			☆☆☆☆☆	
12			☆☆☆☆☆	
13			☆☆☆☆☆	
14			☆☆☆☆☆	
15			☆☆☆☆☆	
16			☆☆☆☆☆	
17			☆☆☆☆☆	
18			☆☆☆☆☆	
19			☆☆☆☆☆	
20			☆☆☆☆☆	
21			☆☆☆☆☆	
22			☆☆☆☆☆	
23			☆☆☆☆☆	
24			☆☆☆☆☆	
25			☆☆☆☆☆	
26			☆☆☆☆☆	
27			☆☆☆☆☆	
28			☆☆☆☆☆	
29			☆☆☆☆☆	
30			☆☆☆☆☆	
31			☆☆☆☆☆	
32			☆☆☆☆☆	

TARGETING HOMEWORK 6 © PASCAL PRESS ISBN 9781925726480

Answers - Homework Year 6

Unit 1 ENGLISH: Grammar & Punctuation

1 <u>Luke was voted captain this year</u> because he is a great runner.
2 <u>We aren't allowed to eat the apples hanging over the fence</u> until they are ripe.
3 Although Jess is fantastic at cycling, <u>she has fallen off her bike three times.</u>
4 Although we woke up late, we still caught the bus.
5 When we have beach holidays, my family swims in the surf every day.
6 While the scones are baking in the oven, Jack will wash the dishes.
7 **Because** some old people find it difficult to walk, they use the bus.
8 **Since** we make a huge mess in art classes, we have to clean up.
9 I usually sleep in **even though** my dog barks loudly each morning.

Unit 1 ENGLISH: Phonic Knowledge & Spelling

1	transport	5	organise
2	semicircle	6	informant
3	program	7	apprenticeship
4	interstate		

Unit 1 ENGLISH: Reading & Comprehension

1 b. flat, treeless and frozen
2 Khmer, Cham
3 c. They are both about cities.
4–7 In any order: Feudal, Monarchy, Communist, Democracy
8 South Korea
9 Any 3 from: Japan, Indonesia, South Korea
10 15th century

Unit 1 MATHS: Number & Algebra

1 c. {40, 40$\frac{1}{2}$, 50, 50$\frac{1}{2}$, 60, 60$\frac{1}{2}$, 70, 70$\frac{1}{2}$.}
2 c. {-2$\frac{1}{2}$, -2, -1$\frac{1}{2}$, -1, -$\frac{1}{2}$, 0, $\frac{1}{2}$, 1, 1$\frac{1}{2}$, 2, 2$\frac{1}{2}$.}
3 c. 19.5
4 b. -32
5 c. a number that is a decimal fraction but not a common fraction
6 d. 45
7 b. A prime number is a number that can be divided by 2 without a remainder.
8 c. 11

Unit 1 MATHS: Statistics & Probability

1 d. 1 in 2
2 d. the same as the chance of the coin coming up tail because there are only two sides
3 d. to rule out the possibility of a defect in the coin, as well as cheating and anything else that might affect the coin toss

4 c. $\frac{1}{4}$		7 c. $\frac{1}{5}$	
5 a. one in six		8 a. the same as the first go	
6 b. $\frac{1}{6}$			

Unit 1 MATHS: Measurement & Space

1 b. {mm = millimetre, cm = centimetre, m = metre, km = kilometre.}
2 c. {mg = milligram, g = gram, kg = kilogram, t = tonne.}
3 b. {L = litre, mL = millilitre, cL = centilitre, ML = megalitre.}

4	billion	6	kilo	8	mm
5	1 000 000	7	hundred	9	millionth

Unit 1 MATHS: Problem Solving

1	28	4	23	7	13
2	135, 153	5	true		
3	10	6	false		

Unit 2 ENGLISH: Grammar & Punctuation

1 My brother used to love climbing trees, **but** he fell and broke his arm.
2 Baking cakes at school is easy, **so** when I got home I tried a recipe.
3 Fishing off the rocks is great fun **and** I also like beach fishing.
4 These holidays I could go to vacation care, **or** I could stay at Nana's place.
5 Our family has a boat near the river, so we try to catch crabs during crabbing season.
6 Summer is becoming hotter, but some people don't believe it's because of global warming.
7 Serina is learning ballet, and her younger sister is learning hip-hop.
8 Our black stallion was a racehorse and he won lots of races. (no comma because same subject)
9 Eric could go surfing with Dad on Sunday, or he could go to the movies with Mum.

Unit 2 ENGLISH: Phonic Knowledge & Spelling

1	lessen	4	court	7	cheap
2	grate	5	hoarse	8	cereal
3	packed	6	board	9	right

Unit 2 ENGLISH: Reading & Comprehension

1 It was somewhere to send British prisoners.
2 Tasmania, Queensland
3 Catholic, Protestant
4 c. ordered
5 c. governor
6 c. All of the colonies joined to form our country, Australia.
7 b. No

Unit 2 MATHS: Number & Algebra

1	1 and 9, 2 and 8, 3 and 7, 4 and 6	9	8 2, 8 2
2	5 3 2, 3 7, 8 2	10	4 2 4, 3 1 6
3	6 4, 8 1 1	11	3 1 6, 8 2
4	5 2 3, 3 7	12	4 0 6, 9 0 1
5	8 2, 6 2 2	13	2 2 6, 3 7
6	3 2 5, 6 4	14	2 1 7, 9 0 1
7	2 8, 9 1	15	127, 136, 235, 451
8	4 5 1, 5 2 3		

Unit 2 MATHS: Statistics & Probability

1 b. $\frac{3}{5}$	2 d. not sure	3 c. $\frac{4}{5}$	

4 Yes. The more times a chance event is studied, the more accurate will be the analysis of probability.
5 c. fairly sure
6 c. $\frac{4}{5}$
7 Yes. The more times a chance event is studied, the more accurate will be the analysis of probability.
8 b. very sure

Unit 2 MATHS: Measurement & Space

1	d. 3500 m	9	a. 3.75 cm
2	b. 350 cm	10	d. 4850 g
3	c. 65 mm	11	b. 1550 mg
4	b. 225 000 cm	12	d. 4.736 kg
5	a. 1500 mm	13	c. 1 200 000 mg
6	d. 0.5 km	14	a. 2340 mL
7	c. 7.25 km	15	b. 1 mL
8	b. 17.25 km		

Unit 2 MATHS: Problem Solving

1	2 7 13	5	1 1 8 1, 1 4 2 4, 9 7 4
2	2 6 12	6	40 centimetres
3	3 1 16	7	2.5 grams
4	6 9 5, 9 3 8	8	250 millilitres

Unit 3 ENGLISH: Grammar & Punctuation

1–7 loudly, quickly, tomorrow, secretly, cheerfully, speedily, now

8 <u>After lunch</u>, Dan ran to join his friends on the basketball court.

9 Rabbits ran around the paddock <u>during the night</u>.

10 Lightning cracked directly above our heads <u>during the fierce storm</u>.

11 Monstrous squid live kilometres <u>below the ocean surface</u>.

12 Tigers <u>in the zoo</u> pace their cages from dawn until dusk.

13 We race <u>around our town</u> when our annual bicycle race is held.

14 The last swimmer pulled herself out of the water <u>very slowly</u>.

15 <u>With great difficulty</u>, the mountain climber climbed up the rock wall.

16 Riding <u>very carefully</u>, the girl nursed the tired horse home.

Unit 3 ENGLISH: Phonic Knowledge & Spelling

1 patient
2 direction
3 paradise
4 special
5 geologist
6 monocycle
7 biologist

Unit 3 ENGLISH: Reading & Comprehension

1 Antarctica
2 diseases
3 b. taking gold and silver using weapons
4 In any order: land, food, gold, silver
5 In any order: Great Britain, France, Spain, Portugal
6 c. fought the foreigners
7 1400s to 1700s
8 a. related to

Unit 3 MATHS: Number & Algebra

1 F
2 Negative
3 Positive
4 3
5 1
6 5
7 3
8 6 (Note: technically not -6 because the difference is $0 - (-6) = 6$.)
9 4 (That is: $-3 - (-7) = -3 + 7 = 4$)
10 7
11 13
12 16
13 b. They are added.
14 c. They are subtracted.
15 b. They are added.

Unit 3 MATHS: Statistics & Probability

1 b. 0.5 chance
2 d. 75% chance
3 a. 0.8 chance
4 c. a one in four probability
5 b. two in five probability
6 b. a ten in one chance
7 c. 5% probability
8 d. 0.4 probability

Unit 3 MATHS: Measurement & Space

1 B
2 A
3 b. no
4 B
5 A, D
6 C
7 B
8 4 cm^2
9 1 cm^2
10 B
11 A, D
12 8 cm
13 6 cm
14 26 cm

Unit 3 MATHS: Problem Solving

1 -1
2 C
3 -5
4 2
5 4
6 2, positive
7 3, negative
8 20%
9 0.1
10 $\frac{3}{10}$
11 50%
12 0.3

Unit 4 ENGLISH: Grammar & Punctuation

1 babble
2 plod
3 spotted
4 gazed
5 running
6 weeping
7 yelling
8 giggle
9 chase
10 talk
11 grab
12 cry

Unit 4 ENGLISH: Phonic Knowledge & Spelling

1 omnivorous
2 forearm
3 submerge
4 predict
5 tripod
6 admit
7 shelves
8 rooves
9 scarves
10 wolves
11 spa<u>gh</u>etti
12 ca<u>l</u>m
13 lam<u>b</u>
14 sof<u>t</u>en

Unit 4 ENGLISH: Reading & Comprehension

1 Aboriginal and Torres Strait Islander peoples
2 Indigenous Australian culture
3 Any one from: suffer diabetes, lower life expectancy, less likely to have a job
4 on their country
5 c. They could not use their country to find food.
6 tens of thousands
7 their law and language
8 a. Still happens and is going well.

Unit 4 MATHS: Number & Algebra

1 d. A = $\frac{1}{2}$, B = $\frac{1}{3}$, D = $\frac{1}{5}$, E = $\frac{1}{6}$
2 2
3 4
4 2
5 4
6 4
7 a. one part of A
8 a. two parts of C
9 b. three parts of F
10 =
11 <
12 =
13 <
14 >

Unit 4 MATHS: Statistics & Probability

1 b. no
2 a. yes
3 $\frac{1}{2}$
4 c. $\frac{1}{16}$
5 b. 25%
6 b. 0.125

Unit 4 MATHS: Measurement & Space

1 0.1
2 0.5
3 30
4 0.025
5 4000
6 525
7 2
8 1.25
9 0.025
10 5000
11 0.001 3
12 10 000
13 0.05
14 1000
15 1.2

Unit 4 MATHS: Problem Solving

1 c. $\frac{6}{24}$
2 a. $\frac{1}{4}$
3 b. $\frac{1}{3}$
4 d. $\frac{1}{8}$
5 b. $\frac{1}{24}$
6 yellow, blue
7 red, green, white
8 green, white
9 $\frac{1}{5}$
10 0.25
11 4

Unit 5 ENGLISH: Grammar & Punctuation

1 Ali loves his skateboard, **but he is** not allowed to ride it on the road.
2 We can go and watch a movie, **or we can** go out and have dinner.
3 They happily pulled up the boat anchor, **yet they** didn't catch any fish on that trip.
4 but
5 nor
6 yet (but)
7 or
8 yet
9 but
10 for
11 so

Unit 5 ENGLISH: Phonic Knowledge & Spelling

1 The gold miner wanted to **possess** a piece of gold. (have)
2 We needed to **obtain** a passport for our trip. (get)
3 Do not **remove** sand from the beach. (take)
4 People were asked to **place** their jewellery in the box. (put)
5 cheerful
6 cruel
7 calm
8 arrive
9 cheap
10 bent
11 absent
12 combine

Unit 5 ENGLISH: Reading & Comprehension

1 western lowland, eastern lowland, mountain
2 Gorillas have a slow rate of reproduction.
3 Any one from: increase the rate of reproduction, increase their life span, prevent life-threatening diseases
4 60 years
5 c. only eats plants
6 a. copy something.
7 False

TARGETING HOMEWORK 6 © PASCAL PRESS ISBN 9781925726480

ANSWERS

Unit 5 MATHS: Number & Algebra

1 J	5 G	9 H	13 $2\frac{1}{4}$
2 G	6 H	10 I	14 $2\frac{3}{4}$
3 $1\frac{1}{2}$	7 $1\frac{1}{2}$	11 O	15 J
4 I	8 B, P	12 A	

Unit 5 MATHS: Statistics & Probability

1 a. 2, b. 1, c. 3, d. 4   2 a. 4, b. 3, c. 1, d. 2

3–9 Answers are matters of opinion, general knowledge and local climate type but they must be logical and consistent with one another.

3 H	6 I	9 H	11 25%
4 H	7 D	10 $\frac{1}{2}$	
5 A	8 F		

Unit 5 MATHS: Measurement & Space

1 0.1	6 1	11 10.065 km
2 0.001	7 500	12 1250 mg
3 20 000	8 250 cm	13 2200 g
4 0.08	9 12.5 mm	14 500 kg
5 10 000	10 5725 m	

Unit 5 MATHS: Problem Solving

1 c. $\frac{1}{4}$	4 c. $\frac{1}{3}$	7 50
2 d. $\frac{2}{5}$	5 d. $\frac{1}{6}$	8 25
3 a. $\frac{1}{2}$	6 20	9 40

Unit 6 ENGLISH: Grammar & Punctuation

1 **Because** she slept in, Abbey was late for the bus.
2 All seemed calm **until** the lightning began.
3 We looked at the swans **while/whilst/when/whenever** we waited for the bus.
4 Eve was invited to the party, **but** she couldn't go.
5 **Once** we had had our lunch at the fair, we visited the horror house.
6 There was little rain this year, **therefore** farmers planted fewer crops.
7 **Although** the bike race is dangerous, we will let you compete.
8 Come to the forest centre **while** you are visiting the area.
9 You can't do the mountain climb **unless** you have trained first.
10 Amy was taken to the doctor **before** her cough got any worse.

Unit 6 ENGLISH: Phonic Knowledge & Spelling

1 believe	7 stage	13 sa**l**mon
2 thief	8 ginger	14 e**d**ge
3 ceiling	9 language	15 complex
4 receipt	10 allergic	16 crooked
5 achieve	11 **k**night	17 innocent
6 chief	12 **g**naw	

Unit 6 ENGLISH: Reading & Comprehension

1 b. She spoke nastily.
2 a. change her body
3 Little witches
4 c. make sure she was seen and heard
5 Meg trudged off, more than a little hurt.
6 She was lonely.
7 a. She was overly nice to adults.
8 She definitely looked different to every other student

Unit 6 MATHS: Number & Algebra

1 K	5 J	9 B/C	13 G/H
2 E/F	6 F/G	10 G/H	14 D/E
3 K	7 J/K	11 F/G	15 H/I
4 I/J	8 P	12 H/I	

Unit 6 MATHS: Statistics & Probability

1 c. an elephant in your garden
2 b. a traffic light turning green
3 c. a giraffe wearing an Easter bonnet
4 b. a doctor seeing a patient

5 a. 3, b. 4, c. 1, d. 2	9 green and yellow
6 a. 2, b. 4, c. 1, d. 3	10 red
7 a. 3, b. 1, c. 4, d. 2	11 yellow and green
8 a. 3, b. 4, c. 2, d. 1	12 likely

Unit 6 MATHS: Measurement & Space

1 N	8 Y	15 N	22 Y
2 Y	9 N	16 N	23 N
3 N	10 Y	17 N	24 Y
4 N	11 N	18 N	25 N
5 Y	12 N	19 Y	26 Y
6 N	13 N	20 Y	
7 Y	14 Y	21 N	

Unit 6 MATHS: Problem Solving

1 20 km	4 C or E	7 E	10 120 mL
2 70 km	5 B, D, F	8 C, E	
3 50 km	6 B	9 B, F	

Unit 7 ENGLISH: Grammar & Punctuation

1 She <u>dived</u> in the competition. (past)
2 Jenna always <u>sleeps</u> during the news. (present)
3 The group <u>made</u> the largest sandcastle in the world. (past)
4 It's quite a gift that he <u>sings</u> so beautifully. (present)

5 rode	9 past	13 present
6 fought	10 past	14 present
7 told	11 past	15 present
8 slept	12 past	

Unit 7 ENGLISH: Phonic Knowledge & Spelling

1 we had	9 hall
2 when is	10 audience
3 we have	11 fork
4 who had	12 Pouring

5–8 a. delicious, b. cautious, d. spacious, e. suspicious
13–14 a. witch/craft, d. rain/bow

Unit 7 ENGLISH: Reading & Comprehension

1 Perth   2 c. none
3 In any order: touch football, swimming, cricket
4 b. Nova Peris was able to give time to all of these things.
5 Atlanta Olympic Games (Atlanta, USA)
6 c. kangaroo
7 She dreamed of one day running at the Olympic Games.
8 b. athletics for small children

Unit 7 MATHS: Number & Algebra

1 a. {1, 2, 3, 5, 7, 11, 13, 17.}

2 83	7 b. 2, 2, 2	12 3, 3, 3, 3
3 41, 47	8 2, 2, 2, 3	13 2, 2, 3, 3, 5
4 12	9 2, 3, 5	14 a. yes
5 99	10 2, 2, 7	15 a. yes
6 c. 2, 3	11 2, 2, 2, 5	16 b. no

Unit 7 MATHS: Statistics & Probability

1 B	6 B, C	11 48
2 B	7 B	12 40
3 B	8 21	13 flea
4 flea	9 7	14 mosquito
5 A, C	10 B	

Unit 7 MATHS: Measurement & Space

1 A	5 A	9 B, D	13 3
2 C	6 A	10 27 cm	14 6
3 A	7 12 cm^2	11 A	15 B, D, F
4 C	8 7 cm^2	12 area	

Unit 7 MATHS: Problem Solving

1 c. $3 \times 3 \times 7$	6 24
2 c. $16 \times 3 \times 7$	7 54
3 a. $8 \times 3 \times 3 \times 5$	8 B
4 c. $24 \times 3 \times 5 \times 3$	9 spider bites
5 b. $17 \times 3 \times 11$	10 C

Unit 8 ENGLISH: Grammar & Punctuation
1. The friends **chase** each other to the top of the sandhill. (chased)
2. You **cook** for at least ten extra people each night. (cooked)
3. After the storm we **walk** through the park. (walked)
4. Builders **shout** to each other over the noise of the tractor. (shouted)
5. stayed
6. visited
7. laughed
8. waited
9. danced
10. placed
11. baked

Unit 8 ENGLISH: Phonic Knowledge & Spelling
1. whoop
2. frown
3. cry
4. laugh
5. a florist
6. a plumber
7. an acrobat
8. an accountant
9. beautiful
10. envious
11. application
12. business

Unit 8 ENGLISH: Reading & Comprehension
1. c. Sammy wrote letter 1.
2. because
3. angry
4. lovely
5. b. She is clever.
6. She didn't have time to do her homework before school in the morning.
7. after school tonight
8. Any one from: it got wet; it was put in the oven to dry; it caught on fire; it had tea spilt on it
9. The family was out late last night.

Unit 8 MATHS: Number & Algebra
1. Z/AA
2. G/H
3. No
4. V/W
5. FF/GG
6. N
7. I
8. E
9. H/I
10. S/T
11. I
12. Y
13. N
14. D
15. FF/GG

Unit 8 MATHS: Statistics & Probability
1. Jane
2. Jane
3. Xuan
4. Jane
5. C
6. G and I
7. A
8. J
9. B
10. F and H
11. B
12. Jane

Unit 8 MATHS: Measurement & Space
1. three-dimensional
2. 6
3. c. rectangle
4. 5
5. a. square, b. triangle
6. 3
7. c. rectangle, f. circle
8. two-dimensional
9. two-dimensional
10. 12
11. 8
12. 2
13. 8
14. 5
15. 0

Unit 8 MATHS: Problem Solving
1. b. 4001
2. b. 67
3. b. 3
4. a. 12 700
5. a. 1
6. resting
7. D
8. C
9. 1.5 hours
10. 10.5 hours
11. 13.5 hours
12. 3 hours

TERM 1 REVIEW

Term 1 ENGLISH: Grammar & Punctuation
1. <u>Trish was voted as school councillor</u> because she is now in year six.
2. <u>Over the next few weeks we will see many places</u> as we have no school.
3. Because our alarm clock doesn't always go off, we miss the bus.
4. While Trent loves to go snow skiing, there isn't always good snowfall.
5. When it is overcooked, fish can sometimes become soft and mushy.
6. Toddlers find it difficult to walk <u>as</u> their muscles are not strong.
7. Every year one student gets a book prize <u>because</u> they are good at maths.
8. Every summer the shark alarm sounds <u>but</u> usually the shark swims away.
9. Sam <u>walked</u> in the race today. (past)
10. Mrs R Ose <u>spent</u> time in her garden. (past)
11. Jen often <u>dozes</u> through the news on TV. (present)
12. chatter
13. dawdle
14. observed
15. sprinted

Term 1 ENGLISH: Phonic Knowledge & Spelling
1. waist
2. great
3. packed
4. caught
5. octogon
6. monologue
7. geologist
8. biologist
9. awful
10. interesting
11. bright
12. new

Term 1 ENGLISH: Reading & Comprehension
1. b. hulk
2. thirteen
3. c. sails did not fill
4. He stole three handkerchiefs.
5. It seemed they were made of wood.
6. The convict would get a whipping.

Term 1 MATHS: Number & Algebra
1. d. 555.5
2. c. $999\frac{4}{5}$
3. a. $88\frac{1}{2}$
4. 8 and 7
5. 6 and 9, 5 and 10, 4 and 11
6. 13 and 2, 1 and 14
7. 13 and 2, 9 and 6, 15 and 0
8. 11 and 4
9. 9 and 6, 7 and 8
10. b. addition
11. a. subtraction
12. a. $\frac{1}{2}$, e. $\frac{2}{4}$, f. $\frac{5}{10}$
13. c. $\frac{7}{8}$
14. d. $\frac{1}{4}$
15. b. 71, f. 97

Term 1 MATHS: Statistics & Probability
1. c. to eliminate the possibility of anything that makes the chance of one thing happening more likely
2. b. $\frac{1}{2}$
3. $\frac{2}{5}$
4. 0.1
5. $\frac{1}{12}$
6. $\frac{1}{2}$
7. c. $\frac{1}{3}$
8. B
9. B and E
10. 100

Term 1 MATHS: Measurement & Space
1. 507 cm
2. 588.5 mm
3. 99 009 m
4. 200.5 L
5. 3.709 t
6. 0.071 kg
7. B
8. C
9. A and B
10. A and C
11. 5 m
12. 20 mm
13. 10 cm
14. 81 mm^2
15. 4 m

Unit 9 ENGLISH: Grammar & Punctuation
1. Jax took his old bike, gas stove and old Digger's hat to the river.
2. To make steamed pudding, you need plain flour, red jam, a sealable tin and lots of butter.
3. Dragsters have huge rear wheels, a powerful motor and a parachute to stop.
4. The witch added bat wings, stirred the cauldron, said a spell and then drank the potion.
5. She sandpapered the wood, sawed another piece and then screwed them together.
6. After swimming in the pool, she climbed the tree, tied a rope to a branch and swung across the water.
7. "Well, Mr Simms, may I have that large watermelon please?" asked Jin.
8. "Gracie, please take out the garbage," asked Mum.
9. "Look, Miah, it is not that your dog smells," commented Sam.
10. "Are you well, Tran?" asked Sia.

Unit 9 ENGLISH: Phonic Knowledge & Spelling
1. –ed
2. –or
3. **train**ing
4. **controll**er
5. **wonder**ful
6. **juice**s
7. common
8. tidy
9. breakfast
10. parade
11. fog

Unit 9 ENGLISH: Reading & Comprehension
1. Any two from: great fun, a place to light fires, hide, store all your valuables, drink soft drink
2. The cubby may collapse / you may die.
3. b. You may die because there is no air.

ANSWERS

4 fingers wriggling
5 police and ambulance
6 Mina, Renee
7 c. fearful

8 a hundred times
9 a. They were remembering it.

Unit 9 MATHS: Number & Algebra

1 proper
2 proper
3 improper
4 improper
5 improper
6 improper
7 6
8 5
9 $6\frac{1}{6}$
10 $3\frac{3}{8}$

11 $6\frac{1}{3}$
12 $1\frac{1}{6}$
13 $13\frac{3}{4}$
14 $19\frac{4}{5}$
15 $\frac{4}{5}$
16 $\frac{1}{32}$
17 $\frac{2}{3}$
18 $\frac{1}{9}$

19 $\frac{4}{5}$
20 $\frac{6}{89}$
21 $\frac{13}{4}$
22 $3\frac{1}{4}$
23 $\frac{9}{2}$
24 $4\frac{1}{2}$
25 $\frac{3}{2}$
26 $1\frac{1}{2}$

27 $\frac{7}{3}$
28 $5\frac{1}{3}$
29 $\frac{7}{3}$
30 $2\frac{1}{3}$
31 $\frac{21}{6}$
32 $3\frac{3}{6}$ $(3\frac{1}{2})$

Unit 9 MATHS: Statistics & Probability

1 There is a great difference in values between some of the entries.
2 The broken bars would be much longer (ten times).
3 It goes above the break without breaking.
4 It breaks too soon.
5 It has two breaks.
6 $35
7 $1170
8 $1045
9 $20
10 $125
11 $1010
12 $1155

Unit 9 MATHS: Measurement & Space

1 1500 mL
2 0.335 kg
3 1.567 m
4 2700 m
5 1.345 m
6 2600 mm
7 3600 g
8 2750 g
9 1250 mL
10 0.375 L
11 527 cm
12 3404 cm
13 0.1 cm
14 869 cm
15 0.0015 L
16 1 000 000 L
17 1.257 L
18 54 690 L

Unit 9 MATHS: Problem Solving

1 $\frac{11}{4}$
2 $\frac{22}{8}$
3 $\frac{9}{2}$
4 $\frac{63}{14}$
5 $\frac{2}{1}$
6 $\frac{18}{9}$
7 $\frac{11}{2}$
8 $\frac{33}{6}$
9 $\frac{3}{1}$
10 $\frac{168}{56}$
11–13 Answers may vary slightly.
11 300, 2900
12 25, 1300
13 10 cm, 300 cm
14 800 mL
15 a. 275 cm b. 2750 mm
16 1125 g

Unit 10 ENGLISH: Grammar & Punctuation

1 "Come over here," said Kyle.
2 "Don't forget," reminded Georgia's father.
3 "His manners were poor," commented Coach.
4 The giant pink rabbit said, "This really isn't a dream."
5 "It isn't fair," complained Ryan, "that Josh can sit up front."
6 "Can I have a turn," asked Shari, "after you're finished?"
7 "Yep," Jeff replied, "I'm up for that."
8 "Wherever or however," the captain commanded, "we will be there."
9 Flying down the sandhill, he yelled, "This is fantastic fun!"
10 "Everything has changed," reminded the coach.
11 She swam the river and gasped, "That was the hardest thing I've ever done."
12 "No," Billy shouted, "I don't want to go!"

Unit 10 ENGLISH: Phonic Knowledge & Spelling

1 telephone
2 difficult
3 perfectly
4 paragraph
5 vacant
6 important
7 plant
8 distant
9 fibre
10 litre
11 metre
12 lustre

Unit 10 ENGLISH: Reading & Comprehension

1 b. Forecasting is difficult to get right.
2 In any order: temperature, rainfall, humidity, wind speed
3 No. They take weather measurements every moment of every day.

4 a. the captain of an aircraft, d. a ship's captain
5 Any two from: artificial satellites, ground-based instruments, fastest computers in the world
6 They study weather.
7 Farmers need to know what season to expect.

Unit 10 MATHS: Number & Algebra

1 10
2 $2\frac{1}{8}$
3 7
4 $19\frac{4}{5}$
5 $9\frac{5}{9}$
6 $10\frac{3}{10}$
7 $15\frac{1}{2}$
8 16
9 3
10 $13\frac{2}{5}$
11 32
12 $2\frac{1}{9}$
13 $30\frac{1}{3}$

Unit 10 MATHS: Statistics & Probability

1 Beethoven
2 Tchaikovsky
3 Wagner
4 no
5 Tchaikovsky
6 Beethoven
7 Mozart and Wagner
8 no
9 approximately two times
10 Mozart and Wagner
11 $\frac{1}{4}$

Unit 10 MATHS: Measurement & Space

1 5
2 Train 623
3 Train 621
4 2:47 am
5 3 hours 47 minutes
6 12 hours 52 minutes
7 1 hour 16 minutes
8 1 hour 17 minutes
9 10 hours 57 minutes
10 10 hours 51 minutes

Unit 10 MATHS: Problem Solving

1 $4\frac{2}{4}$
2 $2\frac{2}{4}$
3 2
4 $2\frac{3}{4}$
5 $1\frac{2}{4}$
6 4:26 am, Albury
7 7:30 pm
8 2 hours 42 minutes

Unit 11 ENGLISH: Grammar & Punctuation

1 There was no sunscreen left, **and** no one had any money to go and buy some.
2 They went to the match early, **so** there weren't many people seated yet.
3 I'm trying to eat healthy, **but** I can't ignore the dessert you made.
4 Tom thought that he'd buy the racer, **so** he could ride in the race.
5 Gemma could study for the test today, **or** she could study tomorrow.
6 Rose is very competitive **and** she enjoys playing most sports.
7 Dogs are great pets **and** they are very loyal and become friends easily.
8 We have never travelled to Japan, **but** we have visited China.
9 Tyler felt really sick, **so** his parents took him to the hospital.
10 Should we go to the kart-racing track, **or** should we stand outside and wait?

Unit 11 ENGLISH: Phonic Knowledge & Spelling

1 build: overweight, slim
2 eyes: clear, sleepy
3 hair: blond, curly
4 chilly
5 overcast
6 blustery
7 scorching
8 muggy
9 careful
10 weak
11 safe
12 costly

Unit 11 ENGLISH: Reading & Comprehension

1 c. More cars would be sold.
2 a. longer pedals
3 around schools
4 b. Bec's time is being wasted.
5 She is forced to travel to school on two buses every day.
6 b. There are fewer bicycle accidents.
7 Adults would enjoy that children take themselves to school.

Unit 11 MATHS: Number & Algebra

1 $\frac{3}{8}$
2 $1\frac{5}{16}$
3 $3\frac{1}{5}$
4 $2\frac{5}{16}$
5 $1\frac{8}{17}$
6 $5\frac{5}{7}$
7 $7\frac{2}{9}$
8 1
9 $16\frac{4}{13}$
10 $4\frac{1}{5}$
11 3
12 2
13 1

ANSWERS

Unit 11 MATHS: Statistics & Probability

1. 40 years
2. constant increase
3. 3 819 000
4. Population
5. Years or Time
6. 200 000
7. 2010 and 1980
8. 3 532 000
9. 4 650 000
10. Around 2 118 000, but it was actually 981 000 in the 1921 census.
11. Around 2027–28, but it actually reached 5 million in 2016.

Unit 11 MATHS: Measurement & Space

1. a. E
2. It doesn't have a point.
3. c. F
4. The sides of the triangles can't meet.
5. A
6. B
7. C
8. D
9. A
10. B
11. C
12. D

Unit 11 MATHS: Problem Solving

1. 3 432 000
2. 1990
3. 169 000
4. 139 000
5. 1985
6. rectangular-based pyramid
7. square-based pyramid
8. pentagon-based pyramid
9. triangle-based pyramid

Unit 12 ENGLISH: Grammar & Punctuation

1. The snake catcher, who had a limp, is an expert.
2. Treehouses, which can be made of wood, should not be too high.
3. Deep space, which is well out of the galaxy, hasn't been reached by humans.
4. In her backyard, which is massive, there's a huge mulberry tree.
5. From our boat, we swam to see the seals.
6. Yesterday afternoon, I was allowed to ride Sarah's horse.
7. With tiny steps, the climber reached the peak of the mountain.
8. Because we had been well behaved, our teacher took us to sport.
9. "Yes, I did borrow the bike," Jake admitted.
10. "Oh, that was so clever," Mrs James said.
11. The scientist proclaimed, "Yes, I have the answer!"
12. "No, you need to do that again," demanded his father.

Unit 12 ENGLISH: Phonic Knowledge & Spelling

1. banjos
2. tomatoes
3. potatoes
4. steep, litre
5. cheap, people
6. Our small plane had a very rough landing. (uff)
7. We had to walk through the raging creek water. (ew)
8. My bad cough kept me awake at night. (off)
9. toothbrush
10. afterlife
11. saucepan
12. bedroom
13. necklace

Unit 12 ENGLISH: Reading & Comprehension

1. a. in exchange or response
2. up to nine metres
3. c. She was thinking to herself.
4. tiny plankton, shrimp
5. the same as a car
6. she panicked
7. massive wings, like graceful birds flying, flapping its mighty wing
8. spinning like clothes in a washing machine

Unit 12 MATHS: Number & Algebra

1. 19.817
2. 7.129
3. 5.296
4. 8.964
5. 128.77
6. 55.037
7. 402.197
8. 971.814
9. 12.1268
10. 158.51
11. 161.367
12. 54.658
13. 162.663
14. 1235.2413
15. 99.999

Unit 12 MATHS: Statistics & Probability

1. $\frac{1}{12}$
2. $\frac{1}{12}$
3. $\frac{1}{2}$
4. $\frac{1}{2}$
5. $\frac{1}{12}$
6. c. 75%
7. b. $\frac{1}{3}$
8. 0.25
9. a. 1.0
10. d. Nine came up nine times.
11. c. Five and ten came up 8 times.
12. a. Seven and ten came up 13 times.

Unit 12 MATHS: Measurement & Space

1. B
2. D
3. C
4. F
5. E
6. A
7. B
8. 8
9. 9
10. 9
11. c. 12
12. b. 18

Unit 12 MATHS: Problem Solving

1. 4.66
2. 7.475
3. 12.17
4. 3.206
5. 13.618

Unit 13 ENGLISH: Grammar & Punctuation

1. Mum took us to the pool on the school holidays. (when)
2. After eating the grass, the old cow mooed. (when)
3. Moonlight was streaming through my window. (where)
4. I dug a huge hole with Grandma's shovel. (how)
5. We're going there for a holiday. (why)
6. The lost pilot trudged slowly **through** the swamp.
7. **Without** enough water, people can only survive two days.
8. The explorers dug **behind** the tree and buried their treasure.
9. **Within** seconds the drone crashed to the ground.
10. Both dragons stood quietly **until** one breathed fire and charged.

Unit 13 ENGLISH: Phonic Knowledge & Spelling

1. mayonnaise
2. mutton
3. spinach
4. orange
5. wombat
6. galah
7. wallaby
8. dingo
9. expensive
10. government
11. factory
12. shortish

Unit 13 ENGLISH: Reading & Comprehension

1. Thousands of settlers moved to the west.
2. British settlers
3. 1874
4. a. People wanted to find gold and ignored the treaty.
5. By the early 1800s, the United States Government was removing Native Americans from their land east of the Mississippi River.
6. the Lakota Nation
7. b. Gold was worth lots of money.

Unit 13 MATHS: Number & Algebra

1. 7.21
2. 0.147
3. 4.076
4. 4.34
5. 9.6
6. 22.11
7. 65.89
8. 3.37
9. 10.2263
10. 82.9
11. 7.69
12. 0.25
13. 4.68
14. 6.8
15. 21.81

Unit 13 MATHS: Statistics & Probability

1. 30/11
2. 19/7
3. 11/1, 20/12
4. 20/3, 22/5
5. 11/1, 31/5
6. 31/5, 19/7
7. 11/1, 20/3
8. 11/1, 20/3, 19/7
9. 20/3, 31/5, 19/7
10. 31/5, 20/12
11. 16
12. 31/5, 20/12

Unit 13 MATHS: Measurement & Space

1. translation
2. rotation
3. reflection
4. translation
5. reflection
6. rotation
7. rotation
8. reflection
9. translation
10. rotation

Unit 13 MATHS: Problem Solving

1. 98.299
2. 99.972
3. 1.972
4. 11.958
5. 80.32

ANSWERS

TARGETING HOMEWORK 6 © PASCAL PRESS ISBN 9781925726480

Unit 14 ENGLISH: Grammar & Punctuation

1 As he sat by the log, the dingo **sniffed** the air.
2 Firemen **burst** through the locked door.
3 Our school choir **sang** beautifully at the concert.
4 Eve **shuffled** into the room with the plaster on her leg.
5 Storm chasers **followed** the huge storms across the state.
6 Emma **admires** the winner of the dance competition.
7 They **rejoiced** for hours after finding all that hidden food.
8 Kangaroos **feared** the wild dogs in the bush.
9 The wombats **wished** to grow a bill like the platypus.
10 The sitter **loves** looking after energetic toddlers.
11 The bear **growled** a warning before attacking.
12 Ethan **whispered** as he tiptoed through the house.
13 The team **grumbled** after their loss.

Unit 14 ENGLISH: Phonic Knowledge & Spelling

1 solar
2 zoologist
3 botanist
4 astronomer
5 scissors
6 senior
7 soften
8 island
9 muscle
10 calf
11 autumn
12 knife
13 h**ay**, tr**ai**n (long a)
14 su**g**ar, ma**ch**ine (sh)
15 du**ck**, **c**limb (k)
16 **j**am, wed**ge** (j)

Unit 14 ENGLISH: Reading & Comprehension

1 b. revolting
2 like the leg of a rotting yak
3 Any one from: They could get very sick. / It could lead to a number of very dangerous illnesses. / They could even go to hospital.
4 They make medicine taste so disgusting that children try very hard not to get the cold or flu in the first place.
5 c. cruelty to children
6 ignored
7 make medicine taste nice
8 Text 2

Unit 14 MATHS: Number & Algebra

1 1
2 $\frac{13}{16}$
3 $3\frac{2}{5}$
4 $4\frac{7}{16}$
5 $12\frac{8}{17}$
6 2
7 $8\frac{5}{11}$
8 100
9 $9\frac{1}{13}$
10 $1\frac{5}{15}$
11 3
12 $4\frac{1}{3}$
13 $3\frac{3}{5}$

Unit 14 MATHS: Statistics & Probability

1 -27.4 °C
2 August
3 -2.8 °C
4 January
5 24.6
6 March and October
7 -23 °C
8 Yes
9 The data just shows one temperature per day.
10 April and June
11 February and July
12 March and November
13 b. centre

Unit 14 MATHS: Measurement & Space

1 5
2 6
3 Maasdam
4 0200
5 1500
6 0100
7 1900
8 2 days
9 3 days 5.5 h
10 *Celebrity Solstice*
11 14
12 *Pacific Jewel*
13 7

Unit 14 MATHS: Problem Solving

1 $1\frac{3}{10}$
2 $\frac{4}{5}$
3 $\frac{6}{10}$
4 $\frac{15}{16}$
5 $\frac{1}{7}$

Unit 15 ENGLISH: Grammar & Punctuation

1 He lifted the bow **before** he took aim at the apple.
2 **During** his performance, the clown fell over his feet.
3 Jason buttered the toast **after** taking it from the toaster.
4 The sky was clear and the sun shone **without** a single cloud.
5 The awards were given out **after** the choir sang.
6 She was thrown **against** the rocks after the explosion.
7 In the **past**, the athletes ran barefoot.
8 **Since** the holidays, I have been ill.
9 James ran quickly **after** dark as he was scared.
10 We all had to climb **through** the muddy tunnel.
11 Gemma won't go camping **without** her own tent.
12 There were massive crowds **at** the fairground.

Unit 15 ENGLISH: Phonic Knowledge & Spelling

1 The **co-pilot** landed the plane during the storm.
2 My dad is using lots of **superfoods** in his cooking.
3 I'm training every day for the **triathlon** next month.
4 We can't get to the next level because this level is **incomplete**.
5 He had to **redo** the test because he got everything wrong.
6 happiness
7 truthful
8 friendship
9 likeable

Unit 15 ENGLISH: Reading & Comprehension

1 a. He made me feel good about myself.
2 Any one from: He was teased. / He felt awful. / He started to hate himself. / He didn't like looking in the mirror. / He cried. / He got ill.
3 The new kid was clever, good at sport, good-looking and made friends easily.
4 c. hurt me deeply
5 The new kid stood up for him.
6 a. He hated seeing his hair.
7 Any one from: be proud of yourself / you are a good person
8 b. He stopped people being nasty.

Unit 15 MATHS: Number & Algebra

1 60 c
2 $3
3 50 c
4 $1.25
5 $1.50
6 $4.50
7 $6
8 90 c
9 $2.25
10 $9

Unit 15 MATHS: Statistics & Probability

1 0.24
2 0.16
3 0.12
4 0.4
5 0.4
6 0.52
7 0.24
8 0.2
9 0.6

Unit 15 MATHS: Measurement & Space

1 6K
2 5C
3 3G
4 3J
5 4J
6 1G
7 2M

Unit 15 MATHS: Problem Solving

1 aeroplane
2 aeroplane
3 $2.50
4 ball and elephant
5 24
6 45
7 36
8 18

Unit 16 ENGLISH: Grammar & Punctuation

1 At the football they cheered **loudly** at the goal.
2 Mr Shand spoke **loudly** over the noise.
3 Rabbits hopped **quickly** through the paddock during the night.
4 Pam swam **poorly** during lessons.
5 Lightning flashed **brightly** during the fierce storm.
6 She ran **quickly** to warn of the fire.
7 Our school fete is always held **inside our gym**.
8 Monstrous squid live **in the deep dark ocean**.
9 Tigers hunt **amongst bamboo** which helps them to hide.
10 Men and women work **over the deep gorge** with no safety harness.
11 Old cars drove **around the streets of our town**.

Unit 16 ENGLISH: Phonic Knowledge & Spelling

1 disappear
2 unlikely
3 invisible
4 incomplete
5 unfortunate
6 discourage
7 noodle
8 waltz
9 hamster
10 spare ribs
11 aren't
12 you'll
13 there's
14 what's
15 they're

Unit 16 ENGLISH: Reading & Comprehension

1 b. Hong Kong
2 It would be difficult to find a park for a car because there's so little space.
3 Melbourne
4 b. No, most people live in high-rise apartments in Hong Kong.
5 b. How many people there are in a space.
6 2030
7 c. People in Melbourne mainly live in houses.

Unit 16 MATHS: Number & Algebra

1 13 7	7 6 14, 5 15	12 9 7 4
2 17 3	8 1 4 15	13 8 3 9, 8 1 11
3 1 19, 18 2	9 10 6 4, 3 12 5,	14 6 7 7
4 3 17, 16 4	5 12 3	15 10 3 7, 3 11 6
5 9 11	10 1 2 17	
6 12 8, 7 13	11 8 9 3	

Unit 16 MATHS: Statistics & Probability

1 170
2 326
3 88
4 brown and mulga
5 copperhead
6 $\frac{1}{4}$
7 more
8 $\frac{3}{4}$
9 copperhead, mulga and taipan
10 The numbers of tiger and copperhead combined equal the number of taipans.
11 no
12 25%

Unit 16 MATHS: Measurement & Space

1 40°
2 120°
3 45°
4 60°
5 45°
6 80°
7 80°

Unit 16 MATHS: Problem Solving

1 13	5 5	9 $44.55
2 3	6 10	10 1372 L
3 10	7 0.04 m³	
4 8	8 0.046 m³	

TERM 2 REVIEW

Term 2 ENGLISH: Grammar & Punctuation

1 Serina found glass floats, cuttlefish bones and dead starfish on the beach.
2 After the storm, they found broken trees, swollen rivers and a tin roof in the paddock.
3 To make banana cake, you will need flour, soft bananas, a long tin and lots of butter.
4 She **laughed** at the silly joke.
5 Finding the treasure, they **rejoiced** for hours.
6 Sheep farmers **feared** the wild dogs.
7 Kangaroos **giggled** at the spiny echidna.
8 Ethan scrubbed his car, washed the dog and mowed the lawn on Saturday.
9 The wizard added snake powder, said a spell and changed himself into a frog.
10 At the concert, she smiled, took a deep breath and sang beautifully.
11 "Go over there," said Kell.
12 "Don't be late," reminded Tom's mother.
13 Henry argued, "I think it's your turn to do the dishes."
14 "She let the team down," commented Coach Simpson.
15 The tired explorer slowly and painfully walked **through** the swamp.
16 **Without** eating much food, people can survive for weeks.
17 **Until** now, finding treasure was difficult but not impossible.
18 Walking **across** the desert was difficult for the explorers.

Term 2 ENGLISH: Phonic Knowledge & Spelling

1 pianos	5 toothpaste	9 telethon
2 mangoes	6 background	10 brunch
3 potatoes	7 afternoon	11 smog
4 stones	8 forecast	

12 My grandmother never answers the tele**ph**one.
13 Walking is di**ff**icult for some older people.
14 I wanted to cou**gh** during the concert.
15 costly
16 weak
17 safe
18 careful

Term 2 ENGLISH: Reading & Comprehension

1 c. shown
2 b. Text 1 says that respect is not important and text 2 says it is.
3 a. show
4 Any one from: You should greet someone first. / Firstly, you could say, "Good morning, Mr/Mrs/Ms/Miss/Sir/Lady …"
5 Manners are important because they show respect.

Term 2 MATHS: Number & Algebra

1 9 16	7 17	14 $\frac{15}{4}$	19 21
2 11 14	8 13	15 $3\frac{3}{4}$	20 $\frac{7}{2}$
3 7 18	9 9	16 $\frac{8}{3}$	21 $3\frac{1}{2}$
4 13 12	10 18	17 $2\frac{2}{3}$	22 $\frac{7}{2}$
5 15 10, 19 6	11 11	18 21	23 $3\frac{1}{2}$
6 5	12 16		
	13 40		

Term 2 MATHS: Statistics & Probability

1 no	4 45	8 2003
2 Year 4	5 200	9 2001
3 Prep, Year 1 and Year 2	6 10	10 4590 km
	7 2000, 2004	11 2000 and 2004

Term 2 MATHS: Measurement & Space

1 7.5 hours	7 4:10 pm
2 Stop 5 and Stop 6	8 20 minutes
3 Stop 6 and Stop 7	9 translation
4 Stop 3 and Stop 4, and Stop 6 and Stop 7	10 reflection
5 20 km	11 rotation
6 12:45 pm	12 translation

Unit 17 ENGLISH: Grammar & Punctuation

1 where	3 how	5 why
2 when	4 when	

6 The balloon flew high **above** the smoke.
7 **Without** warning, the waves crashed around our feet.
8 The storm raged **until** early the next morning.
9 The space ship landed **before** running out of fuel.
10 Huge leaves fell from the tree **during** the hail storm.
11 Mum hid from Dad **behind** the door.
12 The men made their way **towards** the mountain.
13 She couldn't leave the cake **without** tasting the icing.

Unit 17 ENGLISH: Phonic Knowledge & Spelling

1 ate, eight	3 check, cheque	5 rows, rose
2 ring, wring	4 reign, rain	6 flour, flower

7 When I get home from school, I like to have a **snack**.
8 **Cookies** and cream is my favourite ice-cream.
9 For breakfast we sometimes have **waffles**.
10 My mother's new **boss** at work is Mrs Vincent.
11 A number of aeroplanes: aircraft
12 More than one young of an animal: offspring
13 English animals: deer
14 People often play games with these: dice

Unit 17 ENGLISH: Reading & Comprehension

1 c. Cockroaches are useful and would be missed.
2 flies
3 They don't bark.
4 b. Cockroaches don't interfere at barbecues.
5 native creatures
6 They smell a bit.
7 b. a subjective text – opinion, thinking, feeling language

Unit 17 MATHS: Number & Algebra

1 32 ÷ 4 = 8	7 234 ÷ 6 = 39
2 64 ÷ 8 = 8	8 500 ÷ 2 = 250
3 99 ÷ 9 = 11	9 990 ÷ 10 = 99
4 225 ÷ 5 = 45	10 758 ÷ 3 = 252$\frac{2}{3}$
5 56 ÷ 7 = 8	11 407 ÷ 5 = 81$\frac{2}{5}$
6 123 ÷ 3 = 41	

TARGETING HOMEWORK 6 © PASCAL PRESS ISBN 9781925726480

ANSWERS

12 $874 \div 9 = 97\frac{1}{9}$ **14** $1789 \div 4 = 447\frac{1}{4}$

13 $841 \div 6 = 140\frac{1}{6}$ **15** $9008 \div 8 = 1126$

Unit 17 MATHS: Statistics & Probability

1 2012	**4** 31 800	**7** too low	**10** 700
2 26 800	**5** too high	**8** too high	**11** 1700
3 29 000	**6** too high	**9** 1400	**12** 700

Unit 17 MATHS: Measurement & Space

1 acute	**5** right	**9** reflex	**13** acute
2 acute	**6** right	**10** obtuse	**14** reflex
3 obtuse	**7** right	**11** reflex	
4 obtuse	**8** obtuse	**12** reflex	

Unit 17 MATHS: Problem Solving

1 29	**4** 37	**7** E, F, G
2 13	**5** A, D	**8** B, H
3 24	**6** C, I	**9** 2

Unit 18 ENGLISH: Grammar & Punctuation

1 when	**3** how	**5** where
2 why	**4** when	

6 The eagle soared high **above** the desert.

7 **Without** a thank you, the girl snatched back her test papers.

8 Kangaroos gathered **beneath** the trees in fear of hunters.

9 The fighter pilot flew the jet **until** the safe landing zone.

10 **Before** exploding violently, the volcano had only smoked.

11 The surfers made their way **towards** the reef break.

12 They continued their march **through** the lightning storm.

13 Marly couldn't leave her room **without** finishing her homework.

Unit 18 ENGLISH: Phonic Knowledge & Spelling

1 they'll	**10** requiring
2 he's	**11–15** **dis**appear, **dis**respect, **im**possible, **un**happy, **un**believable
3 it's	
4 she'll	
5 I'm	**16** orderly
6 baking	**17** teacher
7 liking	**18** humourous
8 hating	**19** sluggish
9 faking	**20** complicated

Unit 18 ENGLISH: Reading & Comprehension

1 to build a chicken coop	**5** c. He got bored and tired.
2 chook mansion	**6** d. screws
3 Wood, because it was easy to build a strong frame.	**7** He ignored him.
	8 She removed the screw.
4 b. wire netting	

Unit 18 MATHS: Number & Algebra

1 $32 \div 4 \times 3 = 24$	**9** $760 \div 8 \times 3 = 285$
2 $64 \div 8 \times 3 = 24$	**10** $756 \div 3 \times 2 = 504$
3 $99 \div 9 \times 7 = 77$	**11** $405 \div 5 \times 3 = 243$
4 $225 \div 5 \times 4 = 180$	**12** $873 \div 9 \times 6 = 582$
5 $56 \div 7 \times 5 = 40$	**13** $840 \div 6 \times 5 = 700$
6 $123 \div 3 \times 2 = 82$	**14** $1782 \div 11 \times 7 = 1134$
7 $234 \div 6 \times 5 = 195$	**15** $9000 \div 8 \times 5 = 5625$
8 $500 \div 10 \times 7 = 350$	

Unit 18 MATHS: Statistics & Probability

1 2014	**4** 260	**7** 0–25	**10** About 7
2 300	**5** 26–39	**8** 40–64	**11** 25
3 400	**6** 65+	**9** 50	**12** About 7

Unit 18 MATHS: Measurement & Space

1 4 right	**5** 3 acute	**8** 4 reflex
2 4 reflex	**6** 3 reflex	**9** 5 obtuse
3 4 right	**7** 2 acute, 2 obtuse	**10** 5 reflex
4 4 reflex		

Unit 18 MATHS: Problem Solving

1 24	**3** They all got 7 humbugs.	**5** 2013, 26–39
2 60		**6** 40–64 and 65+
	4 9	**7** 40–64

Unit 19 ENGLISH: Grammar & Punctuation

1 We hid the presents before **Billy arrived at the party.**

2 Ships seem very safe, but **there are still accidents.**

3 We found the wrecked car after **it had come off the road.**

4 Gina couldn't go to the carnival because **of her chicken pox.**

5 We were allowed to ride in the park **because** we were wearing helmets.

6 Tilly is allowed to play **after** she finishes her homework.

7 The game was fun, **but** we made a huge mess.

8 People couldn't get to space **until** rockets were invented.

9 Mum was angry **because** the car wouldn't start.

10 The bird picked at the seed **and** it also drank the water.

11 Zookeepers put the snake back in its cage **after** capturing it.

Unit 19 ENGLISH: Phonic Knowledge & Spelling

1 pleading	**6** eyeball	**11** decision
2 shore	**7** babysitter	**12** attention
3 sky	**8** silkworm	**13** confusion
4 feat	**9** hairbrush	**14** division
5 interview	**10** motion	

15 He used his **brake** heavily but didn't **break** a single egg.

16 The plane landed on the edge of the plain.

17 Our postman, a **male**, delivers the **mail** daily.

18 We watched the **poor** lady **pour** out her tea.

Unit 19 ENGLISH: Reading & Comprehension

1 thirteenth century	**5** They farmed vegetables on the North Island.
2 the Māori	
3 b. whanau	**6** The late eighteenth century.
4 Any one from: They earn less. / Their life expectancy is shorter.	**7** c. East Polynesia
	8 may have reached 100 000
	9 a. to settle

Unit 19 MATHS: Number & Algebra

1 N	**5** N	**9** Y	**13** N
2 Y	**6** N	**10** N	**14** Y
3 Y	**7** N	**11** Y	**15** Y
4 N	**8** Y	**12** Y	

Unit 19 MATHS: Statistics & Probability

1 Barbara Millicent	**5** Chelsea	**10** 9
	6 5	**11** 6
2 Tutti and Ken	**7** 1	**12** 24
3 Max	**8** 4	**13** 16
4 Skipper	**9** 18	

14 No. The percentages wouldn't work out as whole dolls.

Unit 19 MATHS: Measurement & Space

1 15 squares	**6** 13 squares	**11** 44 m²
2 32 squares	**7** 15 m²	**12** 30
3 7.5 squares	**8** 16 m	**13** 13 m²
4 25 squares	**9** 25 m²	**14** 20 m
5 44 squares	**10** 20 m	**15** 7.5 m²

Unit 19 MATHS: Problem Solving

1 Yes. The multiplier is doubled and so is the answer.

2 Yes. The multiplier is halved and so is the answer

3 No. The multiplier is not halved but the answer is.

4 10 squares	**7** 10	**10** 4 times
5 11 squares	**8** 8	
6 15 squares	**9** 28	

ANSWERS

Unit 20 ENGLISH: Grammar & Punctuation

1–7 After Nick ate his lunch, he (1) **sprinted** to his best friend's place. Amber had a telescope so that they could (2) **observe** birds out at sea. Where birds (3) **gathered**, there were fish. They (4) **dragged** their canoe into the water. Amber and Nick would paddle out to (5) **trap** fish in a net. They were (6) **delighted** with their catch and they (7) **delivered** their fish to the old people's home.

8 walk: sprint
9 talk: giggle
10 think: look
11 hear: get

Unit 20 ENGLISH: Phonic Knowledge & Spelling

1 My **father** was a soldier for many years.
2 It is better to be a little **later** than coming too soon.
3 Our mare's foal was **born** during the night.
4 Investigators haven't found the **cause** of the car accident.
5 Police took away the **device** because it looked dangerous.

6 enter
7 prevent
8 spend
9 currant
10 patient
11 stable
12 dare
13 spare
14 earn

Unit 20 ENGLISH: Reading & Comprehension

1 risk
2 corridor
3 crucial
4 residential
5 reveal
6 restrict
7 c. good value for money.
8 a. they may not be good value for money.
9 False
10 Any one of the following: The corridors will allow the bandicoots to breed in the gardens and then safely travel to other habitat areas. / The bandicoots will face extinction if their habitats aren't protected.

Unit 20 MATHS: Number & Algebra

1 52.3508
2 1231.352
3 3166.84
4 849.68
5 37.4
6 30.256
7 3840.33
8 107.5191
9 10.8528
10 2709.4
11 68.672
12 26.866
13 57.974
14 341.1984
15 29.0368

Unit 20 MATHS: Statistics & Probability

1 50%
2 $\frac{1}{2}$
3 0.25
4 75%
5 37.5%
6 $\frac{3}{8}$
7 0.125
8 $\frac{3}{8}$
9 0.875
10 50%
11 37.5%
12 0.375
13 $\frac{1}{8}$
14 $\frac{7}{8}$
15 50%

Unit 20 MATHS: Measurement & Space

1 48 cm^2
2 4 m
3 9 mm
4 12 cm
5 42 km
6 63 m^2
7 10 km
8 34 mm^2
9 46 m
10 4 km
11 18 cm^2
12 28 mm

Unit 20 MATHS: Problem Solving

1 14 km
2 2812 km
3 111 m
4 511 km
5 $\frac{1}{16}$
6 $\frac{1}{9}$
7 36
8 $\frac{15}{16}$

Unit 21 ENGLISH: Grammar & Punctuation

1 Shelly was really glad **because** she had been elected councillor.
2 Jed played alone **as** he was new to the school.
3 **Although** playing the drums is noisy, it's also fun.
4 **While** it was tiring climbing up, sliding down the sandhill was worth it.
5 We won't finish on time **unless** everyone pulls together.
6 We got to the cricket **before** the crowd got too large.
7 Seeing the art display was great **although** there was little room.
8 **As** they are rare, rescuers battled the waves to save the whales.
9 **While** building the boat was difficult, it was very rewarding.
10 Sunshine streamed through my window **because** it was morning.
11 **After** the terrible storm, we found a glass jar.
12 **Once** the game started, I calmed down.
13 She rang the bell loudly **until** everyone was at assembly.

Unit 21 ENGLISH: Phonic Knowledge & Spelling

1 madam
2 civic
3 deed
4 refer
5 kayak
6 radar
7 There's a large piece of **granite** rock in the garden.
8 Wool is quite often used to make **carpet**.
9 Scientists are preparing a **rocket** to go to Mars.
10 Sam likes to build **model** trains as a hobby.
11 When putting up a large tent you need to have **cooperation**.
12 You use a **capital** letter to start a name.
13 My favourite animal in the zoo is the **gorilla**.
14 We paddled in the water down at the **creek**.
15 **Lightning** flashed and thunder roared in the sky.

Unit 21 ENGLISH: Reading & Comprehension

1 They skipped meals.
2 c. Hunger was a stabbing pain.
3 in the 1930s
4 a. People were extremely poor.
5 They swam under water using a hollow reed to breathe, grabbed the ducks' legs and pulled them down.
6 He feels ashamed about that now.
7 at least a couple of nights
8 b. No-one could afford a fridge.

Unit 21 MATHS: Number & Algebra

1 $\frac{1}{4}$
2 $\frac{1}{8}$
3 $\frac{1}{16}$
4 8
5 4
6 1
7 2
8 6
9 6
10 4
11 $\frac{3}{8}$
12 $\frac{5}{8}$
13 $\frac{11}{16}$

Unit 21 MATHS: Statistics & Probability

1 6.25%
2 0.375
3 $\frac{1}{4}$
4 0.3125
5 68.75%
6 $\frac{5}{16}$
7 0.031 25
8 $\frac{1}{16}$
9 0.0625
10 81.25%
11 $\frac{1}{2}$
12 $\frac{3}{16}$

Unit 21 MATHS: Measurement & Space

1 65°
2 a. 60°
  b. 60°
3 a. 45°
  b. 45°
4 a. 70°
  b. 110°
5 a. 90°
  b. 90°
  c. 90°
6 acute
7 right
8 straight line
9 obtuse
10 reflex

Unit 21 MATHS: Problem Solving

1 Jack
2 Jill
3 Jack
4 Humpty
5 $\frac{1}{16}$
6 Malakai
7 30%
8 27.5%

Unit 22 ENGLISH: Grammar & Punctuation

1 The beast that **ate** Sydney (eats)
2 She **wasn't** your usual hero (isn't)
3 Mad Frank **was** so creepy (is)
4 Felicia **knelt** for the king (kneels)
5 How I **Make** Millions of Dollars (Made)
6 Teddy Smith **Comes** to Town (Came)
7 They **Go** to War (Went)
8 She **Speaks** to Us from Space (Spoke)
9 We **came** in peace. (past)
10 Our old car **drives** us safely. (present)
11 That meal **comes** with gravy. (present)
12 Jenna **waited** for them for an hour. (past)

TARGETING HOMEWORK 6 © PASCAL PRESS ISBN 9781925726480

Unit 22 ENGLISH: Phonic Knowledge & Spelling

1. rea / son / a / ble
2. op / po / **site**
3. be / ne / fit
4. mur / **mur** / ing
5. con / ver / sa / tion
6. wrestle, answer
7. knobbly, **k**nickers
8. wrinkle, wrong
9. subtle, numb
10. to strongly dislike: hat**red**
11. to smash or break glass: sha**tter**
12. to be talkative: **chatty**
13. when birds come out of their egg: hat**ch**
14. produc**tion** (shon)
15. electri**cian** (shon)
16. spe**cial** (shall)
17. spa**cious** (shus)
18. deli**cious** (shus)
19. educa**tion** (shon)
20. essen**tial** (shall)
21. exhibi**tion** (shon)

Unit 22 ENGLISH: Reading & Comprehension

1. force
2. a. rubbed his eyes
   d. his jaw dropped
3. an ancient pith helmet
4. Any 2 from: grandfather, everyone, shopkeeper
5. a. It cost so little.
6. Like dust being vacuumed up, he was sucked in …
7. b. There were dinosaurs.
8. a strange old shop in London
9. strange little shopkeeper

Unit 22 MATHS: Number & Algebra

1. $4\frac{1}{2}$
2. $\frac{3}{2}$
3. $\frac{19}{2}$
4. $9\frac{1}{2}$
5. $\frac{20}{3}$
6. $6\frac{2}{3}$
7. $\frac{13}{4}$
8. $3\frac{1}{4}$
9. $\frac{63}{4}$
10. $15\frac{3}{4}$
11. $1\frac{1}{4}$
12. 2
13. $2\frac{1}{3}$
14. $1\frac{1}{8}$
15. 2
16. $3\frac{1}{2}$
17. $2\frac{1}{8}$
18. $2\frac{6}{7}$
19. $2\frac{1}{3}$

Unit 22 MATHS: Statistics & Probability

1. 25 m
2. 30 m
3. b. There was a cave-in for 5 metres.
4. 3
5. Fast digging for a quarter of the day, then no digging.
6. 2.5 m
7. Day 17

Unit 22 MATHS: Measurement & Space

1. 1, 2, 1, 0
2. 0, 0, 0, 4
3. 2, 2, 0, 1
4. 0, 1, 0, 4
5. 0, 6, 0, 2
6. 0, 2, 0, 6
7. 2, 0, 2, 0
8. 0, 0, 0, 4
9. 3, 0, 1, 1
10. 1, 0, 0, 4

Unit 22 MATHS: Problem Solving

1. $\frac{11}{16}$
2. $2\frac{1}{6}$
3. $2\frac{2}{5}$
4. $4\frac{1}{4}$

Unit 23 ENGLISH: Grammar & Punctuation

1. During winter we <u>didn't use</u> our pool.
2. My sister <u>is learning</u> to knit with needles.
3. We <u>have paddled</u> to the island for fun.
4. Old gum trees <u>were cut</u> for their wood.
5. I <u>am sleeping</u> over at my friend's house tonight.
6–11 Scientists (6) **had** discovered life on Mars. They (7) **were** looking through powerful telescopes. The army (8) **was** scared that people would panic. That sort of news (9) **had** worried the public in the past. Governments (10) **had** seen what happened when news like that reached the newspapers. People (11) **were** frightened and they tried to escape into the forest.

Unit 23 ENGLISH: Phonic Knowledge & Spelling

1. memories
2. territories
3. donkeys
4. lobbies
5. holidays
6. ferries
7. partnership
8. background
9. seahorse
10. dishwasher
11. bookcase
12. tiger
13. element
14. information
15. The photographer had an expensive **camera**.
16. When gardening, Mr Bib used a **shovel** to dig.
17. Jumping from an aeroplane requires a **parachute**.
18. Fishing boats need to have a heavy **anchor**.

Unit 23 ENGLISH: Reading & Comprehension

1. b. ridiculous, d. stupid
2. b. too bad too sad
3. the writer and their pet dog
4. They may keep the valuables for themselves.
5. Their wallet is missing.
6. How silly is that?

Unit 23 MATHS: Number & Algebra

1. $5894
2. $4165
3. $3154
4. $7899
5. $762
6. $2099
7. $3989
8. $4371
9. $5765
10. $142

Unit 23 MATHS: Statistics & Probability

1. B
2. C
3. E
4. A
5. C
6. A
7. D
8. A
9. E
10. B
11. A
12. E

Unit 23 MATHS: Measurement & Space

1. 38
2. Time zones and daylight savings
3. QF660
4. 1 h 50 min
5. QF6606, QF662
6. 31
7. QF6606
8. QF664
9. 1 h 50 min
10. 1 h 55 min
11. 23 August
12. 20 August

Unit 23 MATHS: Problem Solving

1. 0.249
2. $22.50
3. 25%
4. Dinh $7.00
5. $24.20
6. 0.2
7. 0.2

Unit 24 ENGLISH: Grammar & Punctuation

1. We **were playing** in the pool after school on Tuesday. (past)
2. My class **took** a look at the swamp down the road. (past)
3. I **am going to visit** Asia on the next school holidays. (future)
4. I'm **eating** my favourite meal of stir-fry veges. (present)
5. Jai **trains** for football three times a week. (present)
6. I'll **finish** off my project on the weekend. (future)
7. Jess **loved** her netball club.
8. Mum **drank** heaps of water after her jog.
9. Bella **was training** with her swimming coach.
10. The train **left** at 10.00 pm.
11–17 Tom (11) **walked** to school along the river. He (12) **jumped** the fence and (13) **saw** a large brown snake on the track. He (14) **knew** about snakes but (15) **was** still nervous. Tom (16) **picked** up a stick and (17) **lifted** the snake carefully.

Unit 24 ENGLISH: Phonic Knowledge & Spelling

1. mice
2. women
3. children
4. teeth
5. feet
6. people
7. spag / **het** / ti
8. com / pu / **er**
9. dis / **cov** / er
10. in / for / ma / **tion**
11. un / hap / **py**
12. developer, developing
13. beginner, beginning
14. traveller, travelling
15. villain – hero
16. clever – stupid
17. cheap – expensive
18. dawdle – sprint
19. guardian – enemy
20. awesome – unimpressive
21. argument – agreement
22. confident – shy

Unit 24 ENGLISH: Reading & Comprehension

1. c. They plan buildings.
2. Clancy was designing a Lego building in class for the eighth time.
3. a. You try harder.
4. c. plan
5. It's not cool and they wouldn't be seen dead using it.
6. the old teacher
7. "I made sure that there wasn't a waste of space, or that anybody felt that way," the young man commented.

Unit 24 MATHS: Number & Algebra

1 40.32	6 4032	11 4032
2 403.2	7 4032.6	12 0.042
3 0.40326	8 0.0432	13 4
4 43.2	9 40.3032	14 0.0004
5 4.03232	10 40.3	15 4030

Unit 24 MATHS: Statistics & Probability

Answers may vary, but should be logical.

1 A	10 D	mode = 15
2 I	11 C	18 range = 13, mode = 16
3 E	12 C	
4 G/H	13 C	19 range = 12, mode = 15
5 G	14 F	
6 C	15 no	20 range = 32, mode = 9
7 C	16 range = 13, mode = 9	
8 D		21 9, 17
9 G	17 range = 18,	22 12, 21
		23 7, 23

Unit 24 MATHS: Problem Solving

1 240.5	6 either
2 17.5	7 no
3 0.107	8 • Pure chance
4 0.0111	• The dice were tampered with to make it happen.
5 Yes. There is an equal number of odd and even numbers that can come up.	9 No

---

TERM 3 REVIEW

Term 3 ENGLISH: Grammar & Punctuation

1 The rocket flew high **above** the earth.
2 **Without** warning, the waves crashed around our feet.
3 **During** feeding time, the tigers wowed the audience.
4 The boys jogged **around** the school oval.
5 **Before** the concert started, the singers warmed up their voices.
6 **Although** they don't move, we are still in awe of the plastic dinosaurs.
7 Rescuers battled to save the skiers **until** it became dark.
8 We had fun sailing the boat **before** the race started.
9 The dragon **crushes** Sydney
10 She **isn't** a galaxy soldier
11 Crazy Horse **is** a real leader
12 Our friends <u>are coming</u> to stay with us during Christmas.
13 During the trek we <u>had run out</u> of water.
14 My brother <u>didn't train</u> with his team this week.
15 Bonny <u>is going to have</u> surf lessons this summer. (future)
16 Harry <u>was allowed</u> to watch the game after his chores. (past)
17 More people <u>live</u> in cities than in the country. (present)
18 My parents <u>will take</u> me to Europe to visit our family. (future)

Term 3 ENGLISH: Phonic Knowledge & Spelling

1 motion	4 decision	7 unhappy
2 division	5 disappoint	8 inaccurate
3 attention	6 unloved	

9–13 disappear, disrespect, impossible, unhappy, unbelievable
14 Their **father** was very upset when he found out about the bullying.
15 You have to come **later** as you are too early.
16 In hospital there is a **device** to help people breathe.

17 developer, developing	21 clever – stupid
18 beginner, beginning	22 cheap – expensive
19 traveller, travelling	23 dawdle – sprint
20 villain – hero	

Term 3 ENGLISH: Reading & Comprehension

1 reptile	6 legs
2 b. Her legs were useless.	7 Clarrie saw a snake.
3 c. They flew in a plane.	8 to get the blood to flow
4 bodyboarding	9 insisted
5 a. on their cattle station	10 three weeks

11 wrangle
12 "Currently I am ranked number two in the country as a bodyboarder," she explained.

Term 3 MATHS: Number & Algebra

1 31	9 $927\frac{1}{3}$	15 $\frac{13}{4}$	21 $16
2 30	10 $24\frac{3}{4}$	16 $3\frac{1}{4}$	22 $16
3 315			23 $35
4 1971	11 $\frac{7}{2}$	17 $\frac{7}{6}$	24 $27
5 11 753	12 $3\frac{1}{2}$	18 $1\frac{1}{6}$	25 $3
6 11 737			
7 4777.5	13 $\frac{3}{4}$	19 $\frac{16}{3}$	
8 $33\frac{3}{8}$	14 $\frac{3}{4}$	20 $5\frac{1}{3}$	

Term 3 MATHS: Statistics & Probability

1 80 years	4 2	7 1950
2 1950	5 1940 and 1980	8 1990
3 1970	6 No	

Term 3 MATHS: Measurement & Space

1 obtuse	8 64 cm^2	bed
2 reflex	9 1.5 km	14 11:45 am
3 acute	10 12.5 m	15 1:12 pm
4 right	11 3.5 km^2	16 9 mins
5 acute	12 Visiting Lilly	17 1:52 pm
6 right	13 Waking up and getting out of	18 12:15 pm
7 4 mm		19 11:00 am

Unit 25 ENGLISH: Grammar & Punctuation

1 She <u>will wait</u> for the actor to arrive.
2 Aden <u>must be</u> freezing at the ice rink.
3 Rene <u>could swim</u> but didn't like getting wet.
4 Mum said, "I <u>should listen</u> to you read more often."
5 Zac <u>may go</u> to the match next week.
6 The doctor said I **should** take this medicine.
7 Dad said I **must** do well on my exams.
8 Jenna **will** go to choir practice tonight.
9 Luke **will** heat up the soup because it's cold.
10 People **must** not use so many plastic bags!

Unit 25 ENGLISH: Phonic Knowledge & Spelling

1 dragging, dragged	4 longer, longest
2 hissing, hissed	5 hotter, hottest
3 shopping, shopped	6 thinner, thinnest

7 The baby looked so small in the <u>crib</u>. (cot)
8 Toast and <u>jelly</u> are a popular breakfast food. (jam)
9 She ended the sentence with a <u>period</u>. (full stop)
10 Our <u>vacation</u> was ruined by rain. (holiday)
11 a female person: woman
12 being polite: manners
13 wanting something: demand
14 a type of fruit: mango
15 a person who is a boss: manager

Unit 25 ENGLISH: Reading & Comprehension

1 a teacher	6 kangaroos and donkeys
2 b. travel into the bush	7 her kindness and understanding
3 5	
4 their hide	8 year 6
5 a strong leader	9 c. People looked up to her.

Unit 25 MATHS: Number & Algebra

1 5.69	5 4.34	9 14.7	13 3.505
2 37.1	6 22.08	10 151.4	14 8.23
3 3.03	7 20.01	11 2.5	15 608.407
4 7.007	8 11.5	12 4.74	

Unit 25 MATHS: Statistics & Probability

1 15:00	5 16:00 to 17:00
2 14:00–15:00	6 17:00 to 18:00
3 8 °C	7 20:00
4 15:00	8 18:30

TARGETING HOMEWORK 6 © PASCAL PRESS ISBN 9781925726480

9

Temperature, 16 Jan. 2018	
Time	Temp. (°C)
8:00	18
9:00	20
10:00	22.5
11:00	23.5
12:00	25
13:00	27
14:00	30
15:00	38
16:00	35
17:00	27.5
18:00	27.5
19:00	22.5
20:00	20

Unit 25 MATHS: Measurement & Space

1 90°   4 15°   7 140°   10 145°
2 40°   5 85°   8 40°   11 80°
3 55°   6 40°   9 35°   12 100°

Unit 25 MATHS: Problem Solving

1 9 cm   4 0.355 m   7 140°
2 0.8 m   5 90°   8 20°
3 2.55 cm   6 210°   9 both 180°

Unit 26 ENGLISH: Grammar & Punctuation

1 played   3 found   5 told   7 raced
2 tricked   4 wore   6 sat   8 stood
9 We **flew** for the first time today. (fly)
10 Who **broke** the chair? (break)
11 Coach **yelled** at the kids during the game. (yell)
12 The stockman **tied** the rope. (tie)
13 He **answered** very gruffly. (answer)
14 The officials **told** us that our team was best overall.
15 Our parents **stood** in the rain watching the assembly.
16 Before the race my stomach **churned** with nerves.
17 Many people **heard** the bad news.
18 Birds **drank** deeply from the water trough.

Unit 26 ENGLISH: Phonic Knowledge & Spelling

1 The policewoman was in the **counterterrorist** group.
2 Cars parking over there may **obstruct** traffic.
3 She is playing **midfield** in the football side.
4 Doctor Su used the **thermometer** to check Isla's temperature.
5 You rely on your **parachute** for a safe landing.
6 The wings of any aeroplane need to be **ultra**-**strong**.
7 Trying to find a way out of the maze was **puzzling**.
8 His house was clearly too **small** for family to stay.
9 Getting over the river required a **plan**.
10 When trying to stand for the first time, the foal took a **tumble**.
11 geese   13 plant**s**   15 cod
12 salmon   14 space**s**   16 fish

Unit 26 ENGLISH: Reading & Comprehension

1 in the 1800s
2 Any two from: take out the rubbish; clean your room; set the table
3 chores
4 Any one from: Unkind adults forcing their helpless children to do chores. Sometimes children are bribed with pocket money.
5 scientists
6 b. way for them to learn
7 teaches them how to spend wisely
8 a. used
9 text 1

Unit 26 MATHS: Number & Algebra

1 $\frac{15}{100}$, $\frac{3}{20}$ 5 $\frac{20}{100}$, $\frac{1}{5}$ 9 $\frac{5}{100}$, $\frac{1}{20}$ 13 $\frac{1}{2}$
2 $\frac{75}{100}$, $\frac{3}{4}$ 6 $\frac{75}{100}$, $\frac{3}{4}$ 10 $\frac{95}{100}$, $\frac{19}{20}$ 14 3
3 $\frac{25}{100}$, $\frac{1}{4}$ 7 $\frac{20}{100}$, $\frac{1}{5}$ 11 $\frac{1}{3}$ 15 4
4 $\frac{90}{100}$, $\frac{9}{10}$ 8 $\frac{40}{100}$, $\frac{2}{5}$ 12 $\frac{5}{6}$

Unit 26 MATHS: Statistics & Probability

1 g   5 c   9 40
2 Pie Chart Y   6 Pie Chart Z   10 Pie Chart Y
3 k   7 120   11 150
4 j   8 15   12 c

Unit 26 MATHS: Measurement & Space

1 A   5 E   9 (6, -6)   13 (-1, 5)
2 H   6 0   10 (-3, -2)   14 (5, 6)
3 C   7 B   11 (-1, -6)   15 (3, -5)
4 N   8 (-5, 5)   12 (0, -5)

Unit 26 MATHS: Problem Solving

1 60, 70   3 blue   5 (-2, -4)   7 4 cm
2 250   4 7 cm   6 (-6, -6)   8 3

Unit 27 ENGLISH: Grammar & Punctuation

1 We <u>were eating</u> dinner when the huge storm broke.
2 Lucy <u>was trapped</u> in the cave because of the rockfall.
3 Both horses <u>had galloped</u> away during the night.
4 Harry <u>had played</u> the trumpet solo bravely.
5 Some poor people <u>had eaten</u> only leaves in the past few weeks.
6–12 Our class visited the zoo. We <u>were</u>[6] watching the elephant as she <u>was</u>[7] bathing, while other animals <u>were</u>[8] feeding happily. The lions, antelopes and crocodiles <u>didn't</u>[9] notice us. We <u>had</u>[10] walked for hours, it seemed, to reach the hyenas. They <u>were</u>[11] laughing loudly. Most students <u>were</u>[12] standing on the grass listening. The hyenas seemed to excite and disturb all the other animals.
13 We **are** eating our dinner in front of the television.
14 My sister **is** studying in the spare room again.
15 Jake **has** bought a special fish to help clean the tank water.
16 Despite being blind, Bree **can** play the piano beautifully.
17 Georgia **is** counting her money while she waits in line.

Unit 27 ENGLISH: Phonic Knowledge & Spelling

1 base word: accept, prefix: un, suffix: able
2 base word: murder, suffix: ed
3 base word: deliver, suffix: y
4 base word: agree, prefix: dis, suffix: ment
5 should have: should've
6 should not: shouldn't
7 are not: aren't
8 that will: that'll
9 you have: you've
10 they are: they're
11 signature (3)
12 silence (2)
13 horizon (3)
14 remarkable (4)

Unit 27 ENGLISH: Reading & Comprehension

1 how it might be used
2 her tenth birthday
3 b. Katrin thought to herself.
4 in her lab
5 c. The bubble would not let Katrin get the pot plant.
6 a bubble machine
7 as large as beach balls
8 Katrin's whistle

Unit 27 MATHS: Number & Algebra

1 38
2 46
3 18
4 37
5 410
6 64
7 1250
8 243
9 21 (This is the Fibonacci sequence. Add the first two numbers to get the third number, and so on.)
10 299
11 30
12 19
13 8
14 48

Unit 27 MATHS: Statistics & Probability

1 5	5 2	8 $\frac{11}{25}$	11 $\frac{1}{5}$
2 2	6 1	9 $\frac{1}{25}$	
3 3	7 $\frac{11}{25}$	10 $\frac{3}{25}$	
4 3			

Unit 27 MATHS: Measurement & Space

1 C	4 B	7 (-4, -2.5)	10 (6, -1.5)
2 D	5 P	8 (-7, 0.5)	
3 J	6 A	9 (4, -1)	

Unit 27 MATHS: Problem Solving

1 howdy	5 3 and 9	10 540 km
2 hola	6 1 and King	11 2250 km
3 salaam	7 8 and Queen	12 1440 km
4 namaste	9 1800 km	

Unit 28 ENGLISH: Grammar & Punctuation

1 During the race, competitors had to run, swim, crawl and ride kilometres.
2 Trying to get to school on time, she rode, walked and sprinted through the bush.
3 Whilst painting, the artist sketched, shaded, viewed and selected colours.
4 As we cooked, we separated, beat and whisked eggs for the dish.
5 Waiting for the birth of his son, he strode, walked and examined the floor.
6 They had to **gather** their own fruit from the orchard.
7 We **gazed** out at the spectacular view.
8 Brendon **scaled** the red gum tree.
9 She **chattered** nervously before the exam.
10 King Kangaroo used his strong forelegs to **bound** through the bush.

11 swam – swim	15 wrote – write
12 flew – fly	16 listened – listen
13 drank – drink	17 drew – draw
14 stood – stand	18 walked – walk

Unit 28 ENGLISH: Phonic Knowledge & Spelling

1 Jill's desk was very **untidy** because it was never cleaned.
2 We found the movie to be too long and **serious**.
3 Watching bulls at a rodeo can be quite **exciting**.
4 No one could accuse him of being a **coward** in the battle.
5 The **kind** woman looked after orphaned kittens.
6 a flower: pet**unia**
7 part of a flower: pet**al**
8 fuel for a car: pet**rol**
9 has a winner and loser: **compet**ition
10 may look like a doll: **pup**pet
11 A place that is very dry: desert
12 A small dried grape: currant
13 A paper pouch: envelope
14 A very heavy metal: lead
15 Being properly introduced: formally

Unit 28 ENGLISH: Reading & Comprehension

1 in less than an hour
2 Any two from: local police, emergency services, radio stations, television stations
3 b. lots of people can be warned
4 c. deciding how dangerous the storm is
5 a. People look at the weather.
6 volunteer storm spotters
7 Any two from: radar, satellite imaging, computer modelling systems, observations from the ground
8 b. making a decision
9 They provide information about the strength of the storm and its direction of travel.

Unit 28 MATHS: Number & Algebra

1 197.5	5 1.501	9 6500	13 $34\frac{2}{7}$
2 $61\frac{6}{8}$	6 $125\frac{1}{8}$	10 492.5	14 0.03
3 976.563	7 520	11 32.75	15 99.745
4 $268\frac{5}{16}$	8 778	12 160	

Unit 28 MATHS: Statistics & Probability

1 15	3 50	5 14	7 36
2 18	4 19	6 27	

Unit 28 MATHS: Measurement & Space

1 90°	4 100°	7 45°	10 82°
2 45°	5 45°	8 30°	11 28°
3 100°	6 50°	9 55°	12 32°

Unit 28 MATHS: Problem Solving

1 adieu	3 arrivederci	5 F	7 C
2 totsiens	4 sayonara	6 G	8 D

Unit 29 ENGLISH: Grammar & Punctuation

1 **Before** we went to the party, we had some dinner.
2 Having to do gym was a pain **although** most people did enjoy it.
3 He swam against the tide **until** he could see the mainland.
4 Helping Dad build was easy **because** he did most of the heavy lifting.
5 Before they knew the whole story, people began to judge him.
6 The police officer searched the crime scene while the thief hid in the bushes.
7 Although it was expensive, Tran decided to hire the tools he needed.
8 Emma didn't want to go ice-skating because she was so tired.
9 After we move the furniture, we can clean the carpets properly.
10 Saving the trapped horse was hard as water kept flooding in. (no comma)
11 Because of the accident, drivers were suing the government.

Unit 29 ENGLISH: Phonic Knowledge & Spelling

1 Eggs are sometimes hard to **gather** amongst all of the birds.
2 Water made it hard to **adhere** the sticker on the bin.
3 After falling, the climber had to **seize** his friend's hand.
4 Do not **remove** the glass from the window.
5 People found it hard to **achieve** the target.

6 **party:** gathering	13 windy, calm
7 **sound:** noise	14 depart, arrive
8 **shine:** sparkle	15 expensive, cheap
9 **shout:** yell	16 straight, bent
10 **right:** correct	17 present, absent
11 sad, cheerful	18 separate, combine
12 kind, cruel	

Unit 29 ENGLISH: Reading & Comprehension

1 Any two from: facing the drill, the pain, worry
2 The money could be used to feed the poor people of the world.
3 Kids don't have breath like fire-breathing dragons.
4 sugar   5 c. mad
6 thick, yellow coating on teeth
7 lollies, cool drinks   8 poking and prodding

Unit 29 MATHS: Number & Algebra

1 27	5 7	9 30	13 17
2 10	6 9	10 41	14 6
3 28	7 13	11 480	15 13
4 8	8 790	12 16	

Unit 29 MATHS: Statistics & Probability

1 d. $\frac{1}{2}$	4 c. $\frac{1}{13}$	7 c. $\frac{4}{52}$	10 d. $\frac{5}{26}$
2 d. $\frac{1}{4}$	5 c. $\frac{2}{13}$	8 b. $\frac{7}{13}$	11 b. $\frac{1}{13}$
3 a. $\frac{1}{52}$	6 c. $\frac{3}{13}$	9 d. $\frac{6}{13}$	

TARGETING HOMEWORK 6 © PASCAL PRESS ISBN 9781925726480

Unit 29 MATHS: Measurement & Space

1 a. 30°	4 b. 160°	7 c. 335°	10 u
2 c. 95°	5 c. 320°	8 b. 45°	11 t, v
3 a. 90°	6 b. 180°	9 s, z	12 w, y

Unit 29 MATHS: Problem Solving

1 c. $\frac{1}{21}$

2 b. $\frac{1}{18}$

3 c. $\frac{1}{2}$

5 No

6 The same as when you started

7 The same as when you started

Unit 30 ENGLISH: Grammar & Punctuation

1 Curry, which is very spicy, is enjoyed all over the world.
2 Ships that were wrecked in the storm had to be repaired.
3 The teacher who marked the exams is away today.
4 People **who** donated money received a receipt.
5 The school bus **that/which** comes at 8 am is the quickest.
6 The illness **that/which** my dog had was caused by ticks.
7 The show that I watch every night has just been cancelled.
8 The fire, which had been raging all night, damaged many homes.
9 A biologist is a scientist who studies life.
10 The jockey, who is my uncle, won the horse race.

Unit 30 ENGLISH: Phonic Knowledge & Spelling

1 their, they're, thair
2 toad, tode, towed
3 moad, mowed, mode
4 prophet, profit, profit
5 to grasp: cat**ch**
6 a disaster: cat**astrophe**
7 type of fish: cat**fish**
8 models walk on this: cat**walk**
9 copy: **dupli**cat**e**
10 **sausage**s
11 un**usual**
12 un**employ**ed
13 **wonder**ful
14 **haul**ing
15 **open**ing
16 a taste: flav**our**
17 a fine mist: vap**our**
18 a person who gives: don**or**
19 to eat hungrily: dev**our**
20 a male singer: ten**or**

Unit 30 ENGLISH: Reading & Comprehension

1 c. meadows
2 beginning of the 20th century
3 his razor-sharp diving knife
4 a. barnacle-covered rusting pile
5 the clear water
6 a. excruciating
7 It was trapped in a fishing net.
8 Any one from: It nuzzled him in thanks. / It pushed him upwards to the surface. / It saved his life.
9 Any one from: It was covered in seaweed. / It was hard to find if you didn't know where to look.

Unit 30 MATHS: Number & Algebra

1 677 290	5 9 089 761	9 7 523 116
2 6 024 202	6 2 234 678	10 916 742
3 37 642	7 64 210	
4 500 002	8 9 855 320	

Unit 30 MATHS: Statistics & Probability

1 C	2 B	3 C	4 D	5 E

Unit 30 MATHS: Measurement & Space

1 A	4 6 mins	7 2 hours 2 min
2 J	5 G	8 1 hour 41 min
3 9 mins	6 C	9 11 min

Unit 30 MATHS: Problem Solving

1 Shopping Time and Jack's Show
2 Baby School
3 Cartoon Time
4 Jill's Show
5 Fishing Show and Good Cooking
6 The Hat and Fishing Show
7 The Smiths
8 Fishing Show
9 Shopping Time and Jack's Show

Unit 31 ENGLISH: Grammar & Punctuation

1 Always make sure that you swim **between** the flags at the beach.
2 Our plane flew **into** Perth late at night.
3 Jed's bull broke **through** the fence railings.
4 Swimming **under** the water, the guards did not see him enter.
5 **Without** trying, she passed the leader on the line.
6 **Within** minutes, the entire house was in flames.
7 I'm waiting **for** my parents. (no comma)
8 **Through** my window, I could see the sun come up.
9 **On** Sunday morning, I have my gymnastics competition.
10 Lifeguards dived **beneath** the waves to grab the drowning man.

Unit 31 ENGLISH: Phonic Knowledge & Spelling

1 orderly
2 teacher
3 humourous
4 healthy
5 denti, dentist, **tooth**
6 mono, monorail, **one**
7 hydro, hydroelectricity, **water**
8 geo, geography, **world**
9 octo, octopus, **eight**
10 bio, biology, **life**
11 shortish, shortness
12 dependent
13 sickness, sickish
14 retirement
15 resentment
16 meanness
17 discernment
18 selfish

Unit 31 ENGLISH: Reading & Comprehension

1 b. Eat FLABBO.
2 Any three from: white sugar, pure butter, peanuts, olive oil, flavouring, white chocolate with added lard (pig fat)
3 lard (pig fat)
4 It will give you a million times more energy.
5 c. You will be less unhappy.
6 the company doctor
7 fresh white bread
8 a. cleaning teeth
9 olive oil
10 'death breath'

Unit 31 MATHS: Number & Algebra

1 $\frac{3}{8}$	5 $\frac{1}{16}$	8 $\frac{5}{24}$	11 $1\frac{1}{10}$
2 $\frac{3}{10}$	6 $1\frac{1}{20}$	9 2	12 $2\frac{4}{12}$ or $2\frac{1}{3}$
3 $1\frac{5}{14}$	7 $\frac{3}{100}$	10 $1\frac{11}{12}$	13 $\frac{1}{40}$
4 $1\frac{2}{3}$			

Unit 31 MATHS: Statistics & Probability

1 F	3 C	5 E
2 B	4 A	6 D

7 There is a large difference between the value for A and the other values.

8 Yes	10 E	12 C and D
9 C	11 A	

Unit 31 MATHS: Measurement & Space

1 b	5 a, b, c,	8 0	12 8	16 8
2 d	d	9 3	13 8	17 8
3 b, d	6 d	10 0	14 8	18 10
4 b	7 3	11 0	15 8	

Unit 31 MATHS: Problem Solving

1 $\frac{1}{3}$	3 $\frac{1}{2}$	5 $\frac{3}{4}$
2 $\frac{1}{4}$	4 $\frac{3}{5}$	6 Yes

Unit 32 ENGLISH: Grammar & Punctuation

1 The nurse, who was very kind, took my temperature.
2 My bag, which is old, has a frayed strap.
3 The cat, which was hiding, pounced at the mouse.
4 Sue, who had a headache, went home early.
5 Abul, who loves the rain, went for a walk.
6 The girl, who was only 12, could play the piano.
7 The sun, which was too bright, gave me a headache.
8 My cousin, who went overseas, came back last week.
9 The bananas, which are too ripe, are covered in black spots.
10 My father, who loves to cook, is making dinner.

ANSWERS

Unit 32 ENGLISH: Phonic Knowledge & Spelling
1 little fly – mosquito
2 cucaracha – cockroach
3 small war – guerrilla
4 inner courtyard – patio
5 to load – cargo
6 After working in the sun all day, everyone agreed it had been hard **yakka**.
7 There was lots of **yabber** in the classroom and no work got done.
8 Nanja trapped the fish and used his **gidgee** to spear them.
9 In the comedy he was an absolute **drongo**.
10 While he waited, he acted like a **galah** without its feathers.
11 Gold prospectors often lived out in the **mulga** for months on end.
12 tele**ph**one – stu**ff**
13 **g**iant – bri**dge**
14 mi**ss** – **c**ity
15 fu**zz**y – ho**se**

Unit 32 ENGLISH: Reading & Comprehension
1 Lizard Dinner
2 b. fiery blast
3 spinifex
4 cooling dip
5 b. It was fast.
6 school bus, school
7 racehorse goanna
8 c. a group of Aboriginal students
9 c. the heat was part of their lives
10 c. waterhole

Unit 32 MATHS: Number & Algebra
1 51
2 1.5
3 5616
4 0
5 13.08
6 1000.4
7 0.06
8 42.57
9 45.6
10 10.2
11 53.3
12 94.3
13 100
14 0.5

Unit 32 MATHS: Statistics & Probability
1 50 °C
2 3 °C
3 twice
4 25 °C
5 About 37 °C
6 45 °C
7 37 °C
8 13:00 to 14:00
9 14:00 to 15:00
10 12:00 to 13:00

Unit 32 MATHS: Measurement & Space
1 C
2 G
3 F
4 D
5 C
6 D
7 A
8 E
9 A

Unit 32 MATHS: Problem Solving
1 $963
2 $740.75
3 $8394.75
4 $6640.65

TERM 4 REVIEW

Term 4 ENGLISH: Grammar & Punctuation
1 We <u>stayed</u> at the game after school on Wednesday. (past)
2 <u>I'm competing</u> in the swimming trials today. (present)
3 My sister <u>took</u> a look at the bush near the river. (past)
4 We <u>are going</u> to France next summer. (future)
5 He <u>had waited</u> for the principal to leave.
6 Pam <u>was laughing</u> at her spelling mistakes.
7 Zach <u>has rowed</u> all the way down to the river mouth.
8 Aunty Jan <u>is watching</u> the gymnastics competition.
9 Lamingtons, <u>which I love</u>, are often eaten on Australia Day.
10 Books <u>that were damaged in the flood</u> had to be replaced.
11 The teacher <u>who takes the athletics training</u> is not here.
12 Our music teacher <u>will be</u> late this afternoon.
13 The train to the city <u>should come</u> on time.
14 Emma <u>might take</u> her homework to Grandma's house.
15 <u>Can</u> I <u>give</u> the dog its food?
16 <u>When the snake found the chook run</u>, it ate the eggs.
17 <u>After Ryan came home from school</u>, he relaxed and then made dinner.
18 <u>Because the soup was hot</u>, I put it on the table and waited for it to cool.
19 Whilst building, the lady hammered, sawed, nailed and screwed the wood.
20 As we waited, we played, jumped, skipped and hopped in the playground.

Term 4 ENGLISH: Phonic Knowledge & Spelling
1 should have – should've
2 should not – shouldn't
3 are not – aren't
4 that will – that'll
5 you have – you've
6 they are – they're
7 kind – cruel
8 untidy – clean
9 arrive – depart
10 calm – windy
11 exciting – boring
12 coward – hero
13 hiss, hissing, hissed
14 shop, shopping, shopped
15 long, longer, longest
16 thin, thinner, thinnest
17 geese
18 plant**s**
19 space**s**
20 fish
21 signature (3)
22 silence (2)
23 horizon (3)
24 remarkable (4)

Term 4 ENGLISH: Reading & Comprehension
1 b. die
2 5–7 hours
3 c. large
4 leave your car
5 thirty to fifty litres or more
6 b. important
7 spare tyres, parts
8 Very few trees are able to live in the outback and those that can are spindly and have few leaves.

Term 4 MATHS: Number & Algebra
1 $\frac{3}{8}$
2 $\frac{1}{5}$
3 $\frac{1}{3}$
4 $\frac{7}{18}$
5 $\frac{8}{21}$
6 $\frac{3}{4}$
7 $2\frac{1}{12}$
8 $1\frac{1}{5}$
9 $1\frac{1}{9}$
10 $1\frac{1}{5}$
11 10 080
12 14
13 300
14 90.95
15 66

Term 4 MATHS: Statistics & Probability
1 -10 °C
2 9:00–10:00, 10:00–11:00, 15:00–16:00, 16:00–17:00
3 18 °C
4 1 °C
5 16° C
6 2.5 hours
7 15 °C
8 6.5 hours
9 50%
10 5%
11 25%
12 0.75
13 0.1
14 $\frac{7}{20}$
15 $\frac{1}{15}$
16 5%, 0.05, $\frac{1}{20}$
17 2 and 3
18 1.25%, 0.0125, $\frac{1}{80}$

Term 4 MATHS: Measurement & Space
1 a, c, h, i, l
2 b
3 c
4 f
5 h
6 k
7 j
8 (-4, -5)
9 (-1, -2)
10 (6, 9)
11 (0, 0)
12 (3, 2)

TARGETING HOMEWORK 6 © PASCAL PRESS ISBN 9781925726480